This Spot of Ground

This Spot of Ground

Spiritual Baptists in Toronto

CAROL B. DUNCAN

Wilfrid Laurier University Press
[WLU]

This book has been published with the help of a grant from the Canadian Federation for the Humanities and Social Sciences, through the Aid to Scholarly Publications Programme, using funds provided by the Social Sciences and Humanities Research Council of Canada. We acknowledge the financial support of the Government of Canada through the Book Publishing Industry Development Program for our publishing activities.

Library and Archives Canada Cataloguing in Publication

Duncan, Carol B. (Carol Bernadette), [date]
    This spot of ground : Spiritual Baptists in Toronto / Carol B. Duncan.

Includes bibliographical references and index.
ISBN 978-1-55458-017-0

    1. Spiritual Baptists—Ontario—Toronto—History. 2. Caribbean Canadian women—Religious life—Ontario—Toronto. 3. Black Canadian women—Religious life—Ontario—Toronto. 4. Black Canadians—Race identity—Ontario—Toronto. 5. Women immigrants—Religious life—Ontario—Toronto. I. Title.

BX9798.S6535C3 2008   286'.5   C2008-900387-X

Cover design by Sandra Friesen. Front cover photograph by Carol B. Duncan. Back cover photograph by Walter Singh. Text design by Catharine Bonas-Taylor.

© 2008 Wilfrid Laurier University Press
Waterloo, Ontario, Canada
www.wlupress.wlu.ca

∞
This book is printed on Ancient Forest Friendly paper (100% post-consumer recycled).
Printed in Canada

Contents

Preface

On Labour Day weekend in 1987, I took my first of many bus trips with a group of Spiritual Baptists. Our destination upon leaving the central west area of the city of Toronto was New York City. When I took that trip, little did I know of the impact it would have on my life a few years later. At the time, I had just finished a summer of working two jobs before starting the fourth year of my undergraduate degree in sociology at the University of Toronto. The trip to New York City was a reward to myself for a long summer of work and in anticipation of my upcoming final year. Like many members of the Caribbean community in Toronto, I had family and social networks that extended from Toronto to the United Kingdom, the Caribbean region, and major urban centres in the United States such as New York City. I had taken the bus trip not because I was participating in the pilgrimage of the church members to New York City but out of a need to find an affordable means of visiting New York City on short notice. A family member who attended Spiritual Baptist services alerted me to the bus trip and off I went. I met the church members in front of the church in downtown Toronto late on the Friday evening of the Labour Day weekend. Archbishop Brinsley Dickson, the male leader of the church, stood at the side of the bus and made sure that all who were making the journey had boarded.

When we were finally on the bus, our journey began with songs and sharing of food in the darkened cavity. Saltfish and bake[1] and hot, sweet coffee were passed back in the wee hours of the morning. Hymns were raised in polyphonous harmonies. It became obvious that the bus trip was not only a method of transport to New York City but that the journey itself, and not the destination, was a pilgrimage. I, by virtue of being there, was invited to join in this journeying. I was reluctant at first but eventually joined in the singing of some of the hymns that I knew from the Anglican Church. This was my first trip with Spiritual Baptists. I remember it well.

Five years later, in 1992, while a doctoral student and research assistant on a project about Toronto's Caribbean community, I was asked to do some research on community support networks. I remembered the bus trip I had taken years earlier as well as my relatives' continued involvement with the church. This time I returned not as traveller but as researcher. On this outing, I entered the church rather than waiting outside its doors to be transported to another cross-border destination. I returned for what I initially thought would be a short period of intensive ethnographic research extending over a two-week period in September of 1992. However, within a very short period of time—hours, in fact—of attending my first church service, I knew I wanted to understand more about the Spiritual Baptist religion and its emergence in Toronto. I wanted to pursue this topic, not only for its scholarly contribution to the literature on Caribbean religions in North America and Caribbean immigration to Canada, but also as a community service to Spiritual Baptists in Toronto, many of whom expressed enthusiasm for the project as they desired to have their history documented for future generations. I subsequently declared this as my dissertation topic after consultation with church leaders.

The research I completed in the fall of 1992 on the Spiritual Baptist Church was included in the section "The Fundamentalist Church," in the chapter on religion in Frances Henry's *The Caribbean Diaspora: Learning to Live with Racism* (1994: 158–66). Some of that research is reflected in this study. I continued ethnographic research over the next more than twelve years, especially from 1994 to 2004.

The features of that initial encounter with Toronto Spiritual Baptists in 1987 presaged the themes of this study. For it was in this encounter that I experienced a sense of the sacred as incredibly mobile, actively engaged, and communally created. Although I was on the bus as a passenger travelling to New York City to enjoy a weekend of visiting, I quickly came to realize that the other passengers had taken the church with them on to the bus!

The mobility of the sacred is not only experienced in cross-border voyages by bus and car by Spiritual Baptists to the United States and in airplane flights to the Caribbean, the United Kingdom, and Africa; it is also signalled by the extension of the Caribbean as a geopolitical–spiritual space into the Canadian landscape. That is to say, the mobility of the sacred also includes the capacity to transform, if only temporarily, physical spaces in Canada and thereby extend the Caribbean and African diasporan religious topography into northern metropolitan contexts to which practitioners have migrated.

The cover photograph of this book exemplifies this idea. I took this photograph in August 2003 at ancestral prayers being held by Toronto Spiritual Baptist leader Bishop Queen Mother Yvonne Drakes, at the easterly outskirts of the Greater Toronto Area. The photograph depicts a practitioner in a long white dress edged in green, red, and gold and a white head-tie. We had both temporarily left the open-air pavilion, a wooden structure with roof but no walls or doors, which had been transformed from a park seating area for meal consumption to a space for prayers and singing. She was moving in a meditative slow-quick run-walk-trot at the lake's shoreline, the water lapping gently at her sandalled feet. It was a slightly hazy, warm, late-summer day, and the sky was a blissful blue with a single wisp of cloud. This woman, in her late fifties, described herself to me as a spiritual seeker who has explored a variety of religious and esoteric traditions, including the Spiritual Baptist Church in Canada. She was born in Jamaica and had spent portions of her adolescence and young adulthood in New York City in the 1960s before settling in Toronto, where she completed her university education and established her work life.

Her presence that day, and indeed that of the other practitioners and myself—*our* presence—disrupted the park space as picnic and leisure space. We were made acutely aware of our otherness by other park users who took photographs of us, openly stared, and commented on the presence of a group of about twenty-five Caribbean women, most of us black with one woman of Indo-Caribbean descent, in white dresses and head-ties. We stood out among other users of the park who were clad in swimwear, shorts, and jeans barbecuing food on grills while Frisbees and footballs were tossed through the air. Some Spiritual Baptist women, in turn, took photographs of the picnic and barbecue park users making a cogent critique of being othered through their viewing practices by literally turning the tables, or the cameras, in this case, on their observers. The presence of black women in white dresses, praying and singing, arranging cakes and other foodstuffs on picnic tables used as altars transformed the picnic, leisure space into sacred space. The lake, too, was transformed from a solely Canadian inland, freshwater lake to become a visible extension of the Caribbean sea and Atlantic ocean, those saltwater passages of black migratory experiences of slave trade, cod fish, and rum that were also the domain of the Yoruban water orisha Yemaya and Oshun. The Middle Passage and Black Atlantic, metaphors of African Diasporic experience, were joined to this image of Canadian freshwater lake.

Although not consciously constructed as such at the time, the photograph echoes themes also explored in the work of the British-based black woman photographer Ingrid Pollard. Born in Georgetown, Guyana, in 1953 and raised in England, Pollard uses photography to explore notions of British-ness and racialized identities through revisiting the British pastoral country-side and photographing black subjects in those settings. In doing so, her work in portraiture and landscape photography both deconstructs and suggests alternative constructions of contemporary British identities that include black subjects.[2] In particular, Pollard's black subjects in the pastoral landscapes of Britain subvert commonly held expectations associating blackness with urban spaces while designating natural landscapes as white-only preserves. Relatedly, Jamaican-born Toronto-based photographer Michael Chamber's earlier work in the 1990s, often featured black nude subjects in natural, out-door settings as well as studio settings.[3]

In our discussion about the photograph in August 2007, the woman depicted emphasized the importance of journeying and exploration in her spiritual life, noting that the photograph in capturing her movement at the lakeshore also included the image of a cloud, barely perceptible in the sky. She noted that she saw the cloud's presence as symbolic of problems and challenges that present themselves in everyday life circumstances that can be met and overcome through diligent religious practice. "I keep coming back to the cloud," she said in our conversation. In many ways, her assessment of this photograph and her place in it reflects the viewpoint other practition-ers offered to explain the tradition's persistence from the Caribbean to a Canadian context: the ability to confront daily life challenges in a new con-text from the vantage point of a tradition that makes sense to practitioners from their own historical and cultural reference points. The ground, in this sense, shifts under the feet of the practitioners but their conscious aware-ness of change and flux as an inherent aspect of daily life experiences pre-pares them for creative engagement with their surroundings. It is in this tension, between Caribbean history, including slavery and colonialism, a longer-time African past, and a heightened awareness of the changing and

shifting circumstances of contemporary migration, that the Spiritual Bap-.
tist tradition has emerged in Toronto, Canada.

NOTES

1 A Trinidadian dish that consists of an oven-baked pan bread and salted cod fish.
   Salted cod imported from Atlantic Canada was a staple in the diet of enslaved Africans
   in the Caribbean. In contemporary times, it has become a part of the cuisine of
   Caribbean countries like Jamaica, where saltfish and ackee is touted as a national
   dish.
2 See for example Ingrid Pollard's "Pastoral Interlude" series (1987), exhibited at the
   Victoria and Albert Museum in London, England.
3 See for example Michael Chamber's "Boulder" (1990).

Acknowledgements

There are many to whom my thanks are due as this work, though individual in terms of responsibility, was formed in dialogue and community. Thanks to the Spiritual Baptist men and women and Orisha people of Toronto and Trinidad who generously shared their life stories and insights with me through the years over meals, on buses, in church, at celebrations, and in their homes. Without their generosity, this work would not have been possible. The invaluable support and generous sharing of the following Spiritual Baptist leaders is gratefully acknowledged: Archbishop Brinsley Dickson, Queen Mother Tritsy Payne (1929–2007), Bishop Queen Mother Yvonne Drakes, Reverend Anthony Drakes, the now-deceased Queen Mother Ruby Phillip of Movant, Trinidad, and Bishop Queen Mother Deloris Severeight. Thanks to Dr. Jennifer Richards.

I appreciate the guidance and support of faculty in the graduate program in sociology at York University, where this work first took shape as a doctoral dissertation. Special thanks also, in this regard, to Karen L. Armstrong, who served as dissertation supervisor; Himani Bannerji and Gordon Darroch of the Department of Sociology; and Patrick Taylor of the Centre for Research on Latin America and the Caribbean. I acknowledge my colleagues Wallace D. Best, Yvonne Chireau, George Elliott Clarke, Afua P. Cooper, Lisa M. Jakubowski, Hugh R. Page, Jr., Alton B. Pollard III, and Dianne M. Stewart for engaging in dialogue about black subjectivities, migration, and the African Diaspora that contributed to refining this work.

Thanks to professor emerita Frances Henry and Alan B. Simmons of York University with whom I worked as a research assistant (1988–1992) on a project on Toronto's Caribbean community during the course of my MA degree and early stage of my doctoral degree program. It was in this capacity that I first initiated research on Toronto Spiritual Baptists in 1992. Thanks to my colleagues and students in the Department of Religion and Culture at Wilfrid Laurier University.

This book has been published with the help of a grant from the Canadian Federation for the Humanities and Social Sciences, through the Aid to Scholarly Publications Program, using funds provided by the Social Sciences and Humanities Research Council of Canada. Final work on this manuscript was one of the projects completed while I was a fellow in the Women's Studies in Religion Program and resident of the Center for the Study of World Religions at Harvard Divinity School in 2006–2007; the support of these programs is gratefully acknowledged. Finally, thanks to my family, especially my grandmother, Dorothy Sebastian Prince (1902–1994).

Introduction

… it was through a vision, too, that I got to come to Canada.
—ARCHBISHOP BRINSLEY DICKSON, *leader of a downtown*
Toronto Spiritual Baptist church, September 29, 1992

And when I came to Canada, I realize it [the Spiritual Baptist Church] was the closest thing to home. It make you feel like—you're in Canada, but you're back in Trinidad because of how they worship in the Baptist [church]. It's similar in most ways but, you know, you find, you know, one or two things different, you know. Yeah.
—SISTER ASHA, *member of a downtown Toronto*
Spiritual Baptist church, September 15, 1994

So, I tell meself, ah comin' but ah comin' on a holiday an' ah comin' on a joy spreadin'—ah come to see wha'ah could pick up! Cuz everybody leavin' Trinidad and dey comin' 'Merica to "pick up." But you see, when you is a soldier … Everyone in this church is Trinidadian? Or an outside country? Because you know why? Dey didn't lose di current of di Holy Spirit. Dey didn' make America shine too bright in their way and make them loss their spiritual current nor di zeal of di Spirit. But ah come and meet di zeal whey ah leave in Trinidad!
—MOTHER SYLVIA, *Spiritual Mother, a visitor from Trinidad,*
testifying at a Spiritual Baptist church in suburban
Toronto, May 28, 1995

I

On a Tuesday evening in early autumn, September 29, 1992, Archbishop Brinsley Dickson sits in his office, a small room, in the back of the Spiritual Baptist Church, located in a storefront in downtown Toronto. The room is sparingly decorated with a desk covered by a lace tablecloth and two chairs, which are occupied by the archbishop and myself. Archbishop Dickson, a man then in his fifties from Trinidad, tells me that his journey to Canada in 1973 was initiated by a vision, not through an application for a visa or the purchase of a plane ticket to come to Canada. Nearly two years later on September 15, 1994, Sister Asha, a young woman in her twenties, speaks intently in the living room of her shared east-end Toronto apartment, the television playing softly in the background, as she tells me about the home feeling reminiscent of Trinidad in Archbishop Dickson's church. The following spring in 1995, Mother Sylvia, a visiting elder woman from Trinidad, brings her testimony to a crescendo, at a suburban Spiritual Baptist church, with references to the "zeal of di Spirit" that connects her experiences of worship in Trinidad, Toronto, and U.S. cities she has visited where Spiritual Baptists congregate. How can these experiences be accounted for within the larger histories of migration and religious experiences that they reference—twentieth-century Caribbean migration to Canada, religious experiences of Africans and their descendants in the Americas—and the notion of Spirit that connects religious and cultural expressions of people of African descent in the Americas? This book attempts to answer these questions using a framework that takes into consideration critical perspectives that emerge from African-Caribbean religious and cultural expressions.

Throughout the history of Africans in the Americas, religious and cultural expressions have formed a crucial component of a culture of resistance to enslavement and various forms of European colonialism and American neo-colonialism. While the historical development of African religions in the Americas has been relatively well documented, the subsequent transformation of these religious forms in the context of post–Second World War immigration to industrialized capitalist countries such as Canada is a nascent area of research. It is at this juncture that this study is situated.

This study aims to contribute new information to the existing literature on African-Caribbean religions in the context of migration,[1] Caribbean immigration to Canada and critical perspectives on African Diasporic identities. It is concerned with the ways in which practitioners of the Spiritual Baptist religion, an African-Caribbean tradition that originated in St. Vincent and Trinidad, have negotiated their experiences of migration as well as the ways in which these migratory experiences have affected the formation of the religion in a Canadian context. The vast majority of these practitioners are black Caribbean immigrants who emigrated between 1965 and 1980, the period of greatest Caribbean immigration to Canada in the twentieth century. Over 90 percent of Toronto Spiritual Baptists are women, a significant proportion of whom have been employed in paid domestic service.

The study documents the emergence of the Spiritual Baptist religion over a thirty-year period in Toronto from 1975, the approximate date of the establishment of the first Spiritual Baptist churches, to the present-day, early twenty-first century. It pays particular attention to the ways in which the religion's worldview, rooted in an African-Caribbean cosmos, has shaped Spiritual Baptists' experiences of living in Toronto. Of particular concern here are Spiritual Baptists' perceptions and experiences of race and racism in their daily lives, especially with regards to employment. A focal point of this inquiry concerns Spiritual Baptist women's contradictory experiences of motherhood. On the one hand, as paid domestic workers, their mothering work is devalued. This devaluation is supported not only by exploitative employment practices but, in part, by the perpetuation of ideological images of black womanhood that have their basis in the racial iconography of slavery in the Americas. On the other hand, in their role as "mothers of the church," these women have created a self-defined and empowering identity. For some women, this identity forms the basis of wider activist involvement in the black community in Toronto.

The history of Spiritual Baptists in Toronto is an oral history, existing in the memories and stories of the practitioners as well as in the oral traditions of the church in song, prayer, testimony, and sermon. In addition, practitioners often relayed their stories in patois or Creole, using a variety of rhetorical strategies, including humour and storytelling. Their narratives often switched temporally between past and present occurrences and future possibilities. As such, a crucial component of the study concerns the development of appropriate theoretical and methodological perspectives that are sensitive to orality and its intersection with literary modes of expression. Thus a combination of qualitative research methods was employed. These include critical ethnography, conversational interviews that often overlapped with storytelling, and testimonial forms of oratory as well as participant-observation at churches in Toronto and Trinidad. Epistemological and ethical questions concerning the participation of "insiders" in qualitative research are also addressed in this discussion of critical approaches to research on Diasporic African communities.

The book's main themes necessitate the articulation of a theoretical and methodological framework appropriate to the discussion of the Spiritual Baptist Church as an African Diasporic religion. The Spiritual Baptist Church is usually characterized in the literature on religious experiences of Africans in the Americas as a specifically Caribbean religious phenomenon (Glazier 1991; Simpson 1980: 141; Houk 1995). Like Zane's study of a related tradition, the Converted, in St. Vincent and Brooklyn (1999), I have had to rethink the geographic, historical, and cultural context of the Spiritual Baptist Church in Canada and the Caribbean region utilizing a framework that allowed for discussion and analysis of religious and life experiences that simultaneously straddled "here" (Canada) and "there" (the Caribbean). For example, in the testimonies with which this chapter began, Archbishop Dickson, Sister Asha, and Mother Sylvia all invoked the image of journeying between the Caribbean and Canada. It is in this tension between "here" and "there"—this liminal, border-crossing state that Latina theorist Gloria Anzaldúa points to in her thesis of *la frontera* or the "borderlands"(1987) as a fertile grounding for a critical consciousness specific for the Americas—that this study is situated.

The language of "diaspora" and "diasporic" enables a discussion of community and identity forms that transcend national boundaries (Clifford 1994). The African Diaspora is characterized by movement and fluidity of identities, ideas, and people who have a connection through lived experience and/or memory of a homeland. By "movement," I am referring to several linked historical and contemporary experiences. "Movement" includes forced migration of Africans via the Middle Passage of the Atlantic slave trade as well as travel between different regions, countries, and territories in the Americas, both historically and in contemporary times. "Movement" also includes contemporary twentieth-century migration to metropolitan countries such as the United States, Canada, England, and other Western European nations. Last, in addition to these spatial transitions, "movement" also includes temporal changes between past and present experiences. The fluidity to which I refer concerns the identity categories that reflect the multiple ethnic, racial, and religious histories of the various African peoples who were brought to the Americas through the Atlantic slave trade. It also refers to the subsequent interactions of Africans with other peoples and cultures, including Native American, European, and

Asian, under the conditions of enslavement, indentureship, colonialism, and neo-colonialism. The result is African Diasporic cultures that are marked by a tremendous hybridity in both their content and approach to the creation of cultural and religious forms.

Thus it was necessary to undertake with equal intensity, as the discussion of Spiritual Baptist experiences in Toronto shows, a project of articulation—best described as a process of "discerning"—an appropriate framework of analysis. I use the term "discerning" in much the same fashion as Henry Louis Gates Jr. does in describing the process of developing a critical theory particular to African-American literature (1988). Gates notes that, because the methods of critical inquiry were indigenous to African-Caribbean and Diasporic African religious and cultural experiences, the theoretical project for the academic researcher is therefore not one of "invention" (is it ever?) but rather one of "discernment." This distinction acknowledges the creativity and unique critical stance of the communities and cultures in question. They are positioned, from this perspective, as conscious producers of knowledge rather than objects of investigation.

I also considered how my multiple social locations inform the discerning of the theoretical and methodological perspectives used to discuss the experiences of Spiritual Baptists in Toronto. Included are my locations: as an insider of overlapping Caribbean communities in Toronto, a family member and friend of people who identify as Spiritual Baptists (though I myself am not a practitioner), and a woman of African-Caribbean descent who emigrated to Canada as a child in the early 1970s (arguably the period of heaviest Caribbean immigration to Canada, which coincided with the articulation and practice of multiculturalism as a federal program of nation-building and national identity formation).

In the early stages of my research on the Spiritual Baptist Church, I presented myself as someone who was an academician-in-training, a researcher whose primary reason for being in the church was to conduct research for a doctoral dissertation. It quickly became apparent to me, however, that my multiple identities were all implicated through the interactions I had with members of the church who related to me on both of the aforementioned bases. In many instances, these identities mediated the ways in which they addressed me as a "researcher" and a "scholar."

My multiple identities were often brought together when church members positioned me as a "young" (in relation to the women who were mostly in my mother's age group) woman whose path to becoming a Spiritual

Baptist was one that took the circuitous route through the academy. On several occasions, including interviews with members, I was often approached as a church insider or member. I was variously seen by church members as a candidate for baptism (the initiatory rite of passage to becoming a Spiritual Baptist), a young woman in the church who was presumed already baptized, and as a church sister and member of the congregation, regardless of my baptismal status.

What I initially considered as cases of "mistaken identity," which prompted me to make frequent mention of my status as a researcher, were not mistakes on the part of members of the church community. I came to understand them as their positioning and accepting me in the wider church community. Though I was prepared for, and open to, input from members of the church community with whom I interacted, I was, initially, taken aback at being identified in ways I had not purposefully chosen to be identified and which I perceived as (possibly) counteractive to the aims of my research as an academician-in-training.

In the following research journal excerpt, I describe an instance in which one of the elder women in the church queries me about baptism:

July 18, 1995, 10:45 p.m.

Just now (about 10 minutes ago), the bus stopped near the church. I could see the sisters and mothers outside the church. Two got on the bus. Mother Laura and Mother Ruth. I will be speaking with Mother Ruth next week. She was to call me today and here it is that I buck up on her in the bus. She said she'd call me next week when she's on nights and then I can come down and see her before her 10:00 p.m. shift. There is a novena at the church tonight. Next Tuesday is the "Feeding of the Poor." ...

Mother Laura and Mother Ruth and I got off at the subway station. We took the train northbound after taking the escalator down to the platform. Sister R suggested it to ease Mother Laura's way.

Mother Laura asked me if school was over. I said, yes. She asked me if I had a job. I said, yes, and that I was glad to have it 'cause I know there are plenty who don't have one. She agreed and said that her grandson was back from university and working for the summer.

Both women got off at Eglinton West Station. Before they got off there was discussion of baptism. Mother Laura asked me: "You will baptize next year? When you goin' to baptize?" I said that it was something that I felt you had to have a calling to do and that it was a serious matter. Mother Ruth nodded and said yes, don't let people force you. They will say if things going wrong that you have to baptize but don't let them force you. You will feel a strong calling, she said. Mother Laura said that she took her time, too. Mother Ruth said that she had had her own messages through dreams that she didn't share with anyone but which told her that it was time. I wondered what they would have said about my recent dreams.

I was concerned that being perceived as a new church member or "baptismal candidate" would alter my research. This experience of recognition on the part of the church members triggered powerful memories of childhood religious, familial, and educational-based experiences of my own immigration to Canada. They came rushing to the forefront of my consciousness as I sang hymns and songs in church, conducted interviews, or travelled familiar bus routes in the central west area of Toronto to visit church members in their homes to conduct interviews. This was the area of the city where I had first lived in the early 1970s. As such it had a resonance of "home."

July 27, 1995

Mother Ruth lives in the Toronto central west area. I took the Keele bus south from York University, got off and walked in to the [house] number. It is a hot, hot day. I came home from my secretarial job at York, changed my clothes and prepared for my interview.... I dropped my clothes off at the cleaners at the mall, bought a falafel for my dinner and then waited for the bus. It came in 5 minutes. The driver was a middle aged, black, Caribbean man from Jamaica. He asked me how I was doing. I told him that I was fine and inquired of his well being. He said he was "not as good as me." I ate my falafel on the bus trip down. I felt sick and queasy as I tend to whenever I try to simultaneously read and ride in a bus, train or car. By the time the bus got to my stop I was nauseated with a pounding headache. I had flashbacks to my first bus trips when I came to Canada; the sweltering heat of the summers of 1973, 1974 and 1975 were spent in a nearby neighbourhood.... On Mother Ruth's street I saw a metal screen door with a dog on it. Looked like a Labrador Retriever or Setter. Some type of long-haired beautiful dog with ears that always reminded me of the just loosed-out plaits of some girls I knew as a young child. The dog transported me to our first home in Toronto, which had the identical screen door on the side entrance of the house that led out to the driveway. As kids, we used to use that entrance all the time until we were barred from it when the tenant, a young, Caribbean man, moved in, in 1974....

I took off my shoes and sighed. I still felt dizzy and nauseated and my head ached from my journey. [Mother Ruth] offered me a drink and I accepted. It was

iced tea. She offered cake and I also accepted it. I moved from her large L-shaped
beige sofa to the dining room table.

The sofa, she explained, was to be given to Goodwill. They had come to collect
it and it couldn't fit through the door. So they left it. The Goodwill collectors
explained that the sofa had probably been moved in when there was less stuff in the
apartment. The wall unit with pictures and bric-a-brac was in the way. We talked
about ways of getting rid of it including her suggestion of getting someone with a
saw to cut it in bits in the apartment that could then be easily removed. I suggested
that she unpack her wall unit and move it. She said it was too much trouble.

The significance of the memories lay in understanding the basis of a
critical perspective that was rooted in the intersection of my childhood
experiences of migration and immersion in the worldview and value system
of African-Caribbean communities as well as those of the dominant European-Canadian society primarily through the educational system.

In the following excerpt, from an interview with Mother Patricia, conducted in Toronto in the summer of 1995, we discuss the research process.
Mother Patricia positions my research process as linked to a shared cultural
history, or "African heritage," as she terms it, from which the Spiritual Baptist Church also emerged. This discussion was initiated by Mother Patricia
asking me, "How far again you think you have to go with this?" with regards
to the completion of the research for the study:

CBD: I've come to realize that the more I know in terms of the different services and the more I talk to people, the more I see. You know?
Honestly, the more I know, the more I see and feel, the more I think every
week. I hear more things. Stuff that I didn't even hear before and it
kinda triggers off...

MP: So, it come like, you come a long way now?

CBD: Yeah. I feel so. I feel so. Just things like the different colours—

MP: Mmmmhmmm.

CBD: —that they use.

MP: And then now, you more understanding now?

CBD: Yeah! Yeah! Because I really felt like I—I had the responsibility
to make sure that what I was representing in my work was as for real as
possible, you know? That I couldn't just come in and do like a "drive by."
You know?

MP: [laughter]

CBD: I just quickly kinda pass through—

MP: Oh, yes!

CBD: —or something like that. That it wouldn't be fair for one thing and it wouldn't even be the responsible kinda thing to do. That's what I felt first up. Like, I really just had to—um, take the humble position and just sit back and observe and listen as much as possible. And I feel really grateful that people have opened their lives as much as they have to me and made it possible for me to be here and allowed me to come into a really sacred space, a space of fellowship and worship and be a part of that experience. And so, that's how I feel about it. And in a sense, I feel also like just, um, it's like I'm learning things about myself, as well. Because, even though, I've been just as a researcher and I'm doing my thesis and I'm doing my Ph.D. and so on ... but you can never be outside of something totally.

MP: No.

CBD: You know what I mean? And especially something like this.

MP: Yes. It's—it's already in your roots no matter how you take it!

CBD: Exactly! [laughter]

MP: Because we—we are from African heritage. So it is part of your roots. You know, as you say, you haven't baptize or mourn but that is not your path. You path is from your roots.

CBD: Exactly.

MP: So you are part of it.

This discussion with Mother Patricia points to a notion of research ethics that is shaped not only out of respect for the dignity and subjectivity of the people with whom one is working, but also is an extension of similar attention toward the self as a member of that community as well.

THE RESEARCH SETTING

Permission was granted from the two churches in which I conducted my research. They included a downtown church, whose male leader, Archbishop Dickson, claims to have established the first Spiritual Baptist Church in Canada and another church led by a female leader, Mother Yvonne, located in suburban Toronto with ties to the downtown church. Through familial contacts, I had known Archbishop Dickson for a number of years prior to conducting the research. In the spring of 1994, he introduced me to Mother Yvonne, the leader of the suburban church. I approached the leaders of both churches with my proposed project, to study and document the experiences of Spiritual Baptists in Toronto. They, in turn, discussed the matter with others who held leadership positions in their churches and I was granted permission to do the study.

I approached individual church members with requests for interviews. Some subsequently suggested other church members. While anonymity was discussed with all of the people whom I interviewed, some insisted on using their "real names." The reasoning was invariably based on wanting to "stand by their words" especially as the subject matter was religious and/or spiritual in focus. This perception challenged the conventional social science model of research with which I started the research.

It was clear from this response that these interviews were regarded by almost all of the seventeen people I interviewed as something other than information-gathering sessions; these were regarded as testimonies. My interview experiences included not only the "talk" but also the recitation of Bible passages and singing of songs, wedding album viewing, shared meals, and admiration of one woman's newborn grand-daughter. In several instances, I was asked advice concerning school-related issues for some women themselves or their children. On numerous occasions, I also saw church members in non-church spaces such as public transit buses and trains and a black hairdresser's salon. All of these experiences, which were unplanned, in the context of the research design nevertheless exerted control over the form and content of the interviews. This represented a form of authorial control exercised through orality and the "intentionality" (Beverley 1992) of the speaker.

Sitting in a bus driving on highways connecting Ontario and the province of Quebec, Mother Yvonne and I had our first of many conversations about ethnographic research. On this particular bus trip in the spring of 1994, I was accompanying Spiritual Baptist members from both Mother Yvonne's and Archbishop Dickson's churches on a pilgrimage to Sainte Anne de Beaupré in Quebec. Mother Yvonne was to become one of the people with whom I interacted the most, sharing her knowledge of Spiritual Baptist history in Toronto and the Caribbean and inviting me to Trinidad to "see," as she put it, "another side of the work," referring to the Orisha tradition.

It is significant to note, however, that both church leaders agreed to let me do participant-observation research in their churches because they perceived the research as meeting their needs. These included expressed goals of documenting Spiritual Baptist church history and the experiences of Spiritual Baptists in Toronto for future generations and to further concretely defined goals connected to community development that extended beyond the boundaries of the immediate church community. Thus the research process and themes emerged from a consultative process.

In the following, Archbishop Dickson introduces me to the congregation on my second visit to the church on September 29, 1992. In his introduction, the archbishop links my presence in the church as a researcher to getting "established," interpreted here as represented in the written record of Canadian history and thereby furthering the aims of establishing a nursing home for black people:

> I was telling my sister in the back [the archbishop is referring to me here], the fruits of the church is the young people. We were having an interview because they are going to make a book and I want the Spiritual Baptist to be established in the book because our aim and our goal is to build … is to make sure before my eyes are closed, a home is built called St. Ann's Home for the Aged to shelter the old people in our town.
>
> Watch the world today, you will find a lot of us in Canada in years, but you're not going to find a lot of black people in nursing home, in hospitals and so forth. What happens when we reach to that stage? Our culture, our culture and food, our religion, our way of worship would be taken away from us if we are not watchful and careful.
>
> Let us be wise, let us stand in arms and fear not. Let us commune with our God from within. Let us hold on to the vine, the vine of Almighty God. May God bless you. May God give you peace. May God encourage you to act. May God show you more vision of the vine and make that vine more precise in your life that you will begin to win more souls for the soon coming kingdom of Almighty God.

While my field research was ostensibly based in two churches, as it turned out, I was introduced to a network of churches and prayer groups that were located throughout the city of Toronto in both downtown and suburban locations. Most of these churches were in some way connected to either Mother Yvonne's or Archbishop Dickson's churches. In some cases, leaders were former members of both churches who had gone on to establish their own churches or were linked through attendance and participation in church visitations.

The research was carried out through attending services and other church-sponsored social and fund-raising functions such as dinners, dances, and concerts, and interviewing the members of two Spiritual Baptist churches in Toronto, as well as leaders of two other churches in Movant and Chaguanas, Trinidad. I spoke with, by my estimation, well over 100 Spiritual Baptist men and women in Toronto and Trinidad. However, the material from which this study is largely constructed is the recorded and transcribed extensive interviews with sixteen Spiritual Baptists (five men and eight women in Toronto; two women and one man in Trinidad) and one male Orisha leader in Trinidad. I also attended a pilgrimage of a Toronto Spiritual Baptist church leader, Queen Mother Bishop Yvonne, to Trinidad in late August and early September 1995, during which time the interviews in Trinidad were conducted. My research began in September 1992 with the bulk of the field research taking place between that time and the fall of 1996. Further field research was conducted in Toronto in intervening years, culminating in 2004.

In the time following the primary period of fieldwork, I have attended major church functions and reviewed the extensive research material, including interview transcripts, with church members. This time has also been punctuated by telephone calls from interviewees with additional recollections of incidents that happened following my recorded conversations and interviews. In a sense, I have not left the "research field" as there are many quadrants of that field that continue to overlap and intersect with my "real life." These issues, including the ethics of doing "insider research," are discussed substantively throughout the book.

Storytelling, Memory, and Writing

When I entered a Spiritual Baptist church for the first time in September 1992, I had no words, it seemed, to describe, transform, sing, or pray that experience. *I felt like an outsider at the beginning of the service. For one moment, however, I felt like one of the cells of energy* (Journal, September 27, 1992). All that I had learned in the academy, my careful absorption and repetition of those words and theories punctuated by stops and starts, had not fully prepared me to speak "here" or about "here." I found myself in the paradoxical position of speaking and not recognizing my own words; of speaking and feeling betrayed by the implied meanings of the words; of speaking and being tongue-tied by my hybridity of language and experience.

I was speechless until I began the process of recalling and remembering the fragments of myself that had been marginalized through a process of cultural amputation. A significant aspect of the research process of this study involved finding a voice and language with which to tell and write the story of the Spiritual Baptist Church in Toronto. I was tongue-tied and silenced, not by the stories of the Spiritual Baptist women and men, but by my memories and experiences of particular forms of academic voice that actively negate the experiences of African and other colonized people as self-conscious and creative subjects who can speak their own realities in critical, authentic language that has emerged from their lived experiences and history. I silenced myself and erased every word as "too personal," "too informal," "too emotional," and "not scholarly enough." Feminist scholars such as Susan Farrell (1992) and Lorraine Code (1991) critique the predominant scientific mode of analysis and its valuation of objectivity that informs quantitative sociological analysis as one of the ways in which women's knowledge and experiences are obscured. Farrell also notes that social science research has not been particularly attentive to diverse experiences on the basis of "class, race-ethnicity, sexuality, geographical location; and other variables as well as gender" (58). Like Smith (1988), Farrell stresses the importance of women's "everyday lives" as the locus of "different knowledge and understandings" than those of men (59). However, she points to essentialist tendencies in feminist theorizing and research in which "the experience of white, middle-class, heterosexual, Euro-American women has served as a basis to generalize about the experience of WOMAN" (60). Here Farrell like Spelman (1988) critiques essentialist feminist theorizing in calling for specific analyses of women's diverse experiences in the creation of "inclusive knowledge" (Farrell 1992: 60).

Herb Green, a gay African-American man, in describing his experiences of trying to incorporate his Bahamian childhood in post-colonial critique in the U.S. academy echoes my sentiments concerning the importance of calling into question the relationship of researchers' identities with the subject matter at hand:

> While thinking more and more about what I hoped to achieve via the academy, I constantly examined how the multiple and ostensibly conflicting identities that I occupy informed and helped shape the kinds of academic writing that I produced or desired to produce. I make a distinction

between what I "produce" and what I "desire to produce" because of the academy's false distinction between subjectivity and analysis. For instance, when I try to talk about my interpretation of post-colonial theory and literature in relation to my experience growing-up for the first thirteen years of my life in the Bahamas, I have been told that I am being "anti-intellectual," that I am "privileging my nativism," and that I need to stick to the assigned text. Somehow, the assumption is that I just don't get it. Again, I am the problem. (1996: 255)

Green's comments are particularly relevant for this discussion for his experiences of migration mirror mine as well as his claim for a Caribbean childhood (in the many ways that this identity can be defined) as a valuable critical standpoint for post-colonial studies. They were excerpted from an article written while he was a doctoral candidate in Ethnic Studies at the University of California at Berkeley, co-taught a university course on comparative lesbian and gay ethnic identities in the United States at the same institution, and taught in an academic outreach program for "under-represented minority" junior high school and adolescent students (304). Like myself, Green is engaged in scholarship and teaching that address his multiple identities. The search led to an acceptance of my own voice which encodes my own personal Black Atlantic history[2] of traveling from England to Antigua and then to Canada. This search necessitated a remembrance and embracing of the child I was, am, and became through the transatlantic Middle Passage in the ship's belly, through telling the story.

Historian Elsa Barkley Brown in her essay "Piecing Blocks: Identities" discusses a similar search for a "historiographical tradition" that would allow her to record African-American experiences in a way that was recognizable to the communities themselves (1993: 91). Brown notes that it was through her mother that she learned "the importance of preserving the historical record of the community as the people within it understood it" (91). Her search for a way of writing and teaching history that preserved the subjectivity of black people in a way that was recognizable to the people themselves was initiated by the contradiction she encountered in graduate school when she read books about the African-American community that contradicted what she knew about the lives of people personally as well as "the historical documents my mother had daily laid before me, her record of people's speeches, ideas, and actions" (91).

THE STUDY AS A "TALKING BOOK"

This study is multi-voiced in its construction, reflecting the contrapuntal, polyphonal, double-voiced articulation that characterizes orality in African Diasporic cultures. Literary critic Henry Louis Gates Jr., in his study *The Signifying Monkey*, points to the essentially double-voiced character of West African oral expressions and their influence on modes of expression, both oral and literary, among New World African cultures (1988). Examples from African-American oral traditions include the call and response of black church choirs and the contrapuntal interplay of instruments in a jazz ensemble. Gates suggests that the African-American literary tradition is based on a narrative form that has its basis in oral expression: the slave narrative (1987). Slave narratives, which detailed the experiences of those who had escaped or were manumitted from slavery, often by their own means, were often narrated by the formerly enslaved and then transcribed into written documents. There are important exceptions such as the slave narratives of Olaudah Equiano and Frederick Douglass that were penned by these men, one at the close of the eighteenth century in England and the other in mid-nineteenth-century United States. However, the majority of slave narratives started as oral accounts of enslavement told by formerly enslaved persons, frequently on the anti-slavery circuit of public speaking engagements.

Gates suggests that the slave narrative straddles both the oral and the literary and that this tension between the spoken and the written characterizes African-American literary tradition (1987). The "speakerly text" or the "Talking Book" is the result. Literally, this term refers to a book in which the narrative is constructed through rhetorical forms that have their basis in the oral cultures of African-Americans. The "speakerly text" is evident in the groundbreaking work of Zora Neale Hurston, anthropologist, folklorist, playwright, and performer. Contemporary authors such as Alice Walker and Toni Morrison also reflect this tradition of the "speakerly text" in their fictional writings.

In a Caribbean literary context, scholars such as Edward Kamau Brathwaite (1984), Honor Ford-Smith (1987), and Carolyn Cooper (1993) have pointed to the importance of orality in Caribbean cultures as the locus of self-defined critical perspectives emerging from Caribbean people's experiences. These perspectives are particularly important in the context of the imposition of European languages such as English, Dutch, French, and Spanish, which were imposed during colonial regimes on Caribbean inhabitants, including enslaved Africans. Afua P. Cooper, a black Canadian poet and historian of Jamaican heritage, asserts the importance of orality in the construction of a critical consciousness in the title of her poem "Memories Have Tongue" (1992).

Brathwaite points to the way the colonial context in which the English language was taught in schools produced a focus on experiences external to Caribbean realities and firmly set in England. As a result, the language to describe Caribbean experiences was not readily available (1984: 8). However, as Brathwaite goes on to further discuss, Caribbean people have created an oral mode of expression, "nation language" (5), which "more closely and intimately approaches our experience" (12). Nation language, "the submerged area of the dialect which is much more closely allied to the African aspect of experience in the Caribbean," is particularly expressive and able to provide critical perspectives that emerge from within Caribbean people's experiences (13). Nation language encompasses Caribbean poetry and music as well as jazz and what Brathwaite calls "traditional (ancestral/oral)" influences that include ring games, tea-meeting speeches, and yard theatres, as well as religious traditions such as Shango and Spiritual Baptist services (48).

What I have sought to do in the writing of this study is to employ analytical and narrative strategies that emerge out of nation language as expressed in several linked contexts. Thus my aim, in this regard, parallels Gates's in his exploration of "the relation of the black vernacular tradition to the Afro-American literary tradition" (1988: xix). These linked contexts include the nation language of the Spiritual Baptist Church, which includes the oral expressions involved in ritual and worship such as singing, praying, preaching, testifying, and witnessing. Many of the people I interviewed and spoke with either speak Creole or use Creole expressions along with English, as I do myself. My familiarity with and use of Creole is indicative of my position, straddling as it does usage of European-Canadian, African-American, African-Canadian, and Anglo-Caribbean (specifically Antiguan) modes of expression, reflecting my experiences of migration as well as my academic training within the academy.

The experiences of Spiritual Baptists in Toronto were recorded orally in stories and recollections. I was faced with the task of transforming an oral record into a literary one in the form of a book. This project, aside from the mechanical concerns of transcription of sermons and interviews and other oral forms into written text, also posed the problem of what can only be described as a "lack of transference" of meaning between the orality of nation language and the literary form of a book. To be more explicit, what Brathwaite describes as the "characteristics of our nation language" (1984: 17) are not immediately compatible with conventional forms of an academic exposition or communication.

Nation language is characterized by two traits that are firmly rooted in orality and multi-logic communication. First, nation language emerges from the oral tradition, which is located in the spoken word. The very sounding or "noise" of its expression is a part of the meaning (17). Thus when written, the sounding as well as part of the meaning is lost (17). Second, nation language is a part of what Brathwaite calls a "total expression" (18). That is to say that it exists in communication between a "noise maker" and an audience that is responsive (18). This total expression emerged

> because people be in the open air, because people live in conditions of poverty ('unhouselled') because they come from a historical experience where they had to rely on their very breath rather than on paraphernalia like books and museums and machines. They had to depend on immanence, the power within themselves, rather than the technology outside themselves. (19)

My experiences of Spiritual Baptist services in Toronto and Trinidad, and conversations and interviews with church members, were characterized by both their rootedness in oral tradition and by a "total expression." In these various contexts, the complementary roles of "noise maker" and "audience" were dually played by myself and the person(s) with whom I was interacting.

And here was my dilemma. The conventional mode of expression and discourse in the modern academy privileges writing and reading as solitary expressions. How then could I write an ethnography that reflected, in its construction and mode of expression, this fundamentally oral and multi-logic character of nation language that characterized the oral mode of transmission of information about the church? Given that my study was the first of its kind about the Spiritual Baptist Church in Toronto, this issue was further compounded by the fact that indeed, there were scant written accounts about the community from which I could draw. I had, in fact, no other records on which to rely save those that were orally transmitted in the context of church services and interviews. I felt caught in a theoretical and methodological conundrum. I did not want to misrepresent or lose the richness of the meaning conveyed in those oral transmissions of Spiritual

Baptist experiences. Yet I was faced with having to write an ethnography that is, fundamentally, a literary mode of expression.

What seemed to me at the time to be an insurmountable problem was eventually addressed through an attempt to represent, in written form, the multiple strands of ideas expressed by the Spiritual Baptists. In other words, this book is constructed, drawing on Gates's theoretical characterization, using the trope of the "Talking Book" (1988: xxv) in which the "noise" of the various "noise makers" are represented. The "Talking Book," according to Gates, represents the double-voiced character of the black tradition. The Talking Book trope points to "double-voiced texts that talk to other texts" (xxv).

The multiple voices represented in the book include the people whom I interviewed, the content of worship such as songs and prayers, and my own multi-voiced expressions about my research experiences represented in my journals and notes, much of which was recorded in both Canadian English and Creole, reflecting my Antiguan roots and the influence of Jamaican patois (I grew up in community with Jamaican youths in Toronto).

I was then faced with the task of representing Caribbean Creole, an oral language in written form. Honor Ford-Smith faced a similar dilemma in compiling the autobiographical narratives in *Lionheart Gal: Lifestories of Jamaican Women* (1987). Like Ford-Smith, I use spellings that approximated the pronunciation of words in Caribbean Creole and Caribbean English while punctuating the speech. Most of the words are "visually recognizable" *vis à vis* English words in their representation on the page. The other alternative would have been to focus exclusively on the sounding of the word as Carolyn Cooper does in *Noises in the Blood* (1993). I have incorporated Cooper's critique in my representation while still producing a text that is recognizable. In this way, the text straddles both oral and written expression in its representation.

The solution to my dilemma of writing a book based in large part on sources from an oral tradition lay in allowing for multi-voiced expressions on salient themes of the study. Thus the book chapters are constructed to include text from a number of different sources.

Interviews are used throughout the study, not to provide justification for my own pronouncements, but as critical analytical voices, speaking on key themes. In fact, in an attempt to subvert the tendency to cite short excerpts from interviews as a way of justifying pronouncement, I frequently integrate sections from the interviews that more accurately reflect the dialogic context in which the ideas emerged. Michael W. Harris in writing a history of gospel blues, a form of African-American sacred music, used a similar approach to convey the dialogic context in which the ideas were developed in conversation with participants in his study:

> I have used speech and written sources without regard for their expression of ideas. In doing so, I have rejected the urge to employ the journalistic practice of editing speech into prose. While unedited speech tends to read often as muddled ideas, there is much to argue for the untidiness of spoken thought. For example, the pause or the utterance of several "ah's" as one works through an idea can be read as important nuances; to delete them simply for the purpose of crafting a more pithy statement is to tamper with the subtext of *how* one puts her thoughts into words. (Harris 1992: xxii)

In addition to the interviews themselves, there are several other important documentary sources. These include the "research journal" I kept during the research process that began in September 1992, as well as my own "personal journal," which I started as a child in October 1974, eighteen months after emigrating to Canada, having lived first in England and then Antigua. This journal started as my attempt as a child to make sense of what I perceived as my rapidly changing reality, which had seen me living in three different countries—England, Antigua, and Canada—by the age of seven. Little did I know when I started this journal all those years ago that it would play a crucial role in documenting the development of my own critical consciousness during the time in which I was acutely aware of my newness to Canadian society. During the research process, I attempted to keep these two journals separate but after a while I found that I was writing about the "ethnography" in my "real life" as much as I was addressing my "real life" in the "ethnography."

In addition to these diaries, a collection of letters that my grandmother, Dorothy Sebastian Prince, wrote to me over an eighteen-year period from October 1976 until her death in December 1994 form another important voice in the study. The elder voice of the grandmother was particularly important for me in influencing my critical perspective on issues of identity, migration, and community, which this study addresses. My grandmother's discussion of these issues was epistolary, as these ideas were expressed in her letters to me over the years.

This approach is similar to the one used by educational studies scholar Susan Weil (1996). Weil notes that in writing her dissertation in 1989, she "approached the thesis as a dynamic interplay of multiple voices which jointly constituted the final dissertation" (227). These included Weil's three critical voices as "post-positivist researcher" (227), a second voice that captured her "actively reflexive side" (227), and a "field diary voice." These three voices were "woven" together with those of the participants in the study in a dialogic form (229–230).

This exposition on the multiple voices included in the study, however, does not address the second characteristic of nation language, which is the "total expression." In order to approximate the "total expression" that necessitates acknowledged communication between noise-makers and audience, I have attempted to represent the voices of various speakers in a way that approximates their pronunciation of words by using spelling of words derived from the "sounding" of the word rather than its grammatical English representation. In addition, I invite the reader to read the words of various speakers out loud, thereby creating a context in which there is both audience and noise-maker, although the two are embodied in the single body as reader/speaker/listener. It is hoped that this practice can represent, if only momentarily, the "live" context of oral expression.

TRAVESSAO

With their narrative voices constantly shifting from "here" to "there"—from the Caribbean to Toronto, from past to present, from the spirit world to the material, from "spiritual" to "carnal"—the telling of the story of the Spiritual Baptist Church in Toronto demands that the teller (and the listener) be simultaneously located in several spaces. The stories demand a critic who at once speaks back and listens and moves through discontinuous physical and psychic locations both "here" and "there." They demand a flexibility of speaking and listening that simultaneously witness events in the past and present. The critical stance also necessitates the ability to navigate discontinuous physical locations both spiritually and carnally, including the tracts[3] of mourners, stories of immigration referencing "home" there, in the Caribbean, and "home" here, in Canada.

The *travessao* transgresses barriers between dualistic pairs such as past and present; black and white; listener and speaker. The *travessao* is an inhabitant of the borderlands, the territory Gloria Anzaldúa points to as *la frontera* (1987). The *travessao* is an expression of what Anzaldúa calls *"la conciencia de la mestiza,"* literally "mestiza consciousness," which she describes as a third, intermediary space that embraces contradictions (2003). In Anzaldúa, *la conciencia de la mestiza* was born out of her life as a Latina in the United States facing contradictions of "race," colour, language, and nation (2003). In the following excerpt from a conversation between Queen Mother Ruby and myself in Movant, Trinidad (August 29, 1995), she discusses the figure of the *travessao*, noting its cosmopolitan and mixed nature enabling travel to many nations. While the terminology is different than that used by Anzaldúa, the meaning of "mestiza" and "cosmopolitan" as used by both Anzaldúa and Mother Ruby is synonymous:

> CBD: And what does it mean to be a traverser? We talked about that. Earlier today when we were looking at some of the pictures, you were saying that you were a traverser.
>
> QMR: A *travessao*?
>
> CBD: *Travessao.*
>
> QMR: Well that is when they many nations now.
>
> CBD: Oh, I see.
>
> QMR: You in everyting.
>
> CBD: You're in everything.
>
> QMR: Yes. And sometimes … sometimes, they claim, the people who would do wickedness and they want to find you, they can't find you.
>
> CBD: Uh huh.
>
> QMR: [laughter. CBD joins in] So now it come like if somebody looking for you and even though you were safe and when dey come here, dey ain' see you. They want to know wey gone. Becor dey know you was here.
>
> CBD: Mmmhmmm.
>
> QMR: You know?
>
> CBD: So that's what *travessao*—
>
> QMR: *Travessao.*
>
> CBD: *Travessao.*
>
> QMR: Yes.
>
> CBD: *Travessao.* Hmmm? What language is that word, *travessao*?
>
> QMR: Well they just mainly cosmo—wha' we say, cosmopolitan.
>
> CBD: Cosmopolitan. Okay.

QMR: [Mother Ruby coughs]

CBD: And are there many *travessao* or—?

QMR: Yes. It have many um, spiritual people … well some a' dem wouldn' *travessao*, they say, "mixed nations."

CBD: Mixed nations. I see. I see. So, even though, you are like like spiritually African, you can still be …

QMR: You're Indian. You could be still Chinee.

CBD: I see.

QMR: You understan'?

CBD: I understand.

QMR: Mmmhmm. So in every country, you could be fin' dere.

CBD: I see.

QMR: But is only who would know you would be able to fin' you out.

CBD: Right. I see.

QMR: Because it come … let us say, I know you and maybe if I leave here now and go out from where you may dress up … serve ting dat I wouldn' make you out.

CBD: Mmmhmm. Mmmhmm.

QMR: You understan'?

CBD: Yeah.

QMR: But with you now, you will … "Dis ain't Mother Ruby?"

CBD: [laughs]

QMR: You know?

CBD: Mmmhmm.

QMR: Becor' through curiosity, you will "Come, ain't your name is Mother Ruby?" Ah say, "Well, yes."

CBD: Mmmhmm.

QMR: "But you ain' remember me?"

CBD: Mmmhmm.

QMR: Ah say, "No."

CBD: Mmmhmm.

QMR: "Aah, is Carol."

CBD: Mmmhmm.

QMR: We goin' to greet! Because you know me and I know you!

CBD: I see.

QMR: So when we leave dere now, you go on 'bout your business and I gone 'bout mine.

In the following excerpt, Mother Yvonne, a church leader in Toronto, relates her experience of being a "nation mother" as a *travessao* experience precisely because of the notion of "mixed nations." She also makes connections between the malleable, flexible nature of the *travessao* and my research on the Spiritual Baptist Church as an experience of re-connection and "re-memory" as noted earlier by Carole Boyce Davies.

CBD: What is that? What is a traverser?

MY: Okay, um …

CBD: I have my own understanding but I want to hear from you.

MY: It's on the Orisha. Um … it means that you would be in all different aspects of the spiritual world.

CBD: Oh.

MY: Okay. Like what you are doing it is … it may be a personal thing. But there is a—there is a spiritual drive behind it.

CBD: Mmmmhmmm.

MY: You wanna know more. You're searching for more.

CBD: Mmmmmhmmm.

MY: It is your background. Something inside of you is telling you—that I need to know more of me. I need to know more of what I come from.

CBD: Mmmmhmmm.

MY: I need to know more of where I'm going. I need to know my—my people.

CBD: Yes …

MY: You know? When we talk of versatility as like for me.

CBD: Mmmmhmmm.

MY: I'm gonna use myself again as an example.

CBD: Mmmmhmmm.

MY: I'm what they call a nation mother. I work out of India. I work the—the nation, all the nations. I was given Mother of the twelve tribes. I was given my colours to represent that. I receive it. Some people receive it in flags.

CBD: Mmmmhmmmm.

MY: I receive it in cords of twelve different colours. So, when it was thrown on my shoulders, that's like, every cord was a pound.

CBD: Mmmmhmmm.

MY: On my shoulder. Because I'm nation representing every nation, this is what we call a *travessao* of the spirit.

CBD: So you are as well? That's very big, Mother Yvonne.

MY: It is.

CBD: [laughter with MY]

MY: You know, you're anywhere. Anywhere spiritually. You could be found.

The figure of the *travessao* is identified with movement, mobility, and "versatility," to use Mother Yvonne's term. Both Mother Yvonne and Mother Ruby, who identify with *travessao* experiences, have "mixed nation" experiences in their family histories. Mother Ruby's parents emigrated from Barbados and St. Vincent while Mother Yvonne's father's family came from Grenada. Mother Yvonne herself immigrated to Canada as a young woman and frequently travels back and forth between Trinidad and other areas of the Caribbean, Canada. and the United States. In fact, I first met Mother Ruby when she was visiting Toronto in the summer of 1994.

In the following excerpt, Mother Ruby discusses the dual Caribbean origins of her family and her attendance in a variety of Christian denominations in her youth:

CBD: Now, when you were younger, before you became a Baptist, before you were baptized …

MR: Mmmhmm?

CBD: What kind of church did you go to?

MR: I was an Anglican. But I was an Anglican—but I had friends from all different churches.

CBD: I see.

MR: So if ah come to you, ah go to you Sunday … to your church … the next Sunday ah go wit somebody else and they will in turn come to me wid my church. So … when you sit down and you study dat, from my youth, I was vigilant in churches.

CBD: I see.

MR: [coughs] Ah had a cousin which is me mother aunt …

CBD: Mmmhmm.

MR: … she was going into di Salvation Army and dey have dat Salvation Army hol'ing in Charlotte Street Ground. It still dere. But ah don't know if it in same spirit.

CBD: Mmmhmm.

MR: So, I used to go there?

CBD: Mmmhmm.

MR: And, everyting dey have, ah was present.

CBD: Yes, yes.

MR: Cor me cousin was dere, you know?

CBD: Yes.

MR: Well, ah go to Gospel Hall Sunday school. Ah go to Catholic Sunday school. Ah go to—uh, Grey fire Sunday school, because ah have friends dey go into dere so dey will come wid me when I ready and dere I will go wid dem.

CBD: Mmmhmm.

MR: You know? So … I had no … partiality in churches. I will go to any church.

CBD: I see, I see. And your parents, were they both Anglican, as well?

MR: Mmmmhmmm. Yes, yes, yes. Yes, yes, yes.

CBD: I see.

MR: And they never stop me from going nowhere else where church is concerned.

CBD: I see. Now, were they from dat area from …

MR: Well, my mother was a Barbadian.

CBD: Oh, I see.

MR: And me faada was a Vincentian.

CBD: Ah, I see.

MR: So, I wasn' born in Trinidad! [laughter with CBD]. [Coughs] So sometime I does sit down and—and ask meself what ah really is.

CBD: Mmmhmm.

MR: Right? But dey were nevah—well, dat is one ting wid my parents, as long as you teach dis church business and all dese tings ...

CBD: Mmmhmm?

MR: ... dey would nevah tell you, don' go.

CBD: I see.

MR: You always heard "Ma so, so, so, so, so—"

CBD: Yeah.

MR: —she say, "Well, all right."

CBD: Yeah.

MR: So, sometime when I leave home Sunday—for Sunday mornings have service at Trinity—sometime I ain' reachin' back home until in di evening. 'Cause have dip in here wid me frien' and dis frien' here and dat frien' dere. And is so it go. You understan'? So den we wasn' prejudice of no—no religion.

CBD: I see, I see.

MR: Mmmhmm.

These women's life histories mirror the multiple migrations within the region and especially specific to Trinidad in the early decades of the twentieth century when people from smaller islands such as Grenada, Barbados, and St. Vincent migrated to Trinidad in search of work.

It was my own experience of multiple migration that prompted Mother Ruby to identify *travessao* experiences with my research recounted here in an excerpt from my journal. Here I describe our first meeting in the summer of 1994 when Mother Ruby visited Toronto:

July 11, 1994

[Mother Yvonne] introduced me to Mother Ruby. She said this is Carol, Carol Duncan.... I stretched out my hand and shook Mother Ruby's. It was warm. She said ... "She has a knowing face." Mother Drakes told Mother Ruby that I was doing my PhD and wanted to document what is happening in the Spiritual community. Mother Ruby nodded.... Mother Ruby asked me where I was from.

*I told her, "This is hard to answer. My father is Guyanese, my mother Antiguan,
I was born in England and raised in England, Antigua, and Canada." Before I
could finish, this, my well-rehearsed mini bio, she said, "Ah, she's a* travessao.
She's a travessao," *and nodded....*

This identification based on my personal and familial migratory history
inspired me to think in a self-conscious way about how this movement and
migration had influenced the construction and relaying of knowledge both
in written and oral rhetorical forms. As Ann Game notes (1991), the experience prompted me to think self-consciously about my own agency in writing rather than to focus solely on Mother Yvonne and Mother Ruby's agency
as the subjects of research.

Travessao *Consciousness*

Is the *travessao* a figure with an ontological reality? The use of the term by
Mother Ruby, Mother Yvonne, and other Spiritual Baptists with whom I
spoke pointed to a "*travessao* of the spirit" as a way of being, seeing, and
interacting in the world that encompasses movement, fluidity, and contradictions. To say, then, that an experience is *travessao* is to indicate its
multi-locality and movement; it is to point to discontinuous locations and
identities and importantly the ability to navigate and negotiate these differences. As Mother Yvonne noted, a *travessao* of the spirit would be "ver-
satile." "Not so many ... people would not be able to handle you," she
added. In this way, the figure of the *travessao* defies one, singular definition
and is a figure of resistance as alluded to by Mother Ruby in the following observation:

> So now it come like if somebody looking for you and even though you
> were safe and when dey come here, dey ain' see you. They want to know
> wey gone. Becor dey know you was here.

However, this multi-faceted identity does not mean ontological insecurity.
As Mother Ruby indicated, the *travessao*, while having the ability to travel to
"other" environments and locales, maintains a knowledge of who they really
are, a knowledge of an authentic self that is recognizable to others—safe
others rather than enemies, as it turns out.

The *travessao* is born of the history of movement and migration within
and outside of the Caribbean region. It is a figure that emerges from the discontinuous landscapes of the Caribbean and its littorals. Benítez-Rojo's

discussion of the Caribbean archipelago as a "repeating island" (1996: 3), a "meta-archipelago," "unfolding and bifurcating until it reaches all the seas and lands of the earth, while at the same time it inspires multidisciplinary maps of unexpected designs" (1996: 3) is useful here in constructing the imaginary geography of *travessao* consciousness.

Benítez-Rojo goes on to note that as a "meta-archipelago"

> it has the virtue of having neither a boundary nor a center. Thus the Caribbean flows outward past the limits of its own sea with a vengeance, and its *ultima Thule* may be found on the outskirts of Bombay, near the low and murmuring shores of Gambia, in a Cantonese tavern of circa 1850, at a Balinese temple, in an old Bristol pub, in a commercial warehouse in Bordeaux at the time of Colbert, in a windmill beside the Zuider Zee, at a cafe in a barrio of Manhattan, in the existential saudade of an old Portuguese lyric. But what is it that repeats? Tropisms, in series; movements in approximate direction. Let's say the unforeseen relation between a dance movement and the baroque spiral of a colonial railing. (1996: 4)

Carole Boyce Davies's discussion of the Caribbean also echoes Benítez-Rojo's notion of the Caribbean as a meta-archipelago while cautioning against the invocation of race and colour-based hierarchies in pointing to notions of a mixed identity:

> Caribbean identities then are products of numerous processes of migration. As a result, many conclude that the Caribbean is not so much a geographical location but a cultural construction based on a series of mixtures, languages, communities of people. Thus some speak of "creolization" or "metissage" as a fundamental defining of the Caribbean. Still, "creole" and "mestizo" carry their own negativities and associations with positions in racial hierarchy, if used in relations to Black populations in certain countries like Brazil. (1994: 13)

As Davies cautiously notes, some—not all—speak of "creolization" and "metissage" as defining characteristics of the Caribbean. Her comments here point to the existence of other possibilities for conceptualizing and understanding the history of the region. In Chapter 6, I return to this discussion through a consideration of the meaning of Africa (both historical and imagined Africas) in the Spiritual Baptist Church.

Boundary Crossing and Displacement

Travessao shifts of time and place involve remembering. As noted by Carole Boyce Davies, acts of reconnecting are representative of African people's political, cultural, and social experiences because of a history of separation:

> Because we were/are products of separations and dislocations and dismemberings, people of African descent in the Americas historically have sought reconnection. From the "flying back" stories which originated in slavery to the "Back to Africa" movements of Garvey and those before him, to the Pan-Africanist activity of people like Dubois and C.L.R. James, this need to reconnect and re-member, as Morrison would term it, has been a central impulse in the structuring of Black thought. (1994: 17)

The experiences of *travessao* encompass this desire to reconnect and re-member through time and space.

The *travessao* is both cartographer and geographer drawing and redrawing discontinuous maps. Both Queen Mother Ruby's and Mother Yvonne's descriptions of the *travessao* imply boundary crossing. However, Carole Boyce Davies reminds us of Bernice Johnson Reagon's assertion that "any crossing of boundaries can mean occupying space belonging to someone else" (1983: 356–68). Questions of appropriation and disenfranchisement are implicated here. This notion of displacement takes on an additional significance for the relationship between researchers and the individuals and communities with whom they are working and theorizing.

Figures like the Watchman and the Prover and Diver in the Spiritual Baptist tradition operate as boundary keepers. They are the self-conscious way in which a religious tradition that embraces boundary crossing checks and balances itself.

Prover, Diver, and Watchman

The leadership roles or "offices" of Prover and Watchman point to the ways in which the Spiritual Baptist Church has developed its own internal system of critique. If the *travessao* is the figure that is able to simultaneously exist in multiple locations, the Watchman, Prover, and Diver are the capacities that address veracity and dissemination of knowledge.

In the following excerpt, Mother Ruby describes the role of Prover:

MR: But in dose days, people couldn' do anyting, anyhow and come in a Baptist church. Becor di Prover dere to Prove you. Di Diver dere to dive you out.

CBD: So what does the Prover do?

MR: Well, Prove yuh, nuh? If you do anyting wrong.

CBD: How would he know?

MR: Well, he go down in the Spirit, dey say.

CBD: Oh. I see.

MR: Mmmhmm.

CBD: So, how would that work? Would that be anybody jus' coming into the church or just for the members?

MR: [coughs] No, no. They couldn' uh … well, let us say as how tiefin' is rampant and all dis, now. You couldn' do all dese tings and come in a church long time and get off wid it. Dey will know you. 'Cor dey have di Provers dey. Dey'll only watch you and according to whatever inspire within dem, what dey get, dey will come and dey kick you out.

CBD: And if they do then what happens?

MR: Nothing. The people and dem will satisfy. Because dey are not lying on them.

In Toronto, Mother Ruth, herself a Watchman in the spirit, describes a Watchman in the following:

CBD: I see. So what does it mean for you to be a Watchman?

MR: Ahm, well, it's like you … how should, I say it … it's like if you open in a factory and they have a night watchman in the night, you have to watch the gate to … who entering, you know. Make sure nobody ain' take nothin' or do this and do that, you know? It's like you search. Your eyes have to be all over to notice what's goin' on, you know.

CBD: So, it's not just, as you would say in church, it's not just in carnal, it's also—

MR: Spiritual. Yeah, yeah. Because a Watchman in the church is spiritual. You watchin' … sometimes you're a Watchman in a church and somebody tellin' you well something is wrong and … well they might try to stop you right by the door there, you know. Sometimes you're a Watchman and somebody sick in the congregation.... It's up to you now to search and see to that church member.

These church offices, regarded by members as spiritual gifts, point to a multi-faceted system of knowledge production and verification within the Spiritual Baptist Church. The usefulness from a critical, theoretical viewpoint is to employ this internal critic as a viable, constructive way of accounting for "what happened." It points to a theory of knowledge that allows for various interpretations and questioning.

I am not, however, suggesting a reformulated Caribbean variant of a laissez-faire, cultural relativist approach. What I am suggesting in pointing to multiple points of origin and multiple temporality is an alternative orientation to conceptualizing narrative and history. My task here is not to suggest a wholesale application of Spiritual Baptist ways of knowing within an academic context, but to show the intrinsic, self-defined ways of knowing, the internal criticism that proves useful for discussing the history of the church and the experiences of its members in Toronto. How can one be a Prover and Watchman simultaneously? The research and writing of this book involved this logic through inviting this critique not only from myself but also from members of the church with whom I worked as well as conventional academic critique. Throughout the research, I was "proven," "watched," "taught," "dove out" as well as "prophesied to" on many occasions within both ritual contexts and conversational interviews.

BOOK OVERVIEW

The first chapter, "A Passport to Heaven's Gate," focuses on the significance of journeying in Spiritual Baptist experience. In this way, Spiritual Baptist migration to Canada is characterized within the much longer history of the Middle Passage, slavery, and enforced African migration to the Americas and subsequent movement between territories including the Caribbean, North and South America, Western Europe, and Africa. Of particular concern here is the continued salience of the "North" as a haven for black people—a motif that has its roots in the African-American and African-Canadian experience of moving "North" to freedom via the Underground Railroad in the U.S. antebellum years of the nineteenth century.

Chapter 2, "'This Spot of Ground': The Emergence of Spiritual Baptists in Toronto," discusses the emergence of individual Spiritual Baptist churches in Toronto in the 1970s as a part of the variety of religious practices and strategies that Caribbean immigrants utilized in meeting their spiritual needs. This analysis is extended in Chapter 3, "'So Spiritually, So Carnally': Spiritual Baptist Ritual, Theology, and the 'Everyday World' in Toronto." This chapter discusses Spiritual Baptist ritual practices, the immigration and employment experiences of Spiritual Baptist women and men, and the ways in which ritual practices mediate these experiences. In Chapter 4, "Africaland: Africa in Toronto Spiritual Baptist Experiences," considers the significance of the multiple meanings of Africa as an imagined place in Toronto Spiritual Baptists' experiences of migration and identity construction. Toronto Spiritual Baptists' lives are lived in a tension between maintaining "back home" traditions from the Caribbean and adapting or creating new rituals and beliefs in response to the contemporary, everyday pressures that they confront as immigrant, black people in Toronto.

Chapters 5 and 6 extend this notion of tension between "back home" and life in Canada by focusing on Toronto Spiritual Baptist women's mothering experiences in both sacred and secular contexts. The seemingly contradictory experiences of Toronto Spiritual Baptist women as "mothers of the church" and as paid domestic workers is discussed in Chapter 5, "'Dey Give Me a House to Gather in di Chil'ren': Mothers and Daughters in the Spiritual Baptist Church." In Chapter 6, "Aunt/y Jemima in Toronto Spiritual Baptist Experiences: Spiritual Mother or Servile Woman?" Spiritual Baptist women's subversive reinterpretation of the Mammy/Aunt Jemima stereotype, which has its basis in U.S. Old South racial iconography, is explored.

I have focused on women's experiences of mothering for a number of related reasons. First, the vast majority of Spiritual Baptists in Toronto, over 90 percent, are women. This figure, mentioned by church leaders, was corroborated by my observations at the church services that I attended in the two Toronto churches during my fieldwork. At the downtown church, out of the approximately sixty regular congregation members, there were eight men and fifty-two women. In the suburban church that had a smaller membership, there were about five men and twenty-five women. These figures may reflect Caribbean immigration patterns of domestic workers, many of whom came as "single" women while sometimes leaving partners and children behind in the Caribbean. Many of the Spiritual Baptist women either have worked or continue to work as paid domestic workers. In this capacity, they perform child care, cooking, and cleaning in private homes for low wages. Some of the women I interviewed in 1995 reported wages of about $150 to $200 per week even while "living out" (i.e., outside of the homes of their employers and therefore responsible for their own room and board) as opposed to "living in." Other women perform similar care-taking, cleaning, and food-preparation work in institutionalized settings such as hospitals. Some of the women, a decade later, have moved on to other employment.

The central idea guiding my analysis in Chapters 5 and 6 is as follows: all mothering work, whether paid, unpaid, private, public, sacred, or secular, informs and shapes mothering work in different contexts. Mothering work includes paid domestic work in jobs such as nanny, housekeeper, and baby-sitter; work performed in the context of the women's own "carnal" families; and lastly, the work women perform as "mothers of the church" in their "spiritual" families. The last two categories of work are heuristic, for in many instances "spiritual" and "carnal" families sometimes overlap with women playing mothering roles in both contexts to their "spiritual children." In other words, the work that women do in paid domestic service, as mothers of the church and in their familial and community-based contexts, influences their work as mothers in a myriad of sometimes contradictory, and at other times mutually reinforcing, relationships. Prime among these contradictions is that paid domestic service is one of the lowest-status and poorest-paid occupations in Canada, while at the same time "mothers of the church" are highly regarded within the church community.

Socialist feminist analysis on women's oppression in capitalist societies is a valuable analytical framework for understanding the dynamics of these relationships. Briefly, this perspective locates women's oppression in the intersection of women's largely unpaid reproductive work in supporting production in capitalist societies—the so-called "more than a labour of love" (Luxton 1980). The analysis presented in Chapters 5 and 6 extends this thesis in several important ways. First, the private and the public worlds of work are deeply implicated in a series of interlocking relationships in not only secular but also sacred contexts. That is to say, it is necessary to examine the mothering work that women do, as employees, in the context of their spiritual work, as mothers of the church. Second, it suggests that the private world of women's domestic work can be the locus of an empowering source of identity formation. This particular notion is contrary to most contemporary Western feminist theoretical approaches in which domesticity, or domestic work, is almost always discussed as a site of oppression, particularly if it relates to notions of the "naturalness" of the work that is performed.

What these two interventions underscore is the contributions made by feminist cultural critics such as bell hooks (1981, 1984) and Angela Y. Dickson (1983) in discussing African-American women's experiences, and Thornhill (1989) and Brand (1989) in discussing black women's experiences in Canada, to pay attention to the ways in which race and class differentially shape women's experiences of gendered identities. My analysis, presented in chapters 5 and 6, argues that mothering work for Spiritual Baptist women, as it is performed within the context of their roles as mothers of the church, is an empowering experience while at the same time the mothering work these women perform in paid domestic service places them at the bottom rung of socio-economic and status ladders.

The final chapter, "Conclusion," reflects on the themes introduced in the book and suggests some ways in which these are relevant for sociological and feminist analysis of religions in the African Diaspora.

NOTES

1 See, for example, *Mama Lola*, Karen McCarthy Brown's study of Haitian vodun in New York City through the exploration of a priestess or manbo in the tradition.
2 Paul Gilroy's notion of Black Atlantic cultures is useful here. According to Gilroy, Diasporic African cultures emerged in the context of the movement of peoples between Africa, Europe, and the Americas during the slave trade.
3 Mourning "tracts" are the accounts of experiences that Spiritual Baptists have while travelling "in the spirit." Their significance lies in their contents being interpreted for signs of the person's spiritual "gifts" as well as messages that may be of significance for that individual or others.

CHAPTER ONE

"A Passport to Heaven's Gate"

I have a passport to heaven's gate
I have a passport, I have a passport
I have a passport to heaven's gate
If you don't have one
(Then) go out and get one
I have a passport to heaven's gate

—*song sung in a Toronto Spiritual Baptist church*

INTRODUCTION

I have a passport to heaven's gate. Sitting in a row toward the back of the church, I raise my voice, joining in, tentatively at first, with the rest of the congregation following the visiting minister's tenor voice. He sings the song line by line and the congregation repeats it after him. After a few rounds, we have learned the song without any paper, song sheet, or accompaniment save for the clap of hands and the tapping of feet on the hard floor. In fact, the song is taught as a round with the message of journeying, embodied in the lyrics, emphasized by the very structure of the song itself. The "we" is myself, a new visitor to the church, and the rest of congregation, five men and fifteen women, who are regular members of a Spiritual Baptist church in downtown Toronto. On this Tuesday night, September 29, 1992, most of us are attending church after a long workday elsewhere in the city. I had finished an interview with Archbishop Dickson a short while earlier and then he invited me to join the service.

The song was introduced to the congregation by a visiting minister, the archbishop's brother, from a Protestant denomination in St. Vincent. This song is significant in several respects for it can be seen as a metaphor of Caribbean immigration to Canada as well as an expression of salvation. The dual resonance of the song rests on the notion of heaven representing the salvation of a new life, as well as a veritable heaven on earth, the coming of the kingdom of God through transformed material circumstances.

The passport also has multiple references. It signifies a mode of access to another realm through acceptance of Jesus Christ as saviour but its meaning also points to salvation as expressed in transformed material circumstances. Similar to the continental U.S. Black Church sacred song tradition, many songs have several meanings (Jones 1993: 58). The meaning is placed in the song by the singer(s) (ibid. 58). This tradition allows for the expression of material, temporally specific goals such as escape from bondage to be couched in metaphorical, often religious terms. Often, both meanings could be evoked simultaneously, changing to suit the spiritual and political needs of the singers. Singer and historian Bernice Johnson Reagon explicated this approach in the following statement:

> The songs are free, and they have the meanings placed in them by the singers. So you can't say every song that has "Canaan" means Canada (or) every song that has "crossing over Jordan" means after I die. It means Canada if it meant Canada. It means "crossing over Jordan when I die" if that's what it means. It just as clearly can be a resistance song as it can be this internal nurturing of the soul! (Reagon as cited by Jones 1993: 58)

In this chapter I explore both the "resistance" and the "internal nurturing of the soul," dimensions of "A Passport to Heaven's Gate," by way of discussing the social and political context of Spiritual Baptist immigration to Canada. I suggest that there is a convergence of two myths about Canada that is reflected in the expectations that immigrant Spiritual Baptists have about life in the country. First, there is the historical image of Canada as a free haven, a heaven on earth, for black people fleeing enslavement in the United States during the antebellum period. In contemporary Canada, this meaning is reinterpreted as a fleeing from the bondage of economic hardship in the Caribbean. Second, there is the contemporary image of Canada as a multicultural heaven in which people of all nationalities, races, and ethnicities live peaceably free from discrimination. This latter image has a recent history linked to post–Second World War nation-building in Canada. The convergence of the two myths of Canada is the image of a "multicultural heaven of the North," where material goals are accessible, facilitated by an absence of discriminatory barriers based on race, ethnicity, and religion. Canada from this perspective is an answer to prayers of deliverance from material hardships and promises a remarkable openness that lends itself to a remaking of identity.

In the first section of this chapter, I explore the journeying motif of the passport, taking up Paul Gilroy's notion of the ship as a metaphor of cultural transmission in the African Diaspora (1993). Here, the significance of the physical setting and pattern of worship of Toronto Spiritual Baptist churches as ships that embark on voyages of the spirit is highlighted. I suggest that these spiritual voyages are a subversive re-reading of the historical experience of the Middle Passage by which Africans were transported to slavery in the Americas. In addition to spiritual voyages of contemporary Spiritual Baptists, another form of journeying is salient here: the positioning of the North as a haven for the formerly enslaved during antebellum U.S. history.

This image of Canada and the North as free has always been contradicted by the reality of racial discrimination and economic hardship experienced by the vast majority of black people who have come to Canada from the United States, the Caribbean, and African countries during both the colonial and contemporary periods.

In the next section of the chapter, "Spiritual Baptists in Multicultural Canada: Considering Religious and National Identities in Migration," I develop a critique of Canada as the free, multicultural North. I make the argument that while top-down, state-sponsored multiculturalism has functioned, in many ways, to reinforce existing notions of race and ethnicity as natural differences, there exist non-official discourses of multiculturalism that offer both radically democratic possibilities for the future and imaginative and affirming reconstructions of the colonial past.

In developing this point, I conclude the chapter with a discussion of "Spiritual Baptist Perspectives of Multiculturalism in Canada" by way of examining an alternative that has emerged from the Caribbean region's multi-ethnic, multi-racial, and multi-religious heritage.

"HEAVEN'S GATE": CANADA IN THE NORTH AMERICAN AND CARIBBEAN BLACK IMAGINARY

References to "heaven" and "Canaan" in the religious experiences of Africans and their descendants in North America, especially in the United States during the antebellum period, have identified the North, in general, and Canada, in particular, as a land of freedom from enslavement. During the period between 1834 and 1865, when slavery ended in Canada and all other British territories but continued in the United States, British North America, in particular Upper Canada and Nova Scotia on the Atlantic Coast, became places where people who escaped from slavery in the United States sought refuge. Through the Underground Railroad, a system of safe houses and escape routes, the enslaved made their way into Canada. The communities built by these people and their descendants still survive today in southwestern Ontario and Nova Scotia (Shadd 1994).

In the contemporary twentieth-century discourse of Caribbean migration epitomized by phrases such as "going to Canada" or "going to America" or "going to England," this historically older, notion of heaven as a place of salvation from earthly travails is also referenced. Included in this reference is a notion of heaven as a place in which economic and educational advancement can be pursued.

"A passport to heaven's gate" can be seen as a symbol of the hopes and dreams represented by the journey to Canada. It also points to the liminal and potentially contradictory status of this journey. The voyage brings the traveller to the gate of heaven, itself a transitional point, thereby hinting, perhaps, that other travails await the traveller in order to enter into the heaven that lies beyond the gateway.

This song, introduced as it was from a Vincentian Christian tradition, may have arisen in circumstances in which "heaven" and the "passport" had meanings other than those I have suggested. As singer and historian Bernice Johnson Reagon has noted, in reference to the African-American sacred song tradition, "the songs are free" (Reagon 1997). By this phrase, Reagon means that the songs are open to multiple and, in many cases, simultaneous interpretations. Thus a "passport to heaven's gate," sung in a Spiritual Baptist church in the Caribbean in a differing social and political context than Toronto, could have an alternative meaning.

In the following excerpt from the sermon delivered by the archbishop on that September 1992 night, an interpretation was offered that locates the song in the present-day circumstances of immigrant Caribbean people living in Toronto. In the archbishop's sermon, the metaphor of the passport to heaven's gate was discussed with direct reference to the experience of migration to Canada:

> This [passport] is not the same as the Immigration people give you. This is the gift of the everlasting gate. Your job, your last money to make a car payment can be taken from you. Christ travelled. But I demand it of your young people, hold on to the vine!

Thus the song and the archbishop's explanation point to the experience of journeying spiritually, physically, socially, and politically that is encompassed in immigrating to Canada. The passport has several metaphorical resonances. First, it refers to religious practice as a point of reference that working class immigrant Caribbean people can utilize to overcome the hardships of everyday life. Second, the passport also references the historical legacy of travel that has brought African people to Canada through the Middle Passage of the Atlantic slave trade, forced migrations through the slave trade, and escape from enslavement through the Underground Railroad.

In both the song and the archbishop's statement there is an allusion to "heaven's gate" as a space of survival and resistance in which dominant power relations, referred to as the taking away of "your job or money for a car payment," are subverted by practitioners. "Heaven's gate" also points to Canada as a "land of milk and honey" in the mythos of both escape from enslavement in the United States during the nineteenth century and as contemporary twentieth-century and twenty-first-century emigration from the Caribbean. The archbishop's statement highlights the recognition that the life that working-class Caribbean people are "given" by the "Immigration people," the representatives of the Canadian federal government, is one that is fraught with instability, powerlessness, and economic deprivation. Thus there is a linking of relationships between the state, individual life experience, the histories of slavery and emigration, and narratives of hope and liberation contained within this song and the archbishop's statement.

A series of questions emerge when contemplating the significance of a "passport to heaven's gate." How do church members in the Spiritual Baptist Church in Canada make sense of their reality in the context of migration to Canada? Is Canada the paradise, the heaven of material culture, the mythical "heaven's gate"? If the quest for liberation was freedom from oppression in the here and now under the colonial and slave regime, would emigration provide a material answer to this quest for freedom in contemporary times? Are these goals subverted and transformed by consumer culture and the acquisitions of material goods as lifestyle?

The new context, life in Toronto, represents a contradictory terrain of possibilities for Spiritual Baptist church members. On the one hand, Toronto and Canada represent new economic and educational possibilities for the immigrants themselves, as well as for their children and future generations. On the other hand, this new context is one in which all respondents reported experiences of racism, classism, and sexism. The vast majority of church members are women who come from working-class and poor backgrounds in the Caribbean. Many have working histories as domestic workers in private homes or as cleaners in larger institutions. Some of the women and men have managed through hard work, educational advance, and fortitude to achieve a better economic standard of living for themselves since coming to Canada in the late 1960s and 1970s. For others, economic hardship remains a day-to-day fact of life.

CHURCH–SHIP: SPIRITUAL VOYAGING

A "passport to heaven's gate" also points to a notion of journeying to freedom. While a journey to heaven's gate might point to death as the portal to salvation in an afterlife, the joyful singing of this song, and its circular structure as a round, point instead to a journey of new life. This journeying motif stands in stark contrast to the historical experience of the Middle Passage that signified a symbolic, if not literal, death via the slave ships that plied the Atlantic. The Middle Passage is the term used to describe the second leg of the transatlantic trade system that developed during the sixteenth to nineteenth centuries. The first leg of the trade involved the transport of manufactured goods from Western European ports such as Bristol, England, to the west coast of Africa, where they were exchanged for captured Africans bound for sale in slavery to the Americas. The second leg of the journey, the infamous Middle Passage, was the voyage across the Atlantic during which an estimated 11.5 million Africans were transported over a 400-year period (Gilroy 1993). The third and final portion of the trade was the transport of the agricultural produce such as sugar, tobacco, and cotton and its byproducts such as rum and molasses back to Western Europe via ship. Also important here is the traffic between North America and the Caribbean of goods and people.

Jack A. Johnson-Hill in his study of the ethics of the Rastafari movement in Jamaica points to the Middle Passage as a 400-year-long experience of liminality (1995: 93). Johnson-Hill notes that the Middle Passage describes the collective experiences of the voyage by slave ship, enslavement in the colonial era, and continuing oppression of the segment of Jamaican society that is broadly of African descent (ibid.).

The idea of the "Black Atlantic," discussed by Paul Gilroy (1993) in his book of the same name, is significant in examining the connections between national, regional, and international migrations of people and cultural forms. Gilroy argues that Atlantic cultures emerged out of the meeting of African, European, and Native American cultures as a result of the slave trade and plantation economies of the Americas. The Atlantic trade, therefore, was not only a trade of commodities such as sugar and cotton and the trade in human beings, but it also engendered various forms of cultural trade and the subsequent emergence of new cultural forms. The ship is the metaphor of this cultural transference for it is the vessel that facilitated this transport of cultural forms. Its liminal status as a vessel travelling from one destination to another is also significant in pointing to the restless movement that characterizes Black Atlantic cultures.

Significantly, in the Spiritual Baptist Church, the ship metaphor is explicitly used to characterize the "spiritual geography" and voyaging explored through worship and symbolized in the physical set-up of the church. The most visible symbol of the ship is the wheel, which is situated at the centre pole in the church. For example, in the suburban church in Toronto, the captress (a female version of the church office of captain) stood at the centre pole, spinning the ship's wheel during the service, guiding the vessel through the spiritual terrain of Africa, India, and China.

It is through trance, or spirit-possession, also referred to as "catching power," in the church that the spirits of the different lands make their presence known. These spirits are also acknowledged through the presence of symbols from religious traditions associated with Africa, India, and China. These respectively are Orisha, Hinduism, and Buddhism, which are represented symbolically through the presence of ritual objects associated with the *orisha*, the divinities of the Orisha religion, which originated with the Yoruba; coloured flags representing gods and goddesses of Hinduism such as Lakshi and Hanouman; and the figure of Buddha.

In the following conversational excerpt from an interview that took place on October 23, 1995, Mother Yvonne, the leader of the suburban

Spiritual Baptist Church in which I did my fieldwork, explains the significance of this form of travel in the spirit for church worship. As we walk around the church, empty except for the two of us, Mother Yvonne discusses the spiritual voyaging of the church as a ship. The tape-recorder, like a permanent extension of my hand, is held between us to record the conversation.

The destinations of this voyage are the ancestral lands of the vast majority of the labouring classes of the Caribbean: Africa, China, and India. The captress and leader of the service are earthly mediators of this voyage navigated, ultimately, by spirit:

MY: Okay. So, um, the corners of the church there is um—although the church is a ship, you know, we have the four corners and we have the bounded centre. And, and in reference that the corners we have, each corner is represented by one of the highest archangel.

CBD: Mmmmhmmm.

MY: We have, you know, Michael, Uriel, Raphael, Gabriel. And then we place other—we ask other—other—other saints to come in, to dwell in those corners also. Then at the—the front of the church, we always have to have a watchman.

CBD: Okay.

MY: Okay. So, you know, we place a watchman in front of there. And in the centre of the church which is with the centrepole. That's the control of the church. Right? That's the centre which is we have all the saints there.

CBD: Okay.

MY: Right? And, well of course, the high altar is the godhead. Right? So, when we use the church in terms of a ship—

CBD: Mmmmhmmm.

MY: —when we start the service, we set the ship out to sail. Because of the spiritual—the way we work spiritually, and we deal with all the different nation. We come to church and when we survey the church, we are acknowledging to the saints that, who are close to church, that we are here and we are ready to take the ship out. So, basically, we—we're telling—we're asking them for their permission, okay? 'Cause we put them in charge, there, right? So, we do a intercessory prayers.

CBD: Mmmmhmmm.

MY: And then we invite the Holy Spirit to dwell during our prayers and we ask for the guidance and different things like that. And it's not every church would um—but my—church we—we start service once you're here or the children enter you will hear "Spirit divine attend our prayers." They know prayers is about to start.

CBD: Mmmmhmmm.

MY: Okay. And that's our—that's one of when we say we talk about our keys, that's one of our key. When we start unlocking. You know? 'Cause after service we dismiss.

CBD: Mmmmhmmm.

MY: So, then we have to open again. You understand? So, we start using the keys to open.

CBD: And this was to open, what?

MY: To let the ship—

CBD: Ahhh ...

MY: —sail.

CBD: I see.

MY: Okay. So once, we open, we invite the Holy Spirit to come in, you know, then we—we—we're—ask for the guidance, you know? ... just guidance of the Holy Spirit. So, we ask for that guidance and then we ask the—the surveying angels to come in and to survey. So then we go to the corners, you know and we survey in acknowledgment that we're here. We will have keys when we go to the corners, you know? We have to use to—in acknowledge that we here and we're ... the true people to take the ship out. [laughter]

CBD: Okay.

MY: All right?

CBD: Mmmmhmmm.

MY: And that we going into intercessory prayers. And paraventure the ship may start to sail. And any port that we land—we could land in India ... China, Africa ... anywhere. You know? This is where the saints will come in, you know? ... We could come in and have a little—completely Indian service.

CBD: Mmmmhmmm.

MY: Ship sails to India and that's where it stay. So, that's basically when we say the ship we sailing. [handclap] Sailing the ship. For instance, Saturday, when this—thanksgiving—we had touched everywhere. You know? Touched everywhere. We—the ship sailed off. It's a nation thanksgiving. It wasn't for any particular—

CBD: Mmmmhmmm.

MY: —you know, we didn't do anything for Indian. It wasn't a Indian table, is a nation. So, we invited the whole nation to come in, you know. Because, too, I am a nation mother. And rightfully, that I have to entertain the whole, the whole nation.

CBD: Mmmmhmmm.

MY: And um … we had the Africans in. And the Indians come in little bit. [laughter] And the Chinese were there, you know?

CBD: Uh-huh.

MY: And all the different manifestation, they all came in, and you know. But, in so doing, we have, what happened … you know, the work is different and it can vary so much because we do not know how the Holy Spirit is gonna work. In certain things there's a set pattern. In certain things, when the spirit come in, they just, you know …

The final comment of this conversational excerpt points to the existence of both fixed and ever-changing spiritual cartographies. These serve as compass and chart for the spiritual voyages of the church-ship in its travels to the spiritual landscape of Africa, India, and Asia. Mother Yvonne's description of the ship's voyage to different lands mirrors Gilroy's notion of the ship as a method of cultural transmission. It also provides an alternative account of the symbolism of ships in the experiences of African peoples in the Americas. Instead of the ship as a slave ship where the voyage is one of captivity, or a ship transporting indentured workers from China and India, in the Spiritual Baptist Church ship, the congregation embarks on freedom-granting voyages of spirit.

SPIRITUAL BAPTISTS IN MULTICULTURAL CANADA: CONSIDERING RELIGIOUS AND NATIONAL IDENTITIES IN MIGRATION

There are a number of historical links between the Caribbean region and Canada. These include their colonial histories, the Atlantic slave trade, and their identification as multicultural or plural societies. Questions of diversity and national identity are recurring themes in both Caribbean and Canadian political and cultural discourses and are engaged in by members of the Spiritual Baptist Church, African-Caribbean men and women, who have emigrated to Canada. In what follows, I explore the multiple contexts in which Spiritual Baptists experience and grapple with multiculturalism.

These contexts include the historical experiences of church members in Trinidad and Tobago, a twin island nation in the English-speaking Caribbean with a multi-ethnic, multi-racial, and multi-religious population. Of equal importance are the contemporary experiences of migration to Canada, a nation with a policy of multiculturalism, and the ways in which the religious beliefs, practices, and symbols of the Spiritual Baptist Church simultaneously reflect and challenge the notions of multiculturalism experienced by the practitioners in Trinidad and Tobago and in Canada.

In developing an analysis, it is necessary to bring in mainstream discourses of national identity and diversity together with perspectives that emerge out of "countercultures of modernity" (Gilroy 1993) such as those forged by enslaved Africans and their descendants in the Caribbean. These perspectives found their expression in oral traditions, including religious forms such as the Spiritual Baptist Church. This dialogue can inform multiculturalism practice and theory through the inclusion of perspectives that emerge from those who are often produced as "multicultural others" within the dominant framework.

COUNTERCULTURES OF MODERNITY AND THE PROBLEM OF MULTICULTURALISM

Multiculturalism as a problematic has as one of its ideological starting points ideas about human subjectivity, governance, and society expressed by Enlightenment philosophers. Those expressions of political and philosophical ideals, which were influential in the formation of the modern nation-state, and ideas about humanity, initially stated as "human nature," were then reformulated in twentieth-century social sciences and humanities as questions of identity. These ideas about human subjectivity were also formulated within a related, though not usually referenced, social and political context—the Atlantic slave trade and the New World African cultures that it engendered. But these ideas usually associated with philosophical formulations in late eighteenth-century France, England, and the newly formed

United States were promulgated during a historical period that was also the so-called heyday of the Atlantic slave trade, when "sugar was king" in economic markets. It was a time in which colonial economic, political, and social relations and the attendant discursive apparatus, including racism, which lent them ideological support, were established. All of this took place during a time when the agricultural-based economies of the Caribbean, the Southern United States, and Latin America prospered economically from the sale of sugar, cotton, rice, and indigo produced primarily through the labour of enslaved Africans.

In discussing multiculturalism as a contemporary problematic of Western liberal democracies such as Canada, I suggest that analysis include a consideration of the enmeshed political and philosophical developments in the areas where liberal democracies emerged, as did their counterparts in the so-called Third World. I draw on the theoretical contributions of historian Eric Williams (1964), psychiatrist and cultural theorist Frantz Fanon (1963, 1967), theologian Cornel West (1993), and anthropologist Eric Wolf (1982), who have pointed to the dialectical relationship between what is essentially the "colonizing Self" and the "colonized Other."[1] In other words, I am suggesting that we look at what Cornel West has ironically called the "dark side of the Enlightenment" (1997), and cultural critic Paul Gilroy has referred to as "countercultures of modernity" (1993) in understanding the problematic of multiculturalism.

Gilroy makes an argument against what he calls "ethnic absolutisms in cultural criticism" (3), which is the tendency to theorize and reflect on culture as if the boundaries between "black" and "white" peoples rendered their cultural development literally "hermetically sealed" (2). Gilroy summarizes his position in the following:

> If this appears to be little more than a roundabout way of saying that the reflexive cultures and consciousness of the European settlers and those of the Africans they enslaved, the "Indians" they slaughtered, and the Asians they indentured were not, even in situations of the most extreme brutality, sealed off hermetically from each other, then so be it. (2)

He notes that a challenge for scholars is to move beyond the "overintegrated conceptions of culture which present immutable, ethnic differences as an absolute break in the histories and experiences of 'black' and 'white' people" to explore another "more difficult option: the theorisation of creolisation, *métissage*, *mestizaje*, and hybridity" (2).

These "countercultures" produced their own ideas about politics, philosophy, and law often in dialectical relationship to those expressed by Enlightenment thought. We must look for the philosophical and political engagements with ideas about national identity and diversity as expressed by those groups of people who were excluded, historically, from the guilds of law, politics, and theology, arenas in which debates about morality, public good, and justice take place. These are issues engaged by the contemporary problematic of multiculturalism. For our discussion here, it means taking into consideration that prior to their emigration to Canada in the post–Second World War years, Caribbean people came from societies that addressed these questions of national identity and diversity, albeit not under the rubric of what became known as multiculturalism in Canada. These questions were engaged by people living in a post–Second World War Caribbean shrugging off the yoke of various European colonialisms while simultaneously becoming enmeshed in neo-colonial relationships with the United States. They were formulated as questions of regional identity and national independence in the Anglo-Caribbean post–Second World War political scene. Through contemporary immigration, different formulations of the problematic of multiculturalism come in to dialogue with each other.

Paul Gilroy discusses "the Black Atlantic" as a "counterculture of modernity" (1993). He underscores the connections between Diasporic African cultures that developed in the Americas, Western Europe, and the Atlantic coast of West Africa through the Atlantic slave trade. Gilroy suggests the ship as a metaphor of cultural transmission since it was ocean voyaging between Western Europe, Africa, the Caribbean, and the Americas that facilitated the spread of diverse aspects of culture.

Drawing on Gilroy's analysis, my analysis takes into consideration the political and philosophical ideas of the enslaved and the colonized and their descendants, as a necessary and integral part of the discussion of multiculturalism in contemporary liberal democracies. To make my point using a historical example, it means examining the implications of the Haitian Revolution for understanding democracy in the Americas as well as the American and French revolutions. The Haitian Revolution took place over a twelve-year struggle in which the enslaved launched a successful military campaign to overthrow their masters in colonial French Saint Domingue to form the independent republic of Haiti in 1804, the only slave revolt in the Americas, and in recorded history, which resulted in the formation of a new country (James 1963: ix). The revolution's *raison d'être* was a reinterpretation of *liberté, égalité et fraternité*, the same banner used by the French revolutionaries who fought to end the stranglehold of the monarchy and *l'ancien régime*. In the context of the revolution led by the rebels of colonial Saint Domingue, this banner was reinterpreted by the life experiences and objectives of the enslaved in Haiti as freedom from bondage in chattel slavery.

To summarize, the problematic of multiculturalism, though often framed in political and philosophical discourse as a problem of Western liberal democracies, should not be extracted from its historical connections with areas of the so-called Third World that have themselves grappled with the key themes included under the rubric of multiculturalism, namely national identity and pluralism. In light of recent post–Second World War migration from areas of the Third World to metropolitan, liberal democracies, this point is especially salient. Through contemporary immigration, different formulations of the problematic of multiculturalism come into dialogue with each other.

But where is the locus of critical engagement with the problematic of national identity and pluralism among members of a religious tradition that has endured a history of persecution as well as systematic exclusion from the arenas of critical discourse? One of the areas to examine, especially in the experiences of African-American peoples, is the religious expressions that emerged from the complex interplay of aspects of African, European, Native American, and Asian religions and cultures. The Spiritual Baptist Church is one of those expressions. It was here that enslaved Africans and their descendants were able to establish the most autonomous institution during slavery, the black church. Religious spaces became an arena of law, theology, philosophy, and ethics through the oral traditions of music, dance, storytelling, and the reinterpretation of the Christian theology introduced by missionaries in the nineteenth century.

A Historical Overview of Multiculturalism in Canada

Multiculturalism in Canada has roots that extend beyond the recent history of the Multicultural Policy of 1971 and the Multicultural Act of 1988. These include a colonial history of French and English settler colonies coupled with discriminatory attitudes and genocidal practices toward Native people, enslavement of Africans, internship of Japanese citizens and Canadians of Japanese descent during the Second World War, and racial tensions in response to late nineteenth- and early twentieth-century Asian immigration. It should be noted that during the Second World War, citizens of Germany and Italy were also interned. However, unlike Germans and Italians, all Japanese descent persons (Japanese and Canadian citizens) had their property impounded and sold. This history of conquest, migration, and settlement informs contemporary notions of national identity and pluralism in the quest to nation build through an official policy of unity in diversity as much as does the national myth of two founding peoples, French and English. Indeed, Bernardo Berdichewsky's notion that multiculturalism is both socio-political process and ideological expression (1994: 66) is useful in understanding the complexity of multiculturalism in Canada.

Intimately tied to the emergence of multiculturalism as a national policy and political practice in contemporary Canada is the history of immigration. During the latter half of the nineteenth century, the immigration policy was one of laissez-faire with regards to immigrants from Europe, in particular, with restrictions on the immigration of Chinese (Driedger 1996: 55). With the offer of free land, especially in western Canada, between 1896 and 1914, immigration from northern, southern, and eastern Europe was encouraged (ibid.). However, there was a lull in the years between the wars and the Great Depression of the 1930s (ibid.). Japanese were deported and/or interred during the Second World War, and anti-German sentiments in some areas resulted in restricted immigration of Hutterites and Mennonites (ibid.). In the years following the war, there was an influx of immigrants as Canadians with relatives in Europe sought refuge for their kin through sponsorship. In addition, others came from Europe as "displaced persons" following the upheaval of the war (ibid.).

Up until this point, Canadian immigration policy was shaped by expressly racially defined criteria. Immigration by people of colour tended to be closely tied to specific economic demands. Examples include the importation of Chinese men for work on mining in the Fraser Valley in British Columbia around 1858 and the Canadian Pacific Railway construction between 1881 and 1885 (Li and Singh Bolaria 1988: 101–105), and black, Caribbean women between 1910 and 1911 and from 1955 to 1967 under the First and Second Domestic Work schemes, respectively, for work in paid domestic service (Calliste 1991: 141, 147–59).

Following a government White Paper in 1966 to determine a more rationalized form of selecting immigrants, the points system was introduced. Under this system, potential immigrants were assessed on the basis of criteria such as facility in English or French, as well as educational achievements and the possession of skills and knowledge relative to high-demand employment sectors such as health care and education, which were in need of workers with specialized training. As a result, there was an influx of people of colour in the late 1960s and 1970s in unprecedented numbers.

In 1971, following the 1969 Languages Act, a federal policy of multiculturalism was introduced under the administration of Prime Minister Pierre Trudeau. This policy focused on bilingualism and on the principle of creating a nation on the basis of two founding peoples, the French and the English, the so-called two solitudes of Canada.

In that context, the multiculturalism policy of the 1970s focused on the preservation of cultural traditions and languages of European immigrant communities. At the same time, race-based ideologies and practices that had their roots in histories of conquest, colonialism, and enslavement continued to influence the emerging Canadian society in interpersonal and institutional contexts. Proponents of anti-racism, in theory and praxis, pointed out that racism was not a "problem of the past," but continued to shape social relations in both interpersonal and institutional contexts. Aboriginal peoples agitated about their historic lack of inclusion in political debate and the federal government's paternalist "internal colonialism" entrenched in the Indian Act, which had effectively wrested self-determination from individuals and communities. These pressures, coupled with the rise of second-wave feminism in North America in the late 1960s and 1970s, which critiqued the androcentric bias of political discourse, posed some serious challenges not only to the content but also the form of political debate (Berdischewsky 1994; Ng 1993).

The 1971 Multicultural Policy was followed by Section 27 of the Charter of Rights and Freedoms in 1982. Together with the 1988 Multiculturalism Act, these pieces of legislation form the core of contemporary federal governmental response to pluralism as defined in specifically ethno-cultural, linguistic, and racial terms in Canada (Berdischewsky 1994: 65). However, these pieces of legislation were not accepted unproblematically as solutions by all sectors of Canadian society. As Berdischewsky notes, from the beginning, in the 1970s, criticisms were raised that the multicultural policy functioned in a way that was consistent with racist ideologies and practices through the focus on "cultural difference" (65). This focus failed to redress exclusion from participation in major institutions and may in fact have highlighted and reconfirmed stereotypical notions of ethnicity and race through this official recognition of difference. Here Charles Taylor's notion of "the politics of recognition" (1992) as they are played out in contemporary Canadian discourse of national identity is most salient.

Briefly, Taylor asserts that recognition, and the lack of it or "*mis*recognition," affects identity formation (1992: 25). He understands identity as "something like a person's understanding of who they are, of their fundamental defining characteristics as a human being" (25). Thus, "if the people or society around them mirror back to them a confining or demeaning or contemptible picture of themselves" (25), the results can be "damaging" (25). "Multiculturalism" for Taylor is understood as one of the contemporary politics, along with feminism, that are waged on behalf of subordinated and subaltern groups.

Indeed, the attendant rise of "race relations" as a practical application of multicultural policy was critiqued as inherently accepting the principle of race as natural. Anti-racism as critical theory and practice emerged in the 1970s and 1980s largely in response to the perceived failure of multiculturalism to redress the problems of racism, which many immigrant people of colour continued to encounter. Anti-racism movements in Canada have tended to be more localized and relatively peaceful in comparison to the civil rights movement in the United States of the 1960s and 1970s (Brand and Sri Bhaggiyadatta 1986: 4).

Scholars such as Zong (1997) and Brand and Sri Bhaggiyadatta (1986) have pointed to the emergence of a "new racism" and a "veiled racism," respectively, that developed within the context of the politics of cultural diversity and national identity in contemporary Canada. Briefly stated, Zong argues that due to recent legal and cultural changes in the fabric of Canadian society, overtly and blatantly discriminatory practices based on racism have been replaced by a more subtle form that is harder to identify and name. She further elaborates that this new racism has emerged in order to avoid social embarrassment and possible legal sanctions. It has also been referred to as "institutional racism" and more popularly as "polite racism" or "racism with a smile," a form of racism that emerged in a country whose national and international image is not usually characterized as racist, especially in comparison with the United States.

In characterizing racism as experienced by non-white people from the black, South Asian, Chinese, and Native communities in Toronto, Brand and

Sri Bhaggiyadatta outlined two factors. The first was a pervasive "culture of racism," which appealed to "common-sense" notions about non-white people often based on stereotypical images that are perpetuated through social institutions such as "the education system, social services, political/administrative bodies, private corporations, and the media" and a host of mutually reinforcing ideological practices (1986: 3–4). The second was the "structuring of economic hardship or disadvantage by the use of racism" (3). Li and Singh Bolaria's discussion of institutional racism resonates with these dual notions. Institutional racism is that which is systematic and legal and justified by an ideology of the supremacy of whites over non-whites (1988: 109). It is distinguished from individual racism that underlies prejudicial actions or behaviours (110). Based on over one hundred interviews, the respondents in Brand and Sri Bhaggiyadatta's study noted that though subtle, the racism they experienced living in Toronto still had a "devastating effect on their lives" (4). The authors suggest that this subtlety or invisibility is a major feature of racism in Canada that often serves to discourage complaints or actions against racism because the burden of proof lies with those who have been victimized (4).

An example of this new racism is recounted in the following description of obstacles encountered in a job search by Brother James, a Vincentian Spiritual Baptist man in his early 40s:

> So, I went there and he send me to this particular guy. So I went there and I ask for the particular guy's name.... Right? So, I ask for him and stuff. Came out and he took me around the shop and stuff like that and told me to call him back between the twentieth and twenty-fourth of March. I did not call him back the twentieth, I wait until the twenty-fourth. When I call, they say they're not hiring right now. Cause the next six weeks ... It continues but I just can't be bothered with those things because I—you ... When you bother with those things you tend to get angry and stuff like that. You just can't do that. You just have to wait until your chance comes. ... But it's all there, it's all there. Whether you like admit it ... it's all there.
>
> There are troubles where they have choice. You will have the equal opportunity. But when they have a choice. Forget it. Notwithstanding that some people has created a bad reputation for the others. I think once they have tasted a bit of paradise they won't give anyone else the opportunity to move themselves up. Mind you, the competition is tight because there are lots of guys out there looking for jobs....

What is particularly notable about Brother James's experience is that one cannot point to a single "racist" actor or action responsible for the lack of job interviews. This incident was only one of several that Brother James shared with me regarding his struggles to gain a job. As a single incident it may seem plausible that Brother James had unfortunate timing with his phone call; however, in incident after incident a pattern of being rebuffed and turned away from jobs for which he was qualified was discernible. The subtlety noted above is evident in the inability to locate the source of discrimination in the behaviour of any single actor.

Another Spiritual Baptist man in his 50s, Brother Tee, reported similar experiences in job searching shortly after his arrival in Toronto from St. Croix (he left Antigua in the late 1960s):

> I started working ... in a little—you know, like a messenger. I did some messenger work in the building and outside. Because in those days, although jobs were begging, it was very difficult as a ... as a person, especially from the West Indies to get the job. 'Cause you go for the interviews and they—oh yes, you read the paper, the jobs are there, by the time you walk in, "Oh the jobs are filled," you know [laughs]. How could they be filled so quickly, you know? Oh! Except the menial jobs, they will give it to you.

When asked about his attendance at an upcoming workshop on anti-discrimination the church had organized, Brother James expressed some doubts about its utility:

> I'm thinking about it, I'm thinking about it. I do not really think that that make any sense because you have to have undoubted proof before you can really bring somebody and stuff up especially if you're applying for the job. The employers have a whole lot of loopholes that he can get away. If you're inside and you're keeping records of things that is happening. See you're applying for a job, the employment, he can vary his theory of hiring to suit the conditions ... But I would like to go.

Brother James expressed great trust in his faith in helping him to understand and counter experiences of racism:

> [S]ometimes you get frustrated and stuff but ... because of what forefathers of old, according to the scriptures, has gone through, you realize that you're not alone. You know? And these things help to bring out

the best in you, help to persevere over the things that is around you. That you yourself can declare that which has happened to you in the past and because what has happened in the past you can be an example to those that is around you. And this is what it's all about.

In sum, a major criticism levelled at multiculturalism policy and emergent praxis is that, though proposed as solutions, they were framed in a discourse of nation-building that had a long history of defining "nation" and "citizen" under very specific, racially informed, and exclusionary ideologies and practices.

MULTICULTURALISM IN THE SPIRITUAL BAPTIST CHURCH

While the Spiritual Baptist Church has not articulated a policy *per se* of multiculturalism, nevertheless some of the crucial questions that have been identified with multiculturalism find expression in its theology and ritual practices as evidenced through "church talk" in sermons, songs, prayers, testimonies. Specifically, the multiculturalism questions addressed by Spiritual Baptist theology and ritual include national identity, diversity, and nation-building.

It should be noted here that there is a long tradition within black churches in North America of using church gatherings as places to address political, economic, and civic matters. In the past, this type of church talk would have revolved around discussions of resisting and managing the rigours of daily life under enslavement and colonial rule, and *de facto* or legalized segregation. Continuing this trend, contemporary black churches engage the social and political issues of the day. This engagement is facilitated by an orientation toward spiritual life in African and African Diasporic religions that sees the sacred and the secular as intimately intertwined. Thus political matters are regularly addressed in church.

It is through this combined sacred-secular worldview, then, that the history of Spiritual Baptist thought in twentieth-century politics in Trinidad and Tobago is connected with the anti-colonialist struggles of the 1950s for the establishment of an independent republic of Trinidad and Tobago. Some Spiritual Baptists at that time saw their quest for liberty intimately tied to the establishment of an independent Trinidad and Tobago free from British rule.[2]

On the question of national identity it should be noted, most importantly, that the establishment of colonial territories in the Caribbean was predicated on the notion of the expansion of European powers beyond their geographical borders, the displacement and dispersement of indigenous people, the transportation of Africans and, later, groups from other areas of the world. So, in this sense, there was in the initial creation of the Caribbean a notion of an expansionist territory, characterized by the movement of people beyond national borders through subsequent migrations from Asia, Europe, and Africa. Cultural theorist Benítez-Rojo in his motif of the Caribbean as a "meta-archipelago," a "repeating island," suggests a postmodernist basis of Caribbean identities (199). Benítez-Rojo's claim is based on the plural origins of Caribbean societies as suggestive of movement and fluidity in characterizing the emergence of Caribbean cultures (2–3).

The notion of a national identity that transgresses borders is evident in the Spiritual Baptist ritual of mourning. Mourning is a period of fasting, prayer, and contemplation usually lasting three to twenty-one days in which the traveller, the "pilgrim," journeys, spiritually, usually to the homelands of the historical migrant labouring classes in the Caribbean as well as "biblical lands." In travel to Africa, China, and India, the homelands of the vast majority of the labouring classes are visited. The pilgrim seeks spiritual guidance from those who reside in this world of spirit, which is intimately linked with the material world. These spirits include their ancestors, biblical figures, and figures from religious and cultural traditions that fall outside of the Jewish and Christian frameworks. It is not uncommon for some Spiritual Baptists to claim that they are Indian or Chinese in the spirit while they are people biologically and culturally of African descent with regard to their family history. From this perspective, the "problem of Others," central to the multiculturalism problematic, is located not only between groups but also within a single individual.

In the following, Brother John, a Trinidadian Spiritual Baptist in his mid-thirties living in Toronto, discussed the presence of Indian, African, and Chinese spirits in Spiritual Baptist worship:

> Di way a' worship and di unity is between Indian, African and Chinese. See, is a unity. Is a unity between Indian, African and Chinese. They all worship together. Even though at home, we can't live together here like we're living here. But on the spiritual realm, they take a different channel. Unity.

He further described this unity in eschatological terms. He went so far
as to refer to the transformation of Malcolm X's political vision following
his pilgrimage to Mecca from a politics of separatist black nationalism to a
multi-racial, multi-religious social justice movement with international significance: "And, when you enter di kingdom a' heaven you would see both
black, white, Indian, Chinee. So, you know, if you go in the East. Da' is
what happen to Malcolm X."[3]

Another way in which claims of national identity are expressed is through
the practice of affiliating spiritually with various "African nations." While not
all Spiritual Baptists participate in this practice, which has its roots in Orisha
and other African-derived religions, it is nevertheless significant for some
members who acknowledge an affinity to different "African nations." Significantly, the nations named are identifiable as those with their roots in the
areas affected historically by the Atlantic slave trade, such as contemporary
Ghana and Nigeria. In the following, Queen Mother Ruby, an elderly
woman who is the head of a Spiritual Baptist church in Trinidad, commented on this aspect of national identity as expressed through a spiritual
association with diverse nations:

> You have ... you—it have people go to mourn ... they come out with
> India ... Indian spirit. Right? Everyting dey do is in India. It have Chi-
> nee—Chinese—will come out. Right? It have the Africans. And dere
> are many tribes in Africa ... Well they ahm ... they have the ahm ... the
> what they call the uh? The Ibo—the Ibo tribe. Well they have a tribe ...
> they—they does have di mark ... in dey face. ... Then they have the
> other tribes ... And dey have di—dey have di tribe wey di men, dey
> wears, di um, di shirts—long shirts, like down to so and di pants. And
> you know, so if everybody, according to your belief, you will get di tribe
> dere. So dey go jus' til you see yourself. But the most important ting is
> life. Dat is di whole foundation. Di life you live. For dese people to stay
> around, you can't live anyhow. You can't do what you want anytime,
> anyhow, so, what you want to do. Because any—you know, you not—
> you not by yuhself alone. Dere's a guard dere wit you. [C: Spiritually?]
> So you have to live di life for he—he or she to remain arung you.

This belief is rooted in the significance of ancestors in African and
African-American religions where ancestors are the community of the elect
who after earthly life reside in a realm of the spirit, which is in constant
awareness of the material world (Hood 1990: 219). The ancestors as the

moral guardians of the community ensure inter-generational continuity (ibid).

This belief in a multi-ethnic spirit world probably emerged in the context of Trinidad and Tobago's post-colonial history as the twin-island nation was the recipient of migrant populations of indentured agricultural workers from India, China, Africa, and Western Europe following the abolition of slavery in all British colonial territories in 1834. It perhaps reflects a further development of the different African "nations" that probably emerged in the earlier history of the transatlantic slave trade. The practice of mixing different cultural and linguistic groups to undercut a basis of solidarity was utilized in slavery. The result was a heterogeneous African workforce. Mintz and Price, for instance, point to the fundamental heterogeneity of New World African religious and cultural traditions as a critique of a monolithic West African origin (Mintz and Price 1997). The task of nation-building in post-colonial Trinidad and Tobago and other Caribbean nations with multi-ethnic populations has engaged this problematic of a unified nation out of diverse constituents. The result is that over the course of the twentieth century, Trinidad and Tobago emerged as a plural society. Granted that there are divisions between Trinidadians of African, Indian, Chinese, Syrian, Lebanese, Spanish and French Creole, and British heritage. These divisions have been played out through class, race, colour, and social status with an exacerbation of existing notions of race that devalue blackness. The result was a situation in which the white British and mixed-race colonial elite gave way to a black and Indian political elite in the post-independence years following the ending of British colonial rule in 1960. And when Spiritual Baptists emigrated to Canada from Trinidad and Tobago they brought with them these experiences of national identity and diversity forged within the recent history of Trinidadian nation-building.

SPIRITUAL BAPTIST PERCEPTIONS AND EXPERIENCES OF MULTICULTURALISM IN CANADA

All of the people whom I have interviewed mentioned multiculturalism in their discussion of their perceptions and experiences of living in Canada. Before they emigrated, nearly all of them thought of Canada as a land of opportunity, sharing in the wider image of America extending north in this case. Some like Sister Maria, a Vincentian woman in her late thirties, compared her perceptions of multiculturalism in Canada with prior experience in the Caribbean:

CBD: So how did you find Canada when you first came?

SM: I found Canada um ... not too bad because what happened ... because I've moved to Aruba and I've get to know the different cultures there, it wasn't really hard for me coming and meeting the same kinda people or just a colour of people here. 'Cause in Aruba I have the people from Holland. You know we have the people from 'statia [St. Eustatia] which is more ... mmmmmm ... kinda Carib-looking, you know, half-bred people, you know, very tan, you know, stuff like that. And they have a mixture of people in Curaçao which is Spanish ... they're from Venezuela. You know, American, Canadian ... so it wasn't really a big chill for me. The only thing that I felt when I came here was the winter. I couldn't take the winter at all.

In mentioning winter, Sister Maria highlights the contrast between, on one hand, her familiarity with the cultural climate of Canada facilitated by a Caribbean experience of multiculturalism in Aruba and on the other her lack of experience with the physical climate.

The view of Canada as a land of opportunity was almost always shattered immediately upon arrival in Canada. In the following, Vincentian Sister Louise, in her early twenties, describes her family's encouragement of her to immigrate to Canada to work as a domestic worker at age nineteen:

Well ... when you're back home, going oversea is like, oh you're going to this rich place. You're going to this gorgeous place. You could do anything you want and you could have anything you want. So they like the idea. And you can send back stuff for them. So they like the idea.

Well! Back home we thought it was like ... oh, we can go here, the stores are all open all night! The clothing store ... you can ... people don't sleep. You meet so many friends. Things like that. But when I got here, the people here ... my godmother picked me up at the airport and we went to Pickering and once we were in Pickering it was in the night. It was a Saturday night ... September ... So ... it was cold. When I got there it was cold. ... So I came and I went there ... we went to bed and in the morning I got up. The place was so quiet because there are houses there and nobody is out who live there because nobody associate with each other like that. They all stayed in their family by themself. When

I get up, I was looking to see the stores here or there. And there was no stores outside. And the people were not on the street. It was so bare. Is not the case that we picture all the time as being so nice like you "walking in gold in paradise" or something like that.

It was not. It's not what I expected. It's like … when I think now, it's like … it's a place where you slow down. You slow life down and think about what you really want in terms of what you want for the future, what are you gonna do because in here you can't do anything without have a job. And in order to have a job here, a proper decent job, you have to have education.

In the above, Sister Louise expressed disappointment followed by frustration between her image of Canada as a land of opportunity and the reality of limited job opportunities she encountered, which was closely allied to educational achievement. Later in this chapter, I cite an interview excerpt in which she expands this analysis with reference to race and class-based power relations that structure access to economic, educational, and cultural resources.

Simultaneous with this critique of life in Canada, following emigration there were other Spiritual Baptists who held fast to ideas about the promise of job opportunities that were closely allied to a perception of a multicultural and by extension egalitarian society. This view is expressed in the following by Sister Asha, a young Spiritual Baptist woman in her late twenties from Trinidad. Sister Asha discussed with me the appeal of living in Canada with specific reference to multiculturalism and ideals of liberal democracies:

[T]he job opportunities. You know, I had the chance to become anything I wanna do or anything I wanna become. You know any field I choose to challenge, you know, I had the opportunity … I realized that it was built up of you know different race. You know, it was like a multicultural place. You know, especially the area where I lived at the time. You know, I saw people from—I didn't even know that you know, these countries existed, you know. And it really did fascinate me.

However, confirming discussions of the critique of multiculturalism as ineffective in confronting racism, nearly all of the Spiritual Baptists living in Toronto whom I interviewed reported experiences of racism and perceptions of Canada as a country that is not welcoming of people of colour, especially black people.

In one instance, a young Spiritual Baptist man, Brother John, who earlier spoke of the spiritual unity of Indian, African, and Chinese cultures, discusses his experiences of racism and locates them within what he considered to be an essential component of the formation of Canada as nation-state expressly developed for Europeans and not for people of African descent:

> You know we—you come here, you see here already build, it's established. I didn't have the idea that I come here to contribute. That never, you know, appear in my mind. Because I more or less, I could give you background in di back seat. If you observe where I am in the church, is in di back seat. Now, there are people who tell me come up to di front. But di Big Man nevah tell me come up to di front. I'm that type a fella. So, if di Big Man nevah tell me come to di front, I would not go to di front. 'Less when I go in front and a guest come to put me to di back. I'm that type a fella.
>
> It's obvious here was very strange, new to me. 'Cause people want you to get in groups, they want you attend here, go here, associate. I was a type a dissociator. I wouldn't associate. So … you know …

Other Spiritual Baptists perceived that non-African people, including other people of colour, classed as "ethnic" within Canada's multicultural framework, were better able to "get ahead" than black people because of favourable class positioning and access to educational opportunities. Using language reminiscent of Charles Taylor's "politics of recognition" (1992), Sister Louise remarks on how she sees her prospects for herself as a young, immigrant, black woman living in Toronto:

> Well … sometime I feel oh, they have us so low down from the beginning, you know, that we have to fight so hard to get something in this world. Even in Canada we have to fight hard. 'Cause—even though we—we are still working hard they don't recognize us as someone who have it and who can do their best—what they want. They don't recognize us as that person. They just bypass us and look us over. I think so. But then, I wanna make the difference. I wanna dwell with them and do the same thing that they do.

Sister Louise continues noting that the "they" she referenced in her previous comments are "all the other races that are making it." She sees her religious practice in the form of "going to church and praying" as "easy" in comparison to the rigours of every day survival:

I look at the white people, the Chinese ... I look at all the other races that are making it, going to school, having their education and getting whatever professional ... I see all of them as different from me because of they getting what they want. They asking they parents for this and their parent are able to give them. Whereas our parents, the black ones, they don't have it to give us. We have to out there and fight for ourself. In the case where my mom is back home, I have to fight here for myself, work— then working, sending money for her, support her and my kids. So, it's like the role of family and everything is on me. It's really hard. I take it— going to church and praying as come easy.

One of the central points of contemporary debates concerning multiculturalism in Canada is the process of inclusion of multiple perspectives and experiences from so-called minority populations who fall outside of the mainstream in their access to power and participation in Canadian institutions (Taylor 1992; Kymlicka 1997; Tully 1997). As noted earlier, it has been suggested that the ideal of multiculturalism—the creation of a liberal democratic society inclusive of the needs of a culturally diverse population—cannot be attained without a simultaneous program of anti-racism.

In the foregoing, Spiritual Baptist men and women expressed frustration and disappointment in light of a perceived failure of the promise of life in a "free" Canada. However, while criticism of racism and its effects on limiting access to cultural, educational, and economic resources was expressed, there was also a reiteration of the ideology of Canada as a land of opportunity. This apparent contradiction can be accounted for in ideas that present a critique of contemporary social reality but also simultaneously embody a hope for the transformation of social relations to create a more just society. Townes in her discussion of womanist theology, which emerges from African-American women's life experiences and interpretation of Christianity, describes a similar perspective as "living into an apocalyptic vision" (1995). Townes's analysis focuses on African-American women's experiences; however, it is notable that Brother John in the context of an African-Caribbean Christian theology expresses a similar sentiment. In addressing this notion of a dual critical/hopeful stance that is focused on the creation of a just society, I will use as an example Brother John's discussion of the problem of the "one" and the "many" expressed as a question of national unity in the face of diversity.

In the following, Brother John refers to Jesus's crucifixion, identifying Simon of Cyrene as a "black man from outta Africa" who helped Christ bear the burden of the cross (Mark 15: 21–32). Simon is positioned as a symbol for the suffering of African, Chinese, and Indian working people of the Caribbean whose labour produced the wealth of the region. He then indicates that conflict also arose between the Taino and Arawak indigenous people in the Caribbean in the pre-Columbian period. These histories, biblical and indigenous pre-Columbian, are referenced in his underscoring of the need for unity in the present day as a "kingdom that divide can't stand":

> They took a man called Simon of Cyrene. It was a black man from outta Africa. Took him to help Christ carry di cross because di cross was too heavy. Right? Okay … these ancient people bear di cross because— maybe they—because of honesty and maybe because they suffer what we Indians, Africans and Chinee suffer: tribalism, differences. 'Cause they were tribal ting between … Carib and Arawaks, native, different tribes, you know, fighting one another. So, di wise man tell himself they who fighting one another, right?—have no unity. And a kingdom that divide can't stand.

Brother John, who was quoted earlier in this chapter discussing the lack of inclusion of black people in decision-making processes in Canada, expresses hope for a unified society that is constituted of diverse people. His commentary draws on a number of reference points including the bible and Caribbean pre-Columbian, colonial, and contemporary socio-cultural history as repository of mythical stories that can be interpreted to make sense of contemporary social reality. This particular narrative strategy draws on two bases. First, it is grounded in New World African Christian approaches to the stories of the bible as an explanatory model as well as a source for articulating a politics of liberation. Second, it draws on the African-American oral tradition in which the storyteller uses repetition to reinforce crucial points. Brother John's statement is excerpted from a longer narrative in which he presents an in-depth discussion and analysis of race and racism in colonial societies and contemporary Canada. In this reflection he drew on stories in the bible and autobiographical references, as well as the biographies of well-known historical figures such as Malcolm X.

CONCLUSION

This chapter has presented a discussion of the song "A Passport to Heaven's Gate" as a metaphor for understanding Spiritual Baptist migration to Canada in both political and spiritual terms. I have suggested that the convergence of national myths of Canada as heaven and a multicultural haven, while significant in expressing Spiritual Baptist desires for emigration, is also challenged by experiences of discrimination that contravene liberal notions of equality.

The chapter then discussed the importance of putting into perspective diversity and national identity, which emerge from countercultural discourses of modernity into dialogue with official policies of multiculturalism in theory and practice in Canada. If one of the proponents of multiculturalism as articulated in contemporary Canada, over the last decade, has been the inclusion of many voices in debates about multiculturalism, then analysis such as this can inform theoretical and methodological approaches to the problematic of multiculturalism.

NOTES

1 Though the foci of their research differ, these authors point to the dynamic relationship between the lifeworlds of the colonizer and colonized. Williams discusses the role of capital from the profits of the Atlantic slave trade as significant in financing the Industrial Revolution in England; Wolf points to "a totality of interconnected processes" (1982: 4) as a key to understanding what he ironically refers to in the title of his book as "Europe and the people without history"; Fanon discussed the way in which internalized colonialism distorted the subjectivity of the colonized, thereby calling for processes of psychological and political decolonization; and finally West calls for an interrogation of the ways in which "race" continues to shape multiple facets of both European and African-American existence in the contemporary United States.
2 See *Joy Comes in the Morning* for a full discussion of the Spiritual Baptists' quest to lift the ban on the practice of the religion in mid-twentieth-century Trinidad and Tobago.
3 See *The Autobiography of Malcolm X* for a discussion of Malcolm X's spiritual and political conversion to a politics of multi-racial societal transformation following his making the Hajj, the pilgrimage to Mecca (Malcolm X and Haley [1964] 1965: 390–93).

"This Spot of Ground"
The Emergence of Spiritual Baptists in Toronto

So there's mergin'! Is a lot of mergin.' Right? Now, what you want to define, is pure Baptistry, Spiritual Baptistry. Right? And, it might be difficult for you to look around and find that.
— BROTHER JOHN, *Toronto*

INTRODUCTION

The Spiritual Baptist Church emerged as a part of a spectrum of religious practices that recently immigrated Caribbean people either created for themselves or adapted to meet their spiritual and social needs while living in Toronto in the 1970s and 1980s. The establishment of the Spiritual Baptist Church in Toronto is also a continuation of a 400-year tradition of heterogeneously adaptive and creative, African-Caribbean religions that emerged during the slavery and colonial periods, in response to the spiritual and political needs of Africans and their descendants. This orientation to religion displays a pragmatic, materialist approach in which religion is used to address issues of secular import while the spiritual is seen as embedded in the everyday, mundane world. The centrality of the experience of slavery must be underscored because for most of the time that Africans have lived in the Americas, they have either lived in enslavement or been faced with its legacy in the form of race and colour hierarchies and racist practices.

In shifting to "this spot of ground," Toronto, the Spiritual Baptist religion was adapted by practitioners to meet their needs. The phrase "this spot of ground," which originates in the churchly expressions of Spiritual Baptists, is often used to denote the sanctified space of the church. The Toronto "ground" has indeed affected the way in which the religion has developed in this context. The spiritual and social needs of contemporary Spiritual Baptists in Toronto, as I will discuss in greater detail in this and the following chapters, were shaped by their experiences of immigration to Toronto. These experiences included race, class, and gender-based discriminatory practices in employment, housing, education, health care, and other aspects of daily life. Chief among these is the impact of race and racism in shaping life experiences and determining choices for Toronto Spiritual Baptists, the vast majority of whom are people of African descent with a small minority of Indo-Caribbean members.

The term Spiritual Baptist Church refers to the religion as a specific tradition rather than to a single overarching organizational structure. There has been a move, initiated in 1997, to organize churches under an umbrella organization with explicit ties to a diocese in Trinidad. However, the current reality is that a number of fairly autonomous Spiritual Baptist congregations exist throughout the Toronto area, ranging in size from as small as a dozen to claims of membership of over one hundred (although all members may not be present at any one time).

Conversations with long-time church members and leaders in Toronto provided much of the information for this chapter. Their comments, though varied in specific detail, indicate that the first Spiritual Baptist congregations emerged as part of a variety of religious practices that were at the same time highly personal and individualized, as well as communal and group-based. These were the practices that recently emigrated Anglo-Caribbean people living in the Toronto area in the 1970s utilized and/or created to meet their spiritual needs as well as their needs for social contact, healing, and the sharing of information and other basic resources.

The chapter is organized as follows: After reviewing the origins of the Spiritual Baptist Church in the Caribbean, I move on to a more detailed account of the church's history in Toronto in the context of 1970s immigration from the Caribbean. Here I cite extensive excerpts from my interviews with long-time church members and leaders such as Archbishop Dickson, the leader of one of the first Spiritual Baptist Churches in Toronto. Among the group of Spiritual Baptists whom I interviewed, Archbishop Dickson and

Bishop Mother Pamela had had the longest history of association with the Spiritual Baptist Church in Toronto. Their accounts corroborate each other as well as those of other church members with whom I had discussions and who passed on their own versions of the church's history as they had heard it through the church's oral tradition.

ORIGINS OF THE SPIRITUAL BAPTIST CHURCH IN THE CARIBBEAN

Brother John, a Spiritual Baptist member in Toronto, expressed the difficulty in categorizing the Spiritual Baptist Church as follows:

> If you sit in the Spiritual Baptist community, right? You sitting on di African people.[1] Right? And dey may confuse you also. Because ... because in di African community—right? You might come across some Muslim. And you might come across Shango. Right? You might come across, you know, some Indians from some ... right? So there's mergin! Is a lot of mergin. Right? Now, what you want to define, is pure Baptistry, Spiritual Baptistry. Right? And, it might be difficult for you to look around and find that.
>
> CBD: [laughter] Yeah, I realize that.

Brother John's suggestion, made as we sat talking in a coffee shop in northern Toronto on a November winter day in 1994, stressing that it might be "difficult for you to look around and find pure Baptistry," proved to be prophetic. "Pure Baptistry" is perhaps best defined in the seemingly paradoxical notion that it is radically heterogeneous in its incorporation of beliefs from other religious traditions and that among individual churches and practitioners there is great diversity. Between the two congregations where I did my fieldwork in Toronto, no two services, even if led by the same person, were ever the same.

This remarkable diversity makes categorization of Spiritual Baptist experiences a difficult task, especially if the criteria of categorization is based on a notion of orthodoxy. Thus, as Glazier noted in his own study of Spiritual Baptists in Trinidad (1982–83: 18), the terms "many" and "some" are used frequently in discussing Toronto Spiritual Baptist experiences to signify the variation of practices and beliefs that most accurately reflect the tradition's orientation.

The question of origin has been paramount in the academic literature about the Spiritual Baptist Church. Several sources of origin, including Africa, St. Vincent, and the United States, have been cited as the starting point of the religion. Clearly, identifying the early formation of the religion is not a straightforward venture.

In attempting to answer questions of origin, researchers often address issues that stem from their own grappling with questions of identity. This concern was reflected in my interviews with church members. At several junctures in the interview process, church members would deconstruct and reconstruct the church's history in telling their own stories of immigration and of their religious lives.

This practice indicates several crucial points. First, in many ways the recounting of the church's history served as the terrain in which new possibilities for that individual could be envisioned, signalling a fundamentally backward temporal look at the future. This perspective on time echoes what John S. Mbiti (1970 as cited by Denniston 1995: 129) refers to as Sasa time or Micro-Time (Little Time) and Zamani (Macro-Time). Sasa time is defined by Mbiti as

> the time region in which people are conscious of their existence, and within which they project themselves both into the short future and mainly into the past (Zamani). Sasa is in itself a complete or full time dimension, with its own short future, a dynamic present, and an experienced past. We might call it the Micro-time (Little Time). The Micro-Time is meaningful to the individual or the community only through their participating in it or experiencing it. (Ibid.)

Second is the acknowledged notion that the history of the church is open to various interpretations within an established parameter of the "story of the church" affirmed and legitimized through numerous tellings in a variety of churchly expressions such as testimonials and sermons. It is from this perspective of the significance of the backward look as encompassing the terrain of possibilities and the "story of the church," which has received multiple tellings, that this history of origin is constructed.

New World societies and the cultures they created were profoundly shaped by the profits generated by the transatlantic slave trade. They were equally shaped by the wealth generated by the labour of the enslaved, the social relations of power that shaped the organization of labour, and by the discursive practices that legitimized and provided ideological justifications for both the slave trade and slavery. The religious experiences of Africans and their descendants in the Americas are best understood in the context of the social and political relations that shaped the lives of individual practitioners and their communities. This legacy includes the subsequent histories of struggles for independence from centuries-old colonial relationships in the post–Second World War years; strategies for economic development aimed at shifting the historical incorporation of the Third World areas of Central and South America and the Caribbean into the global capitalist economy in more equitable relationships; and the discursive apparatus of race, which underpinned the old-style colonial regimes, the slave trade, and the practice of slavery itself.

It is within these wider histories of colonialism and capitalism that the emergence of the Spiritual Baptist Church, a religion forged in exploitation colonies in the Caribbean and then transported to Canada, a former white settler colony, must be contextualized. This history is important because it was constantly referenced by church members in their conversations with me, describing everything from highly personal experiences of racism to reflections on the founding of churches in Toronto.

The Spiritual Baptist Church is a New World African religion that drew on the belief systems of a number of religious traditions in its formation. These traditions include West African religious beliefs; Christianity, especially Roman Catholicism; Islam; Hinduism; Buddhism; and the Kabbalah. While most researchers agree that the Spiritual Baptist Church was developed by Africans and their descendants in St. Vincent and Trinidad and Tobago, they diverge concerning the specific course of development and whether, ultimately, the religion's roots lie in West Africa, St. Vincent, or Trinidad (Houk 1995; Glazier 1983; Zane 1999).

The church was banned in Trinidad and Tobago from 1917 to 1951 by the Shouters Prohibition Colonial Ordinance. In 1994, the Government of Trinidad and Tobago created a national holiday on March 30 commemorating the overturning of the ban. The period of persecution has indelibly shaped the religion. It was referenced by many of the people with whom I spoke as the time when "Baptists were not recognized." Some church members even suggested that the secrecy with which ritual is guarded, particularly those aspects of the religion viewed as "mystery," such as the spiritual quest ritual of mourning and healing traditions, has its roots in this period of persecution as a strategy to preserve the tradition. In the years since the ban was lifted, the religion has spread beyond its initial practitioner base of primarily poor and working-class people of African descent to include a multi-ethnic, multi-racial membership that crosses all class lines. The advent of post-Second World War immigration to Canada and other metropolitan countries has made the religion an international phenomenon and an aspect of Caribbean Diasporic cultures.

The Spiritual Baptist Church can be contextualized in a number of different, and, I suggest, complementary rather than opposing, religious, cultural, and historical trajectories. First, as James Houk notes, it is a part of the "Orisha religion complex" in Trinidad (1995: 36). Houk suggests that the Orisha practitioners and Spiritual Baptists shared and participated in both sacred and secular community life (1995). While these connections exist, it is nevertheless important to note that not all Spiritual Baptists consider themselves allied to the Orisha religion while others, who identify themselves as "Orisha people" or "Shango," also "serve the Spirit" in Spiritual Baptist forms of worship. Spiritual Baptists and Orisha/Shango practitioners I interviewed were both critical, in fact, of terms such as "Shango Baptist" that linked the two traditions without differentiating between them. They preferred to be known as either "Spiritual Baptists" or "Orisha." Trinidadian Orisha leader Shashay, whom I interviewed in August 1995 in Port-of-Spain, Trinidad, remarked: "... bet you bottom dollar it ain' have nutten name Shango Baptist. Is di people call dat like dat."

In cases where individuals participated in rituals of both traditions, they took care to separate the ritual contexts. In this regard, in both churches where I did my field work in Toronto, "African prayers" were held separately, on a once-a-year basis, from the more Christian-based weekly church services.

Second, the church expresses a "Caribbean emancipatory theology" (Davis, 1990) that makes strong connections between spiritual liberation in Christian terms and the transformation of socio-political reality in the contemporary Caribbean. The Spiritual Baptist Church emerged as a part of the culture of resistance that developed during the period of slavery and European colonialism and that reinterpreted Christianity in ways that countered rather than supported the status quo of colonial rule and its supporting discursive ideologies of race and racism.

Third, the Spiritual Baptist Church can be seen as a part of the Sanctified Church in its ritual practices, organization, and patterns of membership. The term is African-American in origin; however, a review of the above reveals the ways in which the church reflects the characteristics of the

Sanctified Church. Gilkes notes that the term Sanctified Church is "an indigenous term African-Americans use to refer to Holiness, Pentecostal, Independent, Community, Spiritual and Deliverance denominations and congregations collectively" (1993: 1005).

Sanctified Churches emerged in the United States during the nineteenth and twentieth centuries (ibid.) with predominantly—over 90 percent—female congregations (ibid.). Salient features of the Sanctified Churches include an emphasis on "some aspect of sanctification and sharing ritual practices emphasizing the Holy Ghost (Spirit) and such activities as 'shouting,' the 'holy dance,' speaking in tongues and other spiritual gifts" (Gilkes 1993: 1005).

Significantly, a group referred to as 'Merikens—a creolized form of American Baptists—is cited in some sources as a possible origin for Spiritual Baptists in Trinidad (Houk 1995). Companies of African-American soldiers, formerly enslaved, some of whom had fought for Britain in the War of 1812–14 in the Corps of Colonial Marines and others who were freed by British soldiers during the war, settled in southern Trinidad after 1816 (Brereton 1981: 68). These men and their families settled in "Company villages," each on sixteen acres of land (ibid.). Former sergeants and corporals exercised some form of community leadership, with a white superintendent holding the bulk of disciplinary power in the "Company villages" (ibid.). The 'Merikens cleared the land in the south during the 1820s. They were largely Baptists and practised the religion that had developed in the southern slaveholding states in the United States among the enslaved.

From my interview experiences and ethnographic work with members of the two churches in Toronto, which involved listening to sermons and prayers in both churches, it became apparent that individual members' life experiences and, indeed, individual church experiences reflected these various theories about place of origin to differing degrees.

In this way, then, Benítez-Rojo's notion of the "repeating island" and Paul Gilroy's of the "Black Atlantic" is especially relevant. It would seem, from the church members' recollections, that the "repeating island" in which the Spiritual Baptist Church developed extended to Toronto, Montreal, New York City, Washington, D.C., Trinidad, St. Vincent, Grenada, Yorubaland in Nigeria, Akan-speaking nations in Ghana, China, India, and Jerusalem and other places of the biblical Holy Lands. In short, I suggest that these different points of origin, outlined by Houk, which place the origin in Trinidad, St. Vincent, the United States, and Africa should also be considered along with members who see themselves as primarily practitioners of a Protestant faith with strong ties to a Euro-American Christian framework in which the place of origin is the Middle East.

It is also important, from this perspective, to take into consideration the landscapes that reflect the Caribbean's labour history. Here I refer specifically to the significance of India and China, as well as Africa, as landscapes that figure prominently in the spiritual lives, particularly in spiritual journeying in dreams and through the spiritual quest ritual of mourning.

Another context of origin for consideration is the relations of power that shaped the emergence of the church. Cultural anthropologists Sidney Mintz and Richard Price suggest that the "birth of African-American culture" must take into consideration the complexities of migration and encounters between African and European people in the Americas (1997). Mintz and Price make a call for a theory explaining African-American culture that is historically specific and that takes into consideration power relations shaped by the fundamental condition of enslavement into which forcibly transported Africans were sold. They argue that the thesis that a homogenous West African culture or shared traits produced African-American cultures once European languages, religions, and other cultural forms were encountered must be critiqued precisely because of the homogeneous origin that is posited as the point of entry. As the authors state:

> Our central thesis is simple: that continuities between the Old World and the New must be established upon *an understanding of the basic conditions under which the migrations of enslaved Africans occurred*. (1997: 49; emphasis added)

I draw on Mintz and Price's thesis in exploring the history of the Spiritual Baptist Church within conditions of migration and a church that was both resistant to and accommodative of power relations under slavery and colonialism in the Caribbean and in contemporary Canadian society. In short, what I am suggesting here is that both perspectives of accounting for the emergence of African-American cultures with regard to "place" and power relations must be integrated.

As discussed earlier, sociologist Dorothy Smith's notion of "the everyday world as problematic" is particularly useful in shedding light on *how* to do such an account of culture that is historically specific and located both spatially and in power relations. Smith argues for a sociology that locates its problematic within the events of people's everyday lives rather than within theoretical constructs that are then imposed from an external position (1988: 89).

It is within these multiple points that I locate the account that follows of the origins of the Spiritual Baptist Church in Toronto, which are both "here" and "there," in Trinidad and Toronto, an African past and a Canadian present. These multiple points of origin are located within the everyday life experiences of the members of the church and include their secular and sacred lives—the spiritual and the carnal.

"THIS SPOT OF GROUND": THE SPIRITUAL BAPTIST CHURCH AS "HOMEPLACE" IN TORONTO

Bishop Dickson, a Vincentian-born, Trinidadian-raised black man who emigrated to Canada in 1973, claims to have founded the first Spiritual Baptist Church in Toronto in the mid-1970s. Following the founding of this church, other congregations emerged in other areas of the city. Many of these churches had links to this initial church through ties of friendship, family, and, in some cases, former membership. What started initially as a prayer group of immigrant Caribbean women who met to worship in "the Spiritual Baptist way" in the mid-1970s eventually became a church under Bishop Dickson's leadership by 1980 with the purchase of a building as a permanent location. Other churches emerged at around the same time. Some were linked to Bishop Dickson's church as a progenitor of sorts, a founding "mother church," while others followed a more autonomous path of development. These other churches followed a similar pattern of practitioners first meeting as prayer groups in members' homes followed by a more formal establishment as a church often in rented commercial space.

The origins of the church in a prayer group that met in the residences of the women members is analogous to the long-standing tradition of black churches in the United States emerging as the so-called "invisible institution" or "church with no walls" (Raboteau 1978). These particular phrases point to a conceptualization of church that is linked intrinsically with a religious community being formed under adverse social conditions that actively prohibited the gathering of black people. This notion of church is further linked to the development of black communities within the context of white supremacist societies where the church was the most autonomous institution occupying an important role as the centre of black civic, social, cultural, and spiritual life.

The churchly expression "this spot of ground," which I heard used in greetings in Spiritual Baptist Churches, resonates with this idea of black churches as the "invisible institution" in a U.S. context, historically (Raboteau 1978). *Happy am I to be here on this spot of ground.* The phrase "this spot of ground," along with "so spiritually, so carnally," is a part of what I refer to as the "spiritual nation language" of the Spiritual Baptist Church. Here I am using Brathwaite's notion of nation language as a part of the self-definition of a people (1984). This "spiritual nation language" expresses the epistemology and worldview of the Spiritual Baptist Church. For the Spiritual Baptists, nationhood is rooted in the spiritual and material worlds, and so "this spot of ground" refers to both the physical and the spiritual location in which people are gathered.

The ground signifies not only the physical world and the earth, but the material conditions in which people live their lives. It also refers to a sanctified space where the spiritual and material meet. Thus the spiritual and material aspects of life inform each other in a complex set of relationships, voiced in the spiritual expressions of the church as "so spiritually, so carnally."

On August 30, 1995, as we sat on her gallery in the countryside just outside of Port-of-Spain, Trinidad, Mother Ruby and I sang:

> You have to rooted and grounded
> in the name of the Lord
> You have to rooted and grounded
> bless his Holy name
> If you want to get to heaven
> You have to rooted and grounded
> You have to rooted and grounded
> In the name of the Lord

To be "rooted and grounded" is understood by church members to be sanctified in the name of Jesus. To be rooted and grounded also points to the need to have connection with the earth and with the ancestors, to have a "solid foundation," as church members often say. This ground can shift in material time and space. One can also be "grounded," meaning that the relationship with the ground, with the earth, with the mother, with the womb, is active.

For example, the ground shifted from Africa to Trinidad and St. Vincent and to Canada. And yet it remained beneath the feet of the travellers through involvement with the Spiritual Baptist Church and other cultural practices that maintain a connection with "home."

"This spot of ground" is also bell hooks's "homeplace" (1990c). hooks discusses "homeplace" as a space of psychic and cultural survival and regeneration created mainly by African-American women for black people facing racism. She asserts that this homeplace was necessary in the context of black people's survival and resistance to racism, and, as such, its construction was shared throughout the Diaspora.

hooks notes the historical importance of the slave hut and the wooden shack as homeplaces for African-Americans. In an African-Caribbean context, the church, the *chapelle*, or Shango yard are also a part of homeplace. Significantly, Spiritual Baptist Churches are often referred to by their members as homes, and the male and female leaders as the mother and father of the home. In the spiritual nation language of the church, friends and visitors, "cousins" and "aunties" from other churches are welcomed to feel at home. Bishop Dickson makes this connection in relation to the Toronto Spiritual Baptist:

> CBD: Yes, I was saying I noticed there was a real feeling of fellowship and community and I am wondering how that translates into …
>
> BD: It's a natural thing amongst the Spiritual Baptist faith or something that I have tried to instill in the people. We're a family; we're not just a church. We're a family and families must be together, linked together, bunched together, be there for each other. If I feel pain, you must feel the same pain. If I am joyous, you must be joyous too. So I tend to focus the fellowship of the church around a family setting. And um, because of the work of the Holy Spirit, everybody tend to come in one accord where we rejoice together, you know.

Homeplace continues to be a vital part of the survival of black people living in North American societies. Thus homeplace, in the context of Caribbean immigration to Canada, extends from the mourning ground of Spiritual Baptist Churches in Trinidad to storefront Spiritual Baptist Churches in Toronto, to the townhouse and apartment in areas of the city associated with working-class and poor people such as Regent Park and Jane and Finch, and to the house in middle-class suburban areas of Pickering, Scarborough, and Thornhill. In this sense, "home" is linked to politics of cultural and economic survival of African-Caribbean people living in Toronto.

"This spot of ground" and "home" are linked to the politics of identity and community formations in Toronto's black and Caribbean communities. The central point here is that there is more than one black community and Caribbean community in Toronto. In defining authentic notions of self and community, questions of inclusion and exclusion arise in relation to both internal (within the individual or community) and external (outside of the individual or community) power dynamics.

Power relations, based on division and exclusion, such as sexism, classism, and homophobia, as well as those based on inclusion such as the notion of an extended, diasporic family "in the spirit," inform community and identity formations around the notion of "home." In other words, the questions of who is welcome as family and in whose home under what conditions are of key importance. I raise them here because an analysis of identity and community formations within African-Caribbean religions in the Americas needs to be linked with these struggles in other areas of social life. I am suggesting this linkage precisely because of the central role that these religious forms have played in social life historically in African Diasporic communities.

THE FOUNDING OF THE FIRST SPIRITUAL BAPTIST CHURCH IN TORONTO (1975–1980)

The first Spiritual Baptist churches established in Toronto during the mid-1970s grew out of prayer groups made up of recently immigrated African-Caribbean people, the vast majority of whom were women, who met in their homes to worship "in the Spiritual Baptist way." Along with these meetings, some individuals also took part in more mainstreamed Christian worship through the Roman Catholic Church as well as Protestant Christian denominations such as the Anglican Church. Other church participation included attendance at other Caribbean-based evangelical congregations, and consulting individual practitioners—"spiritual healers" and "psychic readers"—in accordance with their needs for healing for ailments that manifested a combination of physical, mental, and spiritual symptoms. The latter practice, in particular, reflects a worldview shared by other African and African-American cultures in which the spiritual and material aspects of human existence are perceived as deeply enmeshed.

Bishop Dickson's claim to have founded the first Spiritual Baptist Church in Canada in the mid-1970s is corroborated by the testimony of long-time church members such as Mother Dolores and other Spiritual Baptist leaders such as Mother Patricia and Mother Yvonne. Their testimonies suggest that Bishop Dickson's founding of his church emerged from a loosely linked community of what have been referred to by members of the community as "Spiritualist" churches whose congregations were made up almost exclusively of immigrant Caribbean people. Although no two of these churches are alike, they share characteristics that align them with the Sanctified Church of African American communities. To reiterate, these include an emphasis on spiritual gifts, sanctification through Jesus Christ, ecstatic forms of worship including possession by the Holy Spirit, and movement such as the "holy dance" and "shouting" (Gilkes 1993: 1005).

Although Bishop Dickson played, and continues to play, an important role in the Spiritual Baptist Church community in Toronto, his family did not have a long history of association with the Spiritual Baptist Church. Dickson became a Spiritual Baptist as a young man in his twenties when he lived in Trinidad, after an older sister began participating in the religion:

CBD: You were mentioning earlier that you had a spiritual calling to the Spiritual Baptist faith. Could you tell me a bit about that and when that was?

BD: It was 1967, I lived with a sister in Trinidad that was then a Spiritual Baptist and because of my religious belief in the Gospel Hall. I personally saw the Gospel Hall as the only true religion that was living right. And honest I despised the Spiritual Baptist faith because I deemed them as a downtrodden religion, they had no morals where I'm concerned because they were having boyfriend and girlfriend in the church, having children out of wedlock so I found that their morals was very low. And my sister invited me to one of the services and I said no, I was not gonna go. Because I wanted no part of this type of religion.

And, um, the church usually have what you call a pilgrimage. The Spiritual faith calls it a pilgrimage, our, my background of a religion, the brethren, we call it convention. And the Spiritual faith have their pilgrimage.

Over where we lived we could have stayed there and observed what was taking place so it was two churches meeting and the form of greeting that after I get older I realized was when Abraham and Lot met after they had been separated from each other they hugged each other, they greeted shoulder to shoulder as you see we do now in the Spiritual Church. And the singing was something else, it really got me, and I stayed over where I lived and I was watching at a distance at everything that was taking place. Even the colours that they wore was catching. The way their hymns and everything went on and it was an exciting type of a setting where I was concerned. And I decided I was gonna go one Sunday to see what it was all about after I had stayed that far and saw this carryin' on.

So one Sunday night after the Gospel Hall church I went up to meet my sister in Gonzalez where the church was and I was standing outside at the window and one of the ladies which, at the time I called a madwoman came out, I was dressed in my suit and in the Spiritual faith you don't wear a suit and so forth. She came out and she held on to me and started to shake me and sayin' that the spirit was one in me to be a part of them and I was very annoyed, you know, so I left and I went home.

Times passed, I had a dream about a month or so later that was at the same spot that I observed the pilgrimage from and my sister was there and an Indian man, a very old Indian man came to me and he gave me ten dollars. But they were single dollars but different colours. And they all, at the corner of it where you know where the dollar sign would be indicated one dollar and I questioned her as to why it's ten dollars, ten one-dollar bills but they're different colours. And she pointed up to the church and she said, "Go up there and they will tell you what to do with it."

So in the sleep, I got excited about the money, and I started to run towards the church to take this money for them to give me an explanation. And when I got there I ran straight to a lady in the church and I said an Indian man says to give you this and you will tell me what to do with it. And that was the end of that dream.

I woke out the dream and I told my sister the next day what I dreamt and she was more or less excited because she took it as a spiritual calling and I had to go that route and so forth.

Anyhow, months passed by and I never bothered with it. And I happened to become ill and was very sick for a long time and was not getting anywhere with the medical doctors. So my sister suggested to me, why don't you come to the church and we will pray with you and see if you will get better. So I decided, okay, I was going to go. I went to the church and the night that I went to the church the said lady I saw in the dream I saw the person in the church.

CBD: Really?

BD: Yeah.

CBD: How did you feel?

BD: Terrified, petrified, frightened—mixed feelings. I was not excited. I was actually scared to think I dreamt it and there is—like if I dream you and never met you before and then I walk up and there is this person I saw, exact face, size and everything. So, I told my sister, "There is the woman that I dreamt." And she say, "Well, why don't you go talk to her?" And um, I didn't want to. But I just felt led to do it and I spoke to her and I told her the dream. And she gave me the explanation saying that I had to be baptized in a Spiritual Church. When I am baptized the powers that would be dealing a lot with me would be Indian powers because of the Indian man giving me the money and sending me to the church. The reason why the money was in different colours is because they signifies the bands that is tied on your eyes at the time of mourning. It's one band—one yard to make a band—but it's going to be ten different colours.

CBD: I see.

BD: And I went to, to—I had to mourn for ten days. So, I went home and I thought about it and because I wanted to get better I decided I am going to try this. Not that I had fully believed in what I was told at the time. I decided I was going to try it to see. 'Cause if you're ill you're in a spot. You know, you're going to try anything and I did try. And the experience was—was great. I got baptized and I went straight into what the religious doctrine is calling mourning or fasting. And, um there is where my spiritual growth begin.

CBD: So that was your start in the Spiritual Baptist faith.

Though Bishop Dickson became a member of the religion in 1967, he still attended services at the Gospel Hall Church in which he had grown up. Through healing his mother, spiritually, he revealed his membership in the Spiritual Baptist faith to the rest of his family:

I still went to the Gospel Hall church on Sunday mornings because I am being honest with you, I was ashamed of the religion. I was ashamed of everything that—that people was saying and because the Gospel Hall church was such a dignified religion, I wanted to remain dignified. And I hid it from my parents for many years 'cause I did not want to hurt my mother and father's feelings.[2]

My mother found out about it in 1974. She came to Trinidad to visit; she was ill. And by then I had gone to mourn or fast several times and I had become a healer. But even then, these things were hidden from my parents. My brothers never knew anything about it. But I would go in to mourn or fast, I would lie to them and say I'm going away to Tobago to be with some friends in Tobago.

And um, I was made a healer and my mother had a foot that was giving her problems; a lame foot for many, many years. And through mourning, I was given the things to heal my mother's foot with. But when my mother came to stay in Trinidad, she stayed with me. But I was still petrified of telling her what my involvements were. So when we—she went to the Gospel Hall church with me on Sunday mornings and Sunday night I would not take her. I say well, you know church might finish late, but is because I want to go to the Baptist church. So I left her at home.

And then one day I was coming from work and the power of God manifested upon me in the street and people thought I was crazy. So people that lived nearby that knew that I used to sneak and go to the Baptist faith or even knew about the moving of the spirit in the Baptist faith, told them that I was not crazy, it was power—or I was under the manifestation of the Holy Spirit.

And, um they took me home and then at that time I started to ask in different languages for things that was given to me to heal my mother's foot. And I healed my mother right there and then. And it took about two or three days for the sore that was about that [makes a gesture with his hands indicating a three- to four-inch circle] at the time to come into this [makes a gesture with his hands indicating a circle about the size of a quarter].

And I think God caused it to happen in this way that my mother would not despise me for who I am and what my involvement was because she saw what good it had done for her.... And this is the way my—it came out that my mother knew. And when my mother went back to St. Vincent, she told my father. And um, through correspondence he was not angry at me so I felt more comfortable in getting more involved in the religion.

Dickson's emigration to Canada was precipitated by his Spiritual Baptist sister's vision of his needing to depart Trinidad for Canada:

When I came here I—it was through a vision too that I got to come to Canada. My sister, one of my older sisters, the one that I lived with that was the Baptist at the time she had a dream that um, she had to do a walking mission from Port of Spain to San Fernando which is miles and miles and miles. And she—I was then married and she left to go to this mission. So I took my wife up to her place to keep her kids. And then the Saturday, I said to my wife, let's take the bus and go and see how far we meet her, see if she wants anything 'cause she was a messenger taking message and she had to go by foot.

So when we got off the bus, we saw them walking so we got off of the bus at the next stop. And we walked back to her. And when I walked back to her she—when she saw us coming, she burst into tears.

So, I said to her, if I knew you were going to cry, I wouldn't come. And she said to me, you're going and leave us. And I said, going where? And she said, I was sleeping in some Indian people house and an Indian man came to me gave me a grey suitcase, gave me a plane ticket and told me to tell [you] to leave by the twenty-ninth of March. If he doesn't leave for Canada by the twenty-ninth of March, he will be in a lot of problem.

Bishop Dickson's departure for Canada disrupted professional plans for a career as a police officer:

I was almost into the police force. I had done everything to get into the police force. And um, I was waiting just to go in to get measurement for my uniform and everything. But because of the message that I got from my sister, that if I did not leave Trinidad on that date, I would be in a lot of problem. I didn't have any money 'cause I was young, just married and whatnot. And I borrowed money from an aunt of mine and um, another relative and from my mother-in-law and I made up my passage to come here.

I got here—Canada door was closed November that you couldn't come to Canada to apply. And I came in, in March. I had a very difficult time with the immigration. But because I was sent here, I got through within months. I had a lawyer … and um, he took me up and down, it cost a lot. But in months, I was able to get my landed paper and everything like that. So I felt that was the end of the spiritual affair with me.

While Bishop Dickson initially thought that his coming to Canada would be "the end of the spiritual affair," his decision to come to Canada initiated the beginning of a new spiritual path. In recognition of the securing of his landed immigrant status and that of his wife and child, Bishop Dickson returned to Trinidad in 1975 to ritually thank God through hosting a thanksgiving and feeding the poor. His actions demonstrate that home and homeplace as discussed earlier exists in multiple locales, both here in Canada and there in Trinidad:

> I was going to a church called St. Clair Missionary Church on St. Clair. And um, I had made a promise if God helped me to get my landed paper, get my wife paper—my wife had then had a baby and pregnant with the second child—I would go home and I would—back to Trinidad—I would give a thanksgiving, I would feed the poor and so forth.
>
> And then, my wife who never knew my mother woke up one morning—she was eight months pregnant—and told me your mother came to me and told me you made a promise if you don't fulfill your promise she wouldn't have the baby, she would lose the baby and she probably will lose her life. And that would be through me. I must go and fulfill my promise.
>
> So I remembered what I had promised and I rushed off to Trinidad and I went to mourn then, I fed the poor, I had the thanksgiving and I did everything that was necessary which the Spiritual faith believes is for prosperity, progress, or upliftment. And I did a lot of number of things and I left—I became a baptizer on that throne of grace when I went to mourn. And I was privileged enough to baptize my four nephews, one of my sister's four sons before I left.
>
> I came back and thought that was the end of the Spiritual business with me 'cause there was no Spiritual churches in Canada. I hadn't hear about anything.

Bishop Dickson did not learn about the existence of any other Spiritual Baptists in Canada until his return. Upon his return from Trinidad, he heard from a friend about a group of women who met in each other's homes to worship "in the Spiritual Baptist way." Out of meetings with these women to worship, the seeds of the first Spiritual Baptist church were sown.

> Anyhow, my—I had a friend … who had some friends in Brampton that was having a thanksgiving. And um, he invited me to this thanksgiving. I didn't know that there was any group.

They had a group of ladies that had formed themselves and used to go from house to house to worship in the Spiritual Baptist way. So they were having a thanksgiving and he invited me. I went and at that thanksgiving um, he explained to them that I was a baptizer, I was a leader and they wanted to know if I would speak. I preached at that thanksgiving. And after preaching, they were continuously—everybody was asking me for my number 'cause there was no male involvement in the church and they, I think that they were anxious for a leader. So they ask me if I would go along with them to this house to house prayer group that they were having. I said no, and that was the November of '75.

Although Bishop Dickson did not initially participate in the house-to-house meetings that functioned like mobile home churches on a regular basis, the organization of a Good Friday service in Easter 1976 marked a change in the organization of the home churches. The relatively large number of people—forty—who turned out for this service in a basement apartment demonstrated the interest and support for Spiritual Baptist forms of worship:

BD: Anyhow, the following year, '76 Easter, Good Friday, I called couple of the ladies at work after me to start this church with them. And I said, could we have a Good Friday service? And they were really, really excited and glad and I—they said yes.

One of the girls had lived in a house basement ... and um—Give me one sec, I just want to hear this ... [He then left the room and went out to the front of the church to hear a young woman preach. After about five minutes he returned and the interview resumed.] Yeah so she gladly agreed that we would have a service at her basement. And she phoned around and she invited a lot of people and that first service we had about forty people—

CBD: Oho!

BD: —in a basement, we could not find room to fit people in that basement. Ahm, our first altar was—olden people had what they call a wardrobe.

CBD: Fine.

BD: So she put the wardrobe down on the flat side, she covered it with a solid blue material and white lace. So our first altar was a old wardrobe covered in blue and white. And um, we had our first service that Good

Friday 1976. And um, we started the following Tuesday, they asked me if we would have service every Tuesday and I agreed and that was how the church was formed.

Following this initial meeting, Bishop Dickson took steps to formally create a church. He chose the name St. Michael only to discover that another church leader had already chosen that name for his group. This discovery, of course, raises questions concerning the question of "origin" and "first." In Bishop Dickson's estimation, clearly, the origin of the church preceded any period of formal registration, hence his claim to leading the first Spiritual Baptist Church in Canada.

We had proposed to call it St. Michael but when I went to register I since that—after that—associated myself with a gentleman who had found a group then. And he was a little brisker than I am, and um, found out about registration and he went and he registered his group as St. Michael. So you cannot have two churches register under the same name, so we chose St. Ann, which I am not sorry about. I am glad that we had chosen St. Ann.

When you look into St. Ann is the mother of all nations because it's through her our redemption was paid. Because hadn't St. Ann have Mary, Mary would not have had Jesus, which is the saviour of the world. Mary had to be raised very virtuous by her mother St. Ann in order to be chosen that vessel to bring forth the Saviour of the world.

So we started on a Tuesday, the congregation grew too big for that basement. So we had to move.... And again we grew too big, we grew out the basement because we were having baptisms by the twenty, fifteen, sixteen, nineteen, sometimes three times per year in the summer. They were going to New York to have water baptisms. And um, we decided that we were going to have different functions to raise money to purchase a building. We raised the ten thousand dollars and we purchased this building nineteen-eighty ... eighty ... nineteen-eighty? Nineteen-eighty. Yeah.

So I was then—I was ordained during the process of time as I took out three degrees at the same time I was ordained ... [by a Spiritual Baptist Archbishop] and I was made a Reverend, a High Priest, and a Bishop. Then June 29, '91, I was raised to lay hierarchy of an archbishop.

Mother Patricia's account of the emergence of Spiritual Baptist congregations in Toronto in the 1970s also touches on the significance of house-based prayer groups. Her recollections underscore the significance of a loose network of individual spiritualist churches, prayer groups that met mostly in women's homes and individuals who provided psychic readings.

When we first met in November of 1996, Mother Patricia was then in her forties. She had emigrated to Canada from Jamaica in 1969 when she was in her late teenaged years. Like Bishop Dickson, Mother Patricia did not grow up as a Spiritual Baptist. In seeking a resolution to crises that manifested as physical illness and trance-like states of consciousness, described in greater detail in Chapter 5, Bishop Patricia experienced a "call of the spirit":

CBD: Okay, all right … So, I'm really interested to hear about your own um, history with the faith. How you got into it.

MP: Oh, it's very interesting how I got into it, you know? Um … becor it didn't come by me saying, "Oh I wanna get in religion," or anything like that. I actually was draft into it by the spirit [laughs with CBD].

CBD: How do you mean by drafted into it by the spirit?

MP: Yes! I know, I know, I know it's hard. Because then I had no—I had—I thought I had a choice. I was running away from it but I had no choice. Because during my child days and even when I came to Toronto in the age of nineteen—twenty … I love church, I've grown up in church because I'm always Pentecostal in birth and my aunt was Revivalist but I've never get involved with her that much in Jamaica where I was born. All when I came here I was still spiritual going to church doing everything else because I just wanted to get back into the same custom of the—what I usually do home. Wake up in the morning, dress, and go to church. Feel the proxy of the Holy Spirit, feel everything working for me. And then I come home back and say, well I went to church it's another week.

So coming to Toronto, I wanted to do the same thing. So I start doing it but with the inclination that I wouldn't have to worry about the deep side of it becor nobody wouldn't know [chuckles]. So I keep going to parties, dance and everything and—every time I go into a church to sit down, whether it's a Presbyterian, United, everything, somebody would walk at the back of the church and says to me, "Can you come and help me with Sunday school?" or "Can you come and help me with this?" and then I never show up again because I never wanted to go into it deeply.

So, one—two times or—incident happened to me that I was in my workplace where I work. And I started feeling the spirit call me. I knew it was the spirit but I hide it from everybody else and I didn't want it—to know it was the spirit, so they send and get a taxi home for [me]. And they took me to the hospital. I was in some sort of a trance. So they took me to the hospital, they took me to the hospital, they said, nothing is wrong with her, take her home.

And I rested for three days travelling in the spirit. And if anybody come into my room at the time—I had a little room at the time with a TV because I was going school and I was a new immigrant here, just landed. So it was fascinating. I usually get out and they say, "Oh you tell me this and you do this in the spirit" and I'm going "What?" But then I had to get a paper from the doctor that I was off couple days and I go back to work. And I say, this can't work, I have to do something about it.

Mother Patricia's resolution came through her meeting with two old Caribbean women who were "spiritual women." These meetings were facilitated by friends who were concerned for her welfare and who recognized her as being "called by the spirit":

MP: So I met this lady, she was Guyanese and she said, "Pat, you're crazy." And I was getting sicker and sicker and sicker. And she said "Pat, you're really, really crazy. You don't know what's happening to you?" And I said, "Kind of but I'm not too sure." She said, "You're one of those people!" I said "What do you—those people?" She said, "Those guys that wrap they head and give messages and do different things. You are!" I said, "Me? No way! I'm not doing that. Uh-uh, forget it." She said, "Pat, you have to."

In the United States Mother Patricia met with an old Guyanese woman named Mrs. Hill, an "old spiritual woman" who told her that the spirit was calling her. Following this meeting, Bishop Patricia subsequently met Mrs. Benson in Toronto, a Jamaican woman who was a Revivalist:

MP: Nineteen-seventy-two. So, I told my girlfriend … what was happening to me. And she said, Pat, you gotta—you gotta check this thing out so she took me to the States. There was a old lady named Mrs. Hill. And she was a old spiritual woman. She said, "You'll *never* get better becor the spirit of the Lord need to use you. You're too proud. You're too—" I really never want to get into this. If I had a choice, I would not do anything. But I said to her, "Okay fine, if that's what you want me to do" and stuff like that, "I will go back and I will do it." She said, "You gotta go find that church where you could wrap your head, where you could do stuff." Where you could wrap your head, where you could do stuff, and you could do anything you want. And she says, "You gotta go back and do that 'cause you'd never get better." And my determination is that I could do it. But I don't have to wrap my head. You don't have to do it. I still was stubborn. However, um, I took sick meanwhile.

Doctors didn't know what were happening to me. And somebody took me to this Jamaican lady and she was a Revivalist. And her name was Mother Benson. 'Cause I mention—I think that was in '74 … but … that was in '74, yeah … about '73, '74. Suffering for a year and a half or two. And she look on me and she said to me, "Wow this is ripe! She's just ready to work. She's young, she's vibrant. She have the spirit. But you don't want to go into it." And I said, "No. I'm not wrapping my head. I'm not gonna be crazy like these people. I'm going to be a career woman and I'm not getting involved with this period." And she say, "You gonna have no choice, dear. Else you gonna lose everything." I had a fancy car, I had an apartment. I had everything. I was a spoilt child. An so I make myself spoil. So it was materialistic.

However, Mother Patricia started helping Mother Benson in her spiritual work, which was "partly Revivalist and partly Pocomania."[3] It was during this time that she became aware of the existence of other "Spiritualist Churches" and prayer groups. Accompanied by friends, they would, effectively, "make the rounds" of this loose network of churches:

So I went in to—and I started helping her spiritually. And she—and then I start thinking it was too much of the ancestor type work. It was— when I say ancestor type work, it was Revivalist—but it was partly Revivalist and partly Pocomanian. Sometime you get into the heavy sort of work then people comes. So I know—I know about it, so. And I look at her and said, "I—I don't know if my spirit wanted these type of work." I usually get sick after but I wasn't helping her but I was okay.

So, then I start fishing around for other places to see who and who was there. And then we went to a Spiritualist Church. … And when I went there I met a guy. … And he was doing spiritualist reading from those that passed—psychic reading. And he had a prayer group going and then that was the real um, Spiritual Baptist. It wasn't from Trinidad-type he had going with some ladies. And then I went into his basement at Coxwell and I started worshiping between the two ladies and the two men. ... And then—and then I knew—that was in '74. Then about in '75, I knew of [the Archbishop's Church]. And then there was another Revivalist person at Westmoreland Avenue. And those were the only churches existing at that time for sure within that time.

But nobody was recognized. We were just doing it under the basement in your house—everybody had a house. They were just doing it under ...

So in '75, I had six friends that started going with me back and forth to these churches. And one was a teacher, and couple of them—there was a nurse. And I just finished my Business Administration then ... seventy ... in—at um, [words unclear]. And I was working in accounting then and doing income tax. At the same time, and I look on the whole thing and I says, knowing my background, and the different church whey ah come from and [words unclear] was a minister, we can't keep worshiping like this, we got to have some set up.

Out of this desire to have a church that was "recognized," Mother Patricia and five others organized themselves to establish a church:

So, I took my six friends as a board of directors and we opened the church and I was the secretary and the original person was [one of the two men with whom she had previously worshipped]. ... And we opened that church ..., And we got a little charter in '76 recognized as Spiritual Baptist.

The history of the origin of the Spiritual Baptist Church in Toronto needs to account for two trajectories: One trajectory addresses the formal "recognition" of the church as a registered charitable organization according to Ontario provincial government guidelines. Another trajectory accounts for the informal networks and prayer groups that met in the homes of individuals. "Independent practitioners" such as psychic readers and the "old spiritual women" such as Jamaican Mrs. Benson in Toronto and Guyanese Mrs. Hill in the United States who offer spiritual counselling on an individual basis also played an important role in this community.

Independent practitioners have a long history in black communities in the North American Diaspora of providing "black folk medicine" (Jackson 1997). Described in the title of his article as "the other kind of doctor,"

Jackson points to the crucial role that "medicine men" and "medicine women" have played in Southern American black and white communities since slavery (1997).[4] In fact, a few church leaders with whom I met also did "spiritual work" in which they consulted with individuals, some of whom were not Spiritual Baptists and others who were non-Caribbean, who sought them out for help in health and other matters. One Spiritual Baptist whom I interviewed in Toronto became a member of the religion some time after consulting with a church leader when he was in search of "spiritual work" for help in resolving personal matters.

TORONTO SPIRITUAL BAPTIST CHURCH ORGANIZATION

Spiritual Baptist churches in Toronto emerged as fairly autonomous entities with ties of friendship and "blood" and "spiritual" familial relationships linking churches. By spiritual familial relationships I am referring to the Spiritual Baptist practice of sponsorship for baptism and mentoring beyond this initiatory rite, which fosters bonds between spiritual parents, who are often referred to as spiritual fathers and spiritual mothers, and their spiritual children, who are in turn referred to as spiritual daughters and spiritual sons. Congregations are linked through ties of friendship and family, both "spiritual" and "carnal." Determining exact numbers is also complicated by the fact that there are people who may attend one or more churches. There are also those who worship at mainstream Christian churches and who visit Spiritual Baptist churches from time to time or on special occasions such as a church's anniversary date.

Churches varied in their worship styles and ritual practices from congregation to congregation and from service to service. Not only were no two churches alike, services in individual churches differed from day to day and week to week depending on the interplay between the leaders of the service, the congregation, and, of course, the Spirit. In the next chapter, which discusses the significance of the Spiritual Baptist faith in the lives of Toronto practitioners, I return to a fuller discussion of ritual and its significance in church members' lives.

From my earliest conversations with Spiritual Baptist leaders, the need for more centralized organization of churches was identified. In 1997, a diocese of the Shouters Spiritual Baptist Evangelical faith was established in

Toronto. Archbishop Deloris Seiveright was ordained in June of that year as the archbishop of this diocese by a representative from Trinidad and Tobago. This initiative established a direct organizational link between Spiritual Baptist churches in Trinidad and Tobago and those in Toronto. The implications of this development for Spiritual Baptist churches in Trinidad and Tobago and Toronto deserve further study.

Gender divisions in church leadership and organization feature prominently. In the two churches in which I did my fieldwork, both men and women held leadership roles. Typically men held the highest offices in the church as reverends, shepherds, and leaders while women were mothers of the church, prophetesses, warriors, or teachers.

I met only two female bishops and these were the highest-ranked women in the Spiritual Baptist community in Toronto. In holding these offices, both women remarked that they were "men in the spirit," justifying their occupation of leadership roles with names that draw on the model of the Roman Catholic Church leadership, whose highest offices are occupied exclusively by men. I return to this discussion in greater detail in Chapter 5 when I discuss the role of church mothers in the Spiritual Baptist Church.

Nevertheless, many of the women whom I interviewed noted that they perceived that the work of women in church leadership roles and in other, less prestigious roles in the church, was not given the same recognition and status as those of their male counterparts. While there appears to be a conservative approach to understanding gender in structuring church leadership roles, this conservatism is mediated by the fundamental belief in "spiritual gifts," which, in this case, transcend "carnal" identities. In this way, even identities based on gender and race that have a long history of association with the body as a marker of difference can be transcended. This discussion is revisited at greater length in Chapter 5 with a discussion of "Mothers and Daughters in the Spiritual Baptist Church."

Conclusion

This chapter presents an overview of the emergence of the Spiritual Baptist Church in Toronto during the 1970s and early 1980s. The first Spiritual Baptist communities were prayer groups that met in individuals' homes. From that starting point, highly individualized churches were established starting in the mid-1970s.

Caribbean immigration to Toronto brought together people from various Caribbean islands such as Jamaica, Trinidad, and St. Vincent. Their meeting on religious grounds seems to have fostered a blending and exchange between different African-Caribbean religions that are themselves highly hybrid.

Prior to the establishment of Spiritual Baptist churches in Toronto, Caribbean immigrants whose primary religious affiliation was with Caribbean variants of the Sanctified Church, fulfilled their spiritual needs through a variety of strategies. These included seeking counsel from "spiritual people" who have long ties to the tradition of conjuring in black communities in the Diaspora; participation in mainstreamed Protestant and Catholic churches; the creation of mobile prayer groups that met in the homes of individuals to worship "in the Spiritual Baptist way"; and finally, the establishment of fairly autonomous, though linked, Spiritual Baptist churches with small populations throughout Toronto. Individual Spiritual Baptists also maintained relationships with other Spiritual Baptists in Trinidad and in the United States, creating a transnational network characterized by links of "spiritual families" between churches and individual members. The ordination of Archbishop Deloris Seiveright in 1997 signalled a new chapter in the development of the Spiritual Baptist Church in Toronto. Her ordination created a formal link between Spiritual Baptist Church organizations in Trinidad and Tobago and Canada.

To summarize, it is possible to conceptualize the early history of the Spiritual Baptist Church in a number of historical, political, and cultural histories of related African religious experiences in the Americas. In considering the question of place of origin, however, the historical record also points to a variety of locations, including African, African-American, Trinidadian, and Vincentian origins. Of these four, most researchers are in agreement that Vincentian origins are more than likely for the religion (Houk 1995; Zane 1999; Glazier 1991).

The history of the religion's development in Toronto is intrinsically tied to the everyday life circumstances of its members, both at home in the Caribbean and in the context of immigration and subsequent resettlement in Toronto. As such, I employed a narrative strategy that attempted to show the connections between everyday life experiences and the establishment of Spiritual Baptist churches in Toronto. In many ways, every life story recounted by the practitioners detailed a personal relationship to the establishment of the churches. I have attempted to show through excerpted narratives the intersection of individual auto/biography and the wider history of the religion's development in Toronto. This exploration revealed a great deal of differences between individual participants' experiences. I am in agreement with Glazier, who in discussing his approach to discussing Spiritual Baptist churches in Trinidad discussed his use of the words "many," "some," or "most" in order to point to the variance in approaches and experiences among as well as within churches (1982–83: 23).

The next chapter continues the discussion of the church's history in Toronto through exploring the intersection between the practitioners' experiences of immigration and their religious lives as Spiritual Baptists. The chapter explicitly addresses the ways in which participation in the Spiritual Baptist Church shaped experiences of migration and the ways in which those migratory experiences had an impact on shaping the tradition in Toronto.

NOTES

1 Though Brother John emphasizes the "mergin'" aspects of the Spiritual Baptist faith in this quote, he also notes that the religion is based on African traditions. In Chapter 4, I return to the significance of meaning of "Africa" for Toronto Spiritual Baptists.

2 This quotation appears in Henry (1994: 159).

3 Chevannes in his study of the Rastafari tradition in Jamaica identifies "Revivalism" as the worldview developed by the poor and working class in Jamaica (1994). Revivalism informs not only the Revivalist church, a Caribbean variant of the Sanctified Church, but also Pocomania. Revivalism is characterized by a belief in a hierarchical spirit world over which presides "Massa God" of the Christian tradition. Included here also are spirit beings in Caribbean folk tradition such as "jumbies," as well as the spirits of ancestors and other dead. The spirit world can intervene in human affairs and humans can also interact with the spirit world. Pocomania, also referred to as Pukumina, shares the worldview of Revivalism. It is characterized, however, by an emphasis on connections with ancestors who act as intermediaries in the world of human affairs for their descendants.

4 Jackson argues that there are two types of folk medicine (1997: 420). The first, which is akin to a Western medical model, focused on effecting a cure in an ailing person through the application of a substance to a "somatic problem" (420). The second, Jackson referred to as a type of "religious manipulation," in which the focus is on "attempt[ing] to influence some agent other than the doctor or patient or subject" (420). In an Old World African context, these two approaches often operated together (420). However, in the Southern U.S. black communities, they were often separated with the focus on religious manipulation surviving without an accompanying explanatory framework (420). Religious systems such as Haitian *vodun* feature folk medicine in which both models operate together. Many Spiritual Baptists whom I encountered in Toronto placed some belief in both models of folk medicine.

CHAPTER THREE

"So Spiritually, So Carnally"
Spiritual Baptist Ritual, Theology, and the Everyday World in Toronto

Make a joyful noise unto the Lord, all ye lands. —PSALM 100:1

INTRODUCTION

In Chapter 2, I outlined the emergence of the early Spiritual Baptist churches in Toronto in the mid-1970s. My analysis, based on interviews with a cohort of long-time practitioners, suggested that Spiritual Baptist churches emerged in the mid-1970s as a component of a broad spectrum of religious practices used by recently emigrated Caribbean people to meet their spiritual and social needs. These included attending services in established, mainstream Christian denomination churches such as the Roman Catholic, Methodist, and Anglican; consulting independent spiritualist practitioners; forming home-based prayer groups; and out of these latter establishing churches, frequently in storefronts—commercial property in both downtown and suburban locations.

This chapter continues the discussion of Toronto Spiritual Baptist history by focusing on the ways in which the Spiritual Baptist worldview and accompanying ethics and ritual practices are used by practitioners to make sense of, and negotiate, their everyday lives in Toronto. Included in this discussion is a consideration of how these aspects of the Spiritual Baptist tradition are transformed through the practitioners' life experiences in Toronto. Of critical concern here are the changes and adaptations to the Spiritual Baptist tradition that have taken place in the context of migration to Toronto.

These changes are a point of contention among practitioners. On one hand, some view changes as straying from a notion of "orthodox" Spiritual Baptist practice centred on the perfection of ritual performance. This sentiment was expressed to me on a number of occasions as concern about "things being done right" and "properly." This concern echoes a need, noted by Zane in his study of the Vincentian Converted in Brooklyn, New York, for a Caribbean-based religion to stay the same in the context of migration as it represents "home" (1999). On the other hand, changes are viewed by others as unavoidably necessary given the current circumstances in which church members live their lives. Indeed, the remarks made by Sister Asha, a young, twenty-something Trinidadian woman whom I used to preface the Introduction to this study, point to this dual tension. Sister Asha noted that the Toronto Spiritual Baptist Church she attended made her feel as "if you're in Canada but you're back in Trinidad" and that it was "the closest thing to home." However, in the next breath she noted that "[i]t's similar in most ways but, you know, you find, you know, one or two things different."

This idea that Spiritual Baptist worldview, ethics, and ritual are symbolic of "home" while responding to the challenges of Toronto life is crucial for understanding the development of the religion in the context of migration. However, this assertion is not meant to imply that the Spiritual Baptist tradition is unchanged in a Caribbean context or that its development *there* has followed an *a priori* determined path in a way that it has not in Toronto. Rather, my emphasis in this chapter is to demonstrate the ways in which the tradition in Toronto has been shaped by the circumstances of the practitioners' lives, which simultaneously, for many, include a longing for home. In other words, my claim here, following from earlier discussion, is that a model of cultural development and religious formation that positions the Spiritual Baptist Church in Toronto solely as an extension of the tradition in the Caribbean does not fully appreciate the extent to which Toronto practitioners have contributed to the development of the religion in ways that are unique to their social location. I should reiterate at this juncture that the analysis is presented in fairly generalized terms because in many ways each individual's experience constitutes its own historical trajectory.

Throughout the fieldwork process, it became increasingly apparent through sermons in church services, in conversations with Spiritual Baptist Church members, and in interviews that the ways in which the religion was changing as a result of its practice in Toronto were key points of debate and dialogue. Clearly, practitioners were self-consciously aware of the ways in which the tradition was being shaped, and they held divergent perspectives on the nature and direction of these changes. Queen Mother Pamela, a Vincentian woman elder in the downtown Toronto church in which I did my field research, comments on the significance of these changes using the analogy of "switching furniture around." Through the use of this analogy she indicates this self-conscious awareness as she compares her early upbringing in a Gospel Hall church with her current worship in the Spiritual Baptist Church in Toronto:

> QMP: Then going to the Baptist Church, I still did not forget the teaching that I got from my father and my mother, right. But times pass. I still believe in what my father teach me was the right way, anyway I still believes, yes I still believes. It's only that, ahm, when you come here sometimes you have to change the thing around a little. 'Cause sometimes it's just like a living room. You have you living room and you wouldn't want to have furnitures one way all the time so you change around a little, you know? Sometimes.[1]
>
> CBD: But is the same furniture?
>
> QMP: Yes.
>
> CBD: I understand.
>
> QMP: Right. Same furniture cause you can't go out every time and buy new ones, so is the same. So is the same God we're praying to, right? But is only that it have—you have your morals and I have mine, you know? 'Cause I sure that you go to church whether Baptist, Anglican, Roman Catholic, Evangelist, you go to church. But then your teaching would be different from mine. We all pray in different—we do different things for the same one person.[2]

Concerns about changing rituals were expressed in a variety of ways. These included the already noted concerns about the "proper" performance and the ways in which time constraints, including shift work performed by some members, impinged on participation in church services and other ritual practices.

In discussing the ways in which Toronto Spiritual Baptists have shaped the tradition to meet their own needs, this chapter considers the significance of the "churchly expression" (Cone 1975: 22) "so spiritually, so carnally." This phrase encapsulates a worldview that positions Spiritual Baptists as not solely otherworldly in orientation, although the spiritual predominates, but as also having one foot squarely planted in an explicit concern for material, "this worldly" relations. From this perspective, the spiritual and the material worlds are intrinsically linked in a series of complex relationships. Significantly, as I will argue below, ritual and theology, often conceptualized separately as "action" and "thought," are also deeply linked in ways that transgress this rigid distinction.

The chapter is organized as follows: after outlining Toronto Spiritual Baptists' worldview, I discuss the major rituals of the Toronto Spiritual Baptist Churches. These include weekly church services, baptism, mourning, pilgrimage, thanksgiving, and West Indian Day, a social event/ritual unique, as far as I know, to Toronto. Having set the stage for understanding the worldview and ritual practices that underscore the Spiritual Baptist faith, I then discuss the ways in which Spiritual Baptists engage their daily lives through religious practice and the way in which everyday, "carnal" events influence and shape their religious lives. I also include here a discussion of healing traditions, including spiritual readings.

The everyday events that this chapter discusses include experiences of racism that pervade almost every aspect of daily life, the immigration process of "coming to Canada," and work experiences that for many occur in marginalized occupations such as paid domestic service. I have focused on these experiences because of the central role that they have played in shaping the church members' life experiences in Canada. This assessment is based on the interviews in which these topics tended to dominate even when participants were discussing topics that could be conventionally termed "spiritual" in nature. Many of those whom I interviewed cited employment opportunities and resultant financial reward as the primary reason for immigration to Canada. Even when faced with the harsh realities of Toronto life that quickly dashed visions of Canada as a "paradise" and "land of milk and honey," like many other Caribbean immigrants, Spiritual Baptists remained and fashioned a life for themselves. When educational initiatives and desires were discussed, these were almost always linked with perceptions of affording greater employment opportunities and higher earnings. Chapters 5 and 6 extend this discussion of employment experiences through examining paid domestic service, an occupational area in which many of the women whom I interviewed had worked or continued to work. I have also included an extended discussion of race and racism in this chapter because interviews and conversations revealed that both common sense and institutional ideologies and practices based on race had structured almost every facet of Spiritual Baptist men's and women's lives in Canadian society. The chapter concludes with a discussion of the significance of the church-based support networks that form the basis of a church community.

"SO CARNALLY, SO SPIRITUALLY"

As I have already noted, African religions in the Americas emerged in response to the spiritual, political, economic, and social needs for survival of enslaved Africans and their descendants. While there is tremendous variation among New World African religions, one can point to orientations that both accommodate and resist the hardships of living in societies dominated by racism (Baer and Singer 1992). On one hand, the religions emerged with the dual responses of enabling black people to "git ovah" (Smitherman, 1994: 124), to survive hardships without necessarily transforming existing social relations, while on the other, they also demanded, in explicit terms, the transformation of societies.[3] As it will become apparent in the following, often this dual impulse is expressed simultaneously in a single expression or by a single actor. This seemingly ambiguous approach does not emerge from a lack of awareness or a lack of taking a well-articulated position, but rather underscores a worldview that is both immensely practical in its orientation to the everyday life problems at the same time that it is "otherworldly" in its constant reference to Spirit and spirits. The Spiritual Baptist Church shares this worldview with other African and African Diasporic religions (Hood 1990: 183). This viewpoint underlies perspectives that endorse engagement with carnal, material, or profane matters through the spiritual or sacred, and that see the religious as manifest in seemingly mundane and ordinary everyday events.

The phrase "so spiritually, so carnally" (alternatively voiced by some church members as "so carnally, so spiritually") is a key concept of Spiritual Baptist theology in the two Toronto churches in which I did the bulk of my fieldwork. It was used both in church sermons and testimonies as well as in conversations and interviews with the church members. Briefly, this phrase outlines a worldview in which the spiritual and the material (here referenced as carnal) worlds are intrinsically linked. The Spirit, however, takes precedence over carnal or material world. The Spiritual Baptist conception of the term "carnal" has its basis in the King James Version of the Bible where it means "fleshly" or "physical" (I Corinthians 2:14–15; 9:10–11 as cited by Zane 1999: 33). Spirit is used to refer to "the Holy Spirit of God (in a trinity with the Father and the Son), one's spiritual self; and the spiritual realm in which the Baptists work" (ibid.). These three are related to one another and are distinguished from the fourth meaning of spirit, which is a reference to any spiritual being (ibid.).

"So spiritually, so carnally" resonates with what African-American theologians James H. Cone (1975: 22) and Robert E. Hood (1990: 208) refer to respectively as "churchly expressions" and "noise," and sociologist Cheryl Townsend Gilkes (as cited in Thistlethwaite 1989: 118) calls the "four pillars" of the African-American worship experience: preaching, praying, singing, and testifying.

The Spirit of "spiritual," as it is used here, can be understood as a Diasporic African socio-religious consciousness that is an "untidy, dynamic, and ecstatic power that in part is the legacy of the slaves, who adapted the revelations of their traditional spirits to the biblical Spirit after being freighted to the coasts of the Americas and the Caribbean" (Hood 1990: 204). The Spirit is what moves the worshipper to make "noise" (208) such as singing, amens, hallelujahs, to experience ecstasy in dance, and to talk in tongues.

The Spirit is rooted in conceptions of divinity in the Spiritual Baptist religion that are multiple. Spiritual Baptist cosmology is hierarchical. It includes the Christian trinity conceptualized as Father and Mother God, Jesus Christ, the Son of God and the Holy Spirit, the prophets of the Old Testament and Hebrew Bible, Christian saints of the Roman Catholic Church, and for some worshipers who also practise "African" work, Orisha deities such as Shango, Ogun, Oshun, Oya, and Osain. There are also Spiritual Baptists who include Indian and Chinese powers in their conceptualization of the spirit world. This was evidenced by the inclusion of statues of Buddha, for example, in one church, as well as references to Hindu deities such as Hanouman, Lakshmi, and Durga in another. For some Spiritual Baptists, according to Sister Asha, there is an evil side of the world of spirit, evidenced by the existence of evil spirits or "spirits of illusion and confusion."

Glazier (1980: 90), in his discussion of the Spiritual Baptist worldview in Trinidad, noted there is also a sharing in the belief in the existence of spirit beings that have their basis in Caribbean hybrids and draw on European and African folk cultures. These include the *lagahus* (wolf man), *lajables* or *jables* (a devil woman who appears in the form of a beautiful woman to entrap men), and *soukouyan* or *sukoiyaas* (literally a bloodsucker akin to a vampire that is once again usually associated with women, especially older women). The *lagahus* is the Caribbean variant of the werewolf; the *lajables*, the succubi; and the *soukouyan*, the vampire (Niehoff and Niehoff 1960, as cited in Glazier 1980: 90). In the two churches in which I did my fieldwork in Toronto, I did not hear any discussion of spirit beings such as these. In fact, if anything, in informal conversations with some congregation members there was a definite move to distinguish themselves as "Christian" by disavowing belief in these types of phenomena and ritual practices associated with countering their existence. Nevertheless, this informal talk also revealed a belief in the ability of certain "gifted" individuals to intervene in a shaman role in order to work on their behalf, spiritually. Brother Tee's testimony, included later in this chapter in the discussion of patterns of joining the Spiritual Baptist Church, discusses the continued significance of this belief in Toronto.

The Spirit is a source of continuity between temporal black communities and the community of the ancestors (Hood 1990: 210). It links the religious expressions of black people with cultural products such as art, literature, music, and poetry (210). Spirit is fundamentally diasporic, connecting such seemingly disparate locations as the United States with the Sea Islands along the coasts of Georgia, the Caribbean, urban northern cities, and New Orleans.[4] For the purposes of our discussion, here, Spirit is significant in connecting Spiritual Baptist experiences between Toronto, the Caribbean, and the United States.

The Spirit is rooted in the carnal—material world. It expresses itself materially through the body and actions of people and through social relationships. Thus Christ and the Word constitute transformative moments (Hood 1990). The spiritual and carnal, in this sense, are inextricably linked. This relationship, manifested in everyday life events and ritual, will be discussed later in this chapter.

RITUAL AS PERFORMANCE AND SOCIAL COMMENTARY

One of the most distinguishing characteristics of Spiritual Baptists is their association with ritual that is exuberantly and unabashedly theatrical in its performance. In the two Toronto churches in which I did my fieldwork, on special occasions such as Thanksgivings, it was not uncommon for non-Spiritual Baptist guests to be present not as ritual participants, per se, but as observers. As much as ritual has been a celebratory aspect of Spiritual Baptist worship, there has long been a pejorative, stereotypical notion of "Baptist" identity as associated largely with disorderly ritual. In fact, in the language of the Trinidad Shouters Prohibition Ordinance of 1917, the ritual acts, especially mourning, obliquely referenced in language prohibiting "persons" from being "shut up" in "any Shouters' house for the purpose of initiating such persons," were especially targeted.[5]

Yet what has often been perceived as an endless round of rituals that are repetitive, mimetic, and seemingly disconnected from the religion's symbolic belief are, in fact, part and parcel of the religion. From this perspective, Spiritual Baptist ritual should be conceived of as *religious thought enacted* (Bell 1996). In many ways, the rituals of the Spiritual Baptist Church should be seen as a significant locus of its theology, as much as the King James Bible can be viewed as a scriptural source. As theologian James Cone notes:

> Black theology is not an academic theology; it is not a theology of the dominant classes and racial majorities. It is a theology of the black poor, reconstructing their hopes and dreams of God's coming liberated world. The sources for this theology are not found in Barth, Tillich, and Pannenberg. They are found in the spiritual, blues and sayings of our people. We must go back to black churches so as to authenticate our vocation by helping them to move closer to their calling to be God's instrument of liberation in the world. (1984: 117–18)

This idea of a theology "deeply embedded in black church history" (117) is particularly significant given the important role of the oral tradition in song, sermon, testimony, prayer, and movement that is evident in the church. Cone's emphasis here, however, is on "words": "We must uncover their words about God and make them the foundation of a black theology" (117). I wish to emphasize not only the significance of the content of the spoken, sung, prayed, or testified *word/Word* in ritual but also its performative context. To disconnect ritual action from thought is to effectively deny the notion of embodied thought that is implied by the phrase "so spiritually, so carnally."

Catherine Bell notes that ritual is usually conceptualized as overtly associated with religious "action" as distinguished from the "conceptual aspect of religion" that includes beliefs, symbols, and myths (1996: 22). In discussing Spiritual Baptist ritual, I draw on Bell's call to reconceptualize ritual as something other than "*thoughtless* action—routinized, habitual, obsessive, or mimetic—and therefore the purely formal, secondary, and mere physical expression of logically prior ideas" (ibid.).

Indeed, Bell's claim about ritual being conceptualized as thoughtless is borne out in Staal's notion of the "meaninglessness of ritual" in his article of the same name (1996: 483–94):

> A widespread but erroneous assumption about ritual is that it consists in symbolic activities which refer to something else. It is characteristic of a ritual performance, however, that it is self-contained and self-absorbed. The performers are totally immersed in the proper execution of their complex tasks. Isolated in their sacred enclosure, they concentrate on correctness of act, recitation and chant. Their primary concern, if not obsession, is with rules. There are no symbolic meanings going through their minds when they are engaged in performing ritual. Such absorption, in itself, does not show that ritual cannot have a symbolic meaning. (484–88)

Staal goes on to note, with regards to role of critics and scholars of ritual, that the search for meaning should not be confined to the performers: "If we wish to know the meaning or theory of ritual, we should not *confine ourselves* to practising ritualists; we have learned, after all, that it does not pay to ask elephants about zoology, or artists about the theory of art" (485; emphasis added).

In this section, as I have done throughout the book, I consult with the proverbial "elephants" and "artists" of Staal's metaphor in discussing Spiritual Baptist ritual in theory and practice. Staal's statements are rife with assumptions about the nature of ritual, the role of the researcher, and the nature of sacred space. If the researcher is also a ritual performer and the sacred space is not a confined area but one that "moves" with the ritual performer (as illustrated by the Spiritual Baptist expression "this spot of ground"), a perspective that situates the theorist as an outsider inherently better suited for the thinking role is not the most appropriate framework.

Spiritual Baptist ritual practices are constitutive of both *thought* and *action*. They are an integrative part of the life experiences of church members. In part, this approach is consistent with Tambiah's notion of "ritual as performance" (1996) as well with as Smith's notion of the "everyday world as problematic" (1987) in which she develops a critical feminist sociology that examines power relations in mundane, daily life activities. As Tambiah notes, "[W]e cannot in any *absolute* way separate ritual from non-ritual in the societies we study. But *relative* contrastive distinctions (rather than *absolute* distinctions) help us to distinguish between certain kinds of social activity" (1996: 495). In this way, then, it is possible to conceptualize Spiritual Baptist rituals as an integral component of the practitioners' lives. From this perspective, Spiritual Baptists are self-consciously aware of their roles as ritual participants as well as the ritual activity itself constituting a commentary, or thinking role in the activity.

This approach resonates strongly with the notion of "so spiritually, so carnally," in that the performative aspect of ritual, which can be understood as the carnal, is not distinct from its spiritual, or conceptual/thinking aspect. Nor is it understood as necessarily separate from the ritual participants' everyday lives. As indicated in the very first words with which this book began, the bishop's pronouncement that "it was through a vision" that he got to come to Canada, ritual is clearly deeply implicated in Toronto Spiritual Baptists' everyday lives.

The dynamic of ritual as thought and action, which informs and in many ways constitutes the lived religious experience of Spiritual Baptists, is present in significant events, including church services, baptism, mourning, and pilgrimage, as well as communal meals such as West Indian Day and Thanksgiving.

Services

Church services provide the main occasion for congregational gathering and worship. They are also the space in which information is exchanged both in formal, designated times such as the church secretary's announcements during the service, as well as "informally," in conversations prior to or following church services. On many occasions, I engaged in conversations with church members on the journey home on Toronto public transportation or in church members' vehicles.

Church services in the two Toronto churches in which I did my fieldwork tended to last anywhere from three to six hours. This time frame is consistent with that noted by Glazier in his research on Trinidad Spiritual Baptists in the late 1970s (1980: 94). Church services were held on Sundays and Tuesdays, although the Sunday service was by far the most regularly attended by church members. Occasionally, services were longer, particularly on special occasions such as the consecration of a new church, when a number of guest speakers from other Toronto churches as well as U.S.-based church leaders were present. One such occasion was the consecration of Mother Yvonne's church on May 28, 1995. This service even included a half-hour break for refreshment. On other occasions of lengthy services, the extension in time was due to the "manifestation of the spirit" in one or several church members.

The length and beginning time of church services was sometimes rescheduled to accommodate seasonal shifts in daylight due to Toronto's northern hemispheric location with its characteristic short winter days and early setting sun. On most occasions, services were held in the mid-Sunday afternoon beginning around 3:00 p.m. with a view to ending at 6:00 p.m. However, these services sometimes did not get underway until well after the designated starting time. They were usually preceded by a song service led by a sister, mother, or brother in the church. On one occasion, I was asked by the bishop of the downtown church to lead a song service. Usually, however, I took turns in raising hymns along with the other women who were present.

Young children under the age of twelve participated in a children's Sunday school class in both churches. Children were present for the opening of the service and then left with the Sunday school teacher after a prayer and blessing at the centre pole. These children would rejoin the congregation about two-thirds of the way through a service. Pre-school-aged toddlers and infants usually stayed with their mothers or other caregivers during the service. In the downtown church, one young girl frequently delighted the congregation with her fervent enjoyment of movement when, even as a young toddler, she swayed, clapped, and danced in perfect time to the harmonies of the hymns sung by the congregation.

During my research, the length of the church services emerged as an issue for church members, especially on Sunday nights when there were members who had school-age children or who themselves had to report to their jobs either that evening or very early the next morning. It was not uncommon to observe a member make a discreet exit in order to go to work. In one situation, a church mother who worked night shifts would attend church on Sunday and leave directly from church to go to her job.

A common response to the issue of time (to which I return in Chapter 4 on Africaland), from both speakers in the pulpit and in the congregation, was the notion that appropriate time had to be given to the spirit just as time had been given to the boss on the job. In fact, it was often noted that time spent in church was time meant to fortify the attendees in preparation for the rigours in their work lives, especially in the upcoming week. At one church service I attended, a prayer was offered for bosses.

On other days of the week, regularly scheduled activities were held at the church. These included Bible study meetings and choir practices. In the initial weeks of my research at the downtown Toronto church in the fall of 1992, a youth group comprising young adults in their late teens and twenties met weekly, although the regularity of these meetings varied with the availability of group members.

Services were conducted by a variety of church leaders, including men and women and senior and junior members. A monthly schedule, usually drawn up by the leader of the church and posted within view on the church's notice board, detailed the leaders of the service. Nevertheless, church services were also subject to change, depending on the presence of visiting members and leaders from other churches. It was characteristic for more junior members to appear earlier in the service, when they would read selected biblical passages or preach. More senior members followed later in the service, and the highest-ranking leader of the church would preach last. This pattern conforms to that noted by Glazier in his study of Trinidad Spiritual Baptists (1980: 95).

All services begin with a "surveying" of the church. Surveying is a ritual cleansing of the space that establishes it as sacred, as suggested by Zane, in his description of a similar ritual in Vincentian Converted services (1999: 191). Surveying is performed by the mothers of the church who have received this particular spiritual gift. Perfumed waters are poured along with offerings of milk, grain, and meal at the church's entrance. The bell, representing the voice of God, is rung and incense is burned at the centre pole and the four corners— the veritable "four corners and bounded centre"—often referenced by church members as a representation of not only the physical layout of the church but of Spiritual Baptist cosmology as well.[6] In the services I attended, this surveying took place at the start of the service while the congregation sang the hymn "When I Survey the Wondrous Cross." The Holy Spirit would then be invited into the midst of the congregation and the service would begin.

Contrary to stereotypic images of Spiritual Baptist worship as characterized by spirit possession and other ecstatic forms of worship, services were for the most part "cool." The "ecstatic" parts, in which members would experience "manifestation" of the Spirit, occurred well into the service after the church had been surveyed, and the evening lesson had been read. This pattern, too, corresponds to that noted by Zane (1999).

The services at both churches made room for the inclusion of speakers who were not necessarily connected with worship. These speakers were persons who were overwhelmingly concerned with carnal issues—issues that frequently emerged from the practitioners' everyday life experiences of confronting racism in Toronto. On one occasion in the fall of 1992, I was present at a service in which a church sister noted that there would be a race relations seminar at the church. I was told by a member that past speakers in the downtown church had included a Toronto police officer, and I was present on one occasion when a municipal government member addressed the congregation. I, too, was invited to address the church in this fashion, as "scholar," on my initial visits to the church. Over time, however, the nature of my invitations to speak straddled both carnal and spiritual terrain as I was invited to speak about my research experiences in extemporaneous, testimonial fashion.

Baptism

Baptism is the *rite de passage* (van Gennep 1960 [1909] in Grimes [ed.] 1996) of initiation in the Spiritual Baptist religion. It is one of the most important rituals in the religion as it marks the point of entry of a "new life" in Christ and as a Spiritual Baptist. The lyrics of the Spiritual Baptist song "I Found a New Life" attests to the importance of Baptism as a "new" beginning and "new life," a re-birth for the church member:

I found a new life
I found a new life
If anyone ask you
What's the matter with you my friend?
Tell them that you are saved, sanctified, water-baptized, Jesus is mine
I found a new life

Baptism as an initiatory rite marking the beginning of a new life and new identity as a Spiritual Baptist was often viewed within the wider context of an individual's life as a kind of healing in the face of difficulties. In many instances, Spiritual Baptists spoke of difficult circumstances that they had encountered in their everyday lives of work and relationships that let them know that they "need to get baptize." Many of the Toronto Spiritual Baptist women with whom I spoke noted that the decision to become baptized was an intensely personal one into which one should not be forced by leaders ambitious to increase the size of their congregations or reputations. In the following, Mother Ruth discusses the value of making an independent

decision regarding baptism. She underscores the importance of this independence by noting that her mother, who was a Spiritual Baptist herself,
left the decision to join the church up to her children as they grew into
adulthood. Thus Mother Ruth, whose early childhood coincided with the
period of official banning by colonial ordinance in Trinidad (1917 to 1951),
"grew up" in the faith although she was not baptized until later in her
adult life:

MR: Well, I really grow up in the Spiritual Baptist faith. I born and met
my mom in it and um—although I was christened Catholic at that time,
because in those days the Baptist religion weren't recognized in Trinidad,
right? And so even though you're Baptist you still had to baptize your
children in Catholic or Anglican. So um, I was christened in Catholic
and—but I knew more about the Baptist religion than about the Catholic
religion. And um, I always had liked it, you know? And my mom said
to us, you know, um that she's not going to um … this is something to
get into the religion, this is something you have to do on your own.
Nobody can force you into it. Nobody can make that decision. So, as
children she said she's not going to force us into the religion. It's something that when we get older and understand we have to do on our own.
But I always used to, you know, follow up the religion and so on around.
Even at one time we had a church in the back of our yard you know. And
um … when I left, I always hearing one day I hafta baptize, one day I'm
goin' to baptize but like the time wasn't there yet because like I had
couple friends and they baptize—but they baptize for certain reasons
right? which—in I didn't want to do that, I wanted to do it when the time
was right.

And ahm, I came up here and after I spend, what, four years up here
while's I'm up here [Canada] I started to have like dreams and so on and
I used to find myself walking on the sea, walking by the seashore or
sailin' on a boat or something. And with my belief I think that was my
calling to baptism. And I make that decision there and then. I say, "When
I go home to Trinidad on vacation I'm going and get baptize" and yeah,
and that's where I made my decision.

So, I didn't wait for anyone to say, come and tell me, "Oh you have
to get—" I mean people try that before in Trinidad when I was younger.
I go to like Crusade and the Seven Days' church and so on and they
give you these little […] to do where you mark your name and address
and ting and next thing they show up at your home and try to—and

they show up at your home and just try to, you know, tell you, you have to get baptize and—I went to one crusade once and the minister was preachin' "Now is the time come and do it!" And he had all like little kids, the way he was preachin' kids were getting scared and they were putting down their names ... and "we would provide the towels for you." Little kids, maybe their parents weren't even there and they were just goin' ... But this is not what I wanted people to tell me I have to make a decision. Each and everyone has to make decision. I knew I wanted to be in the Baptist religion.

Baptism for Spiritual Baptists is performed by full immersion of the baptismal candidate in ocean or river water by the leader who is performing the ritual. Male leaders perform baptismal rites exclusively in the Spiritual Baptist Church. In Toronto, Spiritual Baptists are baptized in bodies of water that approximate the ocean and river. Given the geographical location of Toronto in a landlocked area in the centre of Canada bounded by Lake Ontario to the south, a substitute for these natural bodies of water must be found. In Toronto, it is lake water beyond the city limits. Jokes were often made among congregation members about how cold the "Canada water" was compared to the warmth of the Caribbean Sea.

The following description of baptism is based on interviews with Toronto Spiritual Baptists who were baptized in Toronto from the 1970s to 1990s, as well as my attendance at one of the baptism rites held by the suburban church led by Mother Yvonne in July 1994. The actual baptism is preceded by a daylong period of fasting and prayer that approximates a short mourning. Baptism candidates, as they are called, are prepared for baptism by attending a series of classes focused on Bible study. They are sponsored by others who have already been baptized. These spiritual parents, both spiritual mothers and fathers, often go on to play significant roles in the candidates' lives post-baptism.

The night before the baptism, a service is held at the church. The service I attended, in 1994, began around 8:00 p.m. and continued until 2:00 a.m. The baptismal candidates dress in white and wear "bans" (effectively blindfolded by long strips of cloth tied around their eyes) and are brought out into the service by their "nurses." They are made to sit on the "mercy seat," or the "mourning bench," as an act of penitence. There they "tramp" in time to the hymns and songs sung by the congregation. They are encouraged in their tramping and singing by their nurses, who effectively "labour" with them. An image that remains emblazoned in my mind from that July night in 1994 is that of the nurses trampin' and marchin' with the baptism candidates. This period on the mercy seat is meant to be a time in which the candidates ask God for forgiveness of their sins. The baptism candidates are then led to the mourning room, where they remain until the following morning, attended by mothers and nurses. They effectively fast until their baptism is completed the next morning by immersion in water.

In the meantime, the rest of the congregation carries on a service into the early hours of the morning. At the baptism that I attended, the service continued until 2:00 a.m. After a snack and brief period of rest, all those gathered, including the baptism candidates, were transported by chartered bus to a small lake in the Collingwood area in the Ontario countryside for the performance of the baptism. On the bus, songs were sung and a service, complete with lighted candles, was conducted for the baptism candidates. One of the mothers even went into the spirit.

The temperature at the lakeside was cold and chilly. In the windy stillness of the early morning, a temporary altar was made on the sand. The archbishop, the leader of the downtown church, waded into the water in his red cassock. Some of the mothers made offerings to the water. The pilgrims were led out in the water and dunked three times by the bishop. Songs sung at the lakeside included "Leave Your Burden Down by the Riverside." When the newly baptized emerged from the water, they were wrapped in white sheets and escorted back to the bus by their nurses where they changed into white spiritual clothes. After their baptism, others present made an offering to the water using the bread distributed earlier by a mother. On the way back to the church, more songs were sung. When we arrived at the church, a service was held for the newly baptized, and they were instructed on giving the handshake of greeting and on the significance of the four corners of the church and the centre pole. A meal was served after the service. The entire process was a day-long event, taking twenty-four hours from start to finish.

Baptism is, in effect, the initiatory rite, the first step in formal membership as a member of the Spiritual Baptist faith. However, the reasons motivating baptism vary and can include the use of the rite as a way of dealing with negative circumstances in an individual's life. The occurrence of these may be interpreted as a sign that a radical change, literally a "new life" path, symbolized by a ritual of death and rebirth in Christ, should be embarked upon.

Mourning

Mourning is a definitive ritual of Spiritual Baptist worship. It is, perhaps, the one ritual that is associated most closely with the tradition. Like baptism, mourning also includes at its core a concept of symbolic death and rebirth. Mourning, in its simplest terms, is a period of prayer and fasting usually lasting from seven to twenty-one days. During this time the "pilgrim," the term designating one who mourns, "travels" spiritually, experiencing mystical visions and encounters with beings in the spirit world. The travel destinations include the ancestral lands of Caribbean working people—historically, Africa, India, and China, as well as the biblical lands such as Canaan. The ritual is guided by a "pointer," who acts as interpreter of the "tracts," accounts of the pilgrim's spiritual travels. The physical needs of the pilgrim are attended by nurses, women who are church mothers whose spiritual gift is this specific function. Baptism is a prerequisite for mourning, as far as I could determine, among the two Toronto church communities where I did my fieldwork.

African-American mourning rituals have their basis in the Protestantism of the eighteenth-century American plantations and urban areas (Glazier 1985b: 141). Similarities exist between Euro-American and African-American worship traditions. However, there were also differences mediated by the diverse social locations of whites and blacks in the racially segregated slave societies of the eighteenth century (ibid.). Mourning is usually associated with death but also has significance as a "seeking" experience or "vision quest" (ibid.) in the Christian worship experiences of both Southern Baptist African-American and Spiritual Baptist worship.

Although mourning is fundamentally a seeking experience, Spiritual Baptists mourn for a wide variety of reasons that include seeking guidance from the Spirit regarding specific personal problems and crises, as well as a particular spiritual path. It is this latter instance in which "spiritual gifts," which are enacted through various church offices in the hierarchy of leadership, are bestowed by the Spirit. The *interpretation* of symbols from the pilgrim's journey by the pointer determines the pilgrim's spiritual gift rather than the actual symbols themselves. In this way, mourning, as Glazier notes, is deeply related to church organization and advancement in the church's hierarchy (1983, 1985a, 1991). Glazier's analysis points to the importance of the ritual in directly influencing individual members' progress through ranks of leadership in the Trinidad Spiritual Baptist church. He concluded that, through its highly formalized and repetitive structure, the mourning ritual did not leave much leeway for individual members' creative expression (1985b: 155).

While there were sentiments expressed by Toronto Spiritual Baptists that indicated they were well aware of the significant role of the pointer and other senior church leaders in interpreting their mourning tracts, by and large the members viewed mourning as a valuable and profoundly meaningful worship experience. In other words, the experiences of the Toronto Spiritual Baptists whom I interviewed challenged Glazier's conclusion that Trinidad Spiritual Baptist mourning was by and large connected to advancement within church leadership and therefore this association interfered with its value as a worship experience that encouraged self-expression. Interestingly, some church members noted that they preferred to mourn in Trinidad and indeed to do all of their "spiritual work" in Trinidad as their spiritual parents who pointed them still lived in Trinidad. Their participation in Toronto Spiritual Baptist worship was viewed primarily as a necessity due to residence in Toronto.

Glazier compared the mourning rituals of Spiritual Baptists in Trinidad with Southern African-American Baptists and concluded that while they may share historical roots, they were fundamentally different in their relevance to church members' worship experience (1985b). Glazier sees the mourning ritual of African-American Southern Baptists as allowing far greater scope for self-expression for the individual mourner while the latter, in a Trinidadian context, is much more formulaic, or stereotypic (155). Based on the interviews I conducted with Toronto Spiritual Baptists, it seems that, in the context of Canadian immigration, mourning embodies both aspects of Southern African-American "seeking"[7] experiences as well as those of Trinidad Spiritual Baptists that are deeply connected to advancement within the church's leadership structure. Thus it is both a powerful, personal spiritual experience for individual practitioners and an important determinant of position within the church's hierarchy.

Thus far, mourning has been discussed in relation to its socio-historical context and spiritual and political significance for Spiritual Baptists. At this juncture, let us turn to a discussion of the underlying theories of mind/body/spirit relationships out of which the mourning experience emerges. From a "psychoanthropological" perspective (Ward and Beaubrun 1979), drawing on both insights from psychological and anthropological approaches, the mourning ritual is an "altered state of consciousness" that is "naturally occurring" and "self-induced" (487). Ward and Beaubrun note

that in "Western developed societies" there is an "ethnocentric concept of
the mind" that is very "fixed," producing a singular conception of a "normal" experience of consciousness (479). The dominant concept of mind is
characterized as "a state of striving, organized to manipulate the environment
and oriented toward the achievement of personal goals. Its psychological
components include focal attention, object-based logic, heightened boundary perception, and a dominance of formal characteristics over sensory traits"
(Deikman 1971, as cited in Ward and Beaubrun 1979: 479). As a result of
this ethnocentrism, alternative states of consciousness are regarded, generally, as "abnormal or pathological" (479). From this conception, research on
altered states of consciousness, with the exceptions of dreaming and med-
itation, tends to be conducted under laboratory conditions (478). As a result,
any assessments of altered states of consciousness fail to locate them within
lived social contexts (479).

   The study by Ward and Beaubrun of Trinidad Spiritual Baptists, however, locates mourning as an altered state of consciousness that occurs within
a wider social context of Spiritual Baptist experiences (1979). The authors
characterize mourning as a state of consciousness beyond the everyday that
is facilitated by both "sensory bombardment" and "sensory deprivation"
techniques (483–84). Sensory bombardment techniques included activities
such as "singing, clapping, chanting, tromping, shouting and repetitive
preaching" that "engage the sympathetic nervous system" (484), while sensory deprivation is employed through the solitude and darkness of the
mourning room in which pilgrims pray and fast (484). These activities facil-
itate visual and auditory hallucinations (484). In addition to sensory bombardment and deprivation, mourners' visions are facilitated through
"expectation, motivation and demand characteristics" (484), which also
influence experiences of trance and hallucination—otherwise described as
the otherworldly and mystical experiences of the pilgrim. Because pointers
are aware of this tendency of expectation to guide visionary experiences,
they claim to employ checks to verify the truthfulness or falsity of these
experiences, although many pilgrims still achieve their desired outcome (486).

   As I have already noted, Glazier (1985b, 1991) is particularly critical of
the efficacy of mourning as a form of worship for Trinidad Spiritual Baptists that allows for self-expression given its role in securing advanced leadership positions with the church hierarchy. While there is certainly evidence
of this association in the Toronto Spiritual Baptist community, there are
also "psychosocial benefits" (Ward and Beaubrun 1979: 486) of mourning that

underscore its continued significance as worship experience beyond associations with church organization and leadership. Ward and Beaubrun point
to the role of trance as a "tension releasing and anxiety reducing mecha-
nism" (486). In addition, through mourning itself, and the resultant advancement within the church's hierarchy of leadership positions, Spiritual Baptists
are afforded a degree of prestige, accomplishment, and recognition that is
not available to them in the wider society (486).

Subsequent discussion in this and later chapters will show that these
benefits are particularly important in the context of migration to Toronto.
In Toronto, the majority of Spiritual Baptists have encountered racism in
almost every facet of their everyday lives. As well, they are incorporated
into the economy, for the most part, in marginalized employment sectors
such as paid domestic service. Zane notes the irony that while the Converted in Brooklyn are generally of a higher spiritual status due, in large
part, to their economic ability to more readily afford the cost of sponsoring
a mourning compared to their Vincentian counterparts, they are nevertheless largely constrained to positions as "servants to Whites" in their working lives (1999: 166). In Chapters 5 and 6, I revisit the connections between
servitude, particularly paid domestic service, and Spiritual Baptist women's
religious lives as mothers of the church.

While Ward and Beaubrun's article offers insights into the mind/body
connection from an anthropsychological point of view, a view of spirit is
also important here, for the conceptualization of the soul is important in
order to understand mourning from a spiritual point of view. Spiritual Baptists employ a "multiple soul concept." This tripartite view is shared by
other indigenous African-Caribbean religions such as Revival in Jamaica.
From this perspective, a human being possesses a spirit, soul, and shadow
(Chevannes 1994: 27–28). The soul returns to God upon death; the spirit
travels during dreams and in trance; and the shadow is "a reflection of the
self" (28) that can be separated from the self through the practice of obeah.

In my research, this conception of the soul was alluded to in several
instances involving trance. For example, a Spiritual Baptist brother noted on
one occasion following a church service that a woman was "chasing after her
spirit" in explaining why the woman, after going "into manifestation" of
the spirit, then proceeded to run outside of the church clad only in her
church clothing and without outer layers of clothing even though it was a
cold and wintry day with sub-zero temperatures. On that particular occasion, she was followed by another church mother, who brought her back into

the church. From there other mothers in the church and the leader of the service "worked" with the woman to "bring her spirit" back, according to the brother. On another occasion, I heard a Spiritual Baptist leader refer to the care necessary in burial rites to ensure that the person is properly buried. In this instance, ritual care is necessary in order to ensure appropriate transition from earthly to spiritual life.

Pilgrimage

Travel and movement, as I have already mentioned, are fundamental characteristics of Spiritual Baptist experience. It seems as if Spiritual Baptists are always on the move. In Toronto, during the period of fieldwork, I would occasionally meet Spiritual Baptist women on their way to church during the week and on weekends, on subways and buses, identifiable by their tied heads and sometimes fully dressed in their "spiritual clothes," consisting of long skirts and long-sleeved blouses, frequently in white but also in other colours such as pink, blue, and brown, the thick belts worn around their waists and aprons signalling their status as mothers of the church.

Pilgrimage has long been associated with many religious traditions, including the monotheistic Western traditions of Islam, Judaism, and Christianity. Pilgrimage is usually conceptualized as travel to a site or place that is sacred. However, what distinguishes pilgrimage in the Spiritual Baptist tradition is that the destination itself is usually not as significant as making the journey. In this scenario, the journeying itself is a sacred act. The sacredness is embodied by the pilgrim-traveller. Zane (1999) points to the importance of John Bunyan's *The Pilgrim's Progress* as providing a type of meta-narrative for the pilgrimages of the Converted in St. Vincent. Along with the King James Bible, this is one of the most important texts of the Converted. There were no explicit references to *Pilgrim's Progress* by Toronto Spiritual Baptists. However, I do not doubt the importance historically, in the development of the religion in Trinidad by migrants from St. Vincent as the term "pilgrim-traveller" and the use of allegory characterize the interpretation of mourning tracts.

Glazier's typology of Caribbean pilgrimages (1983) is useful for understanding Toronto Spiritual Baptist pilgrimages. Glazier distinguishes between "journeys to sacred fixed *places*" and "sacred journeys" or "flexible pilgrimages" (316). He describes Spiritual Baptist pilgrimages in Trinidad as "flexible" rather than "fixed," and his investigation counters the more widely held view of pilgrimages based on the work of Victor Turner (Turner 1973,

1974, 1978 as cited in Glazier 1983) whose view is that pilgrimages are journeys with fixed destinations.

Among the Trinidad Baptists whom Glazier studied, destination was
not necessarily fixed, while Toronto Spiritual Baptist Pilgrimages embark on
both types of pilgrimages. In the two churches in which I did my fieldwork,
entire congregations or, in some instances, representatives of congregations
made pilgrimages to other Spiritual Baptist churches in Toronto and occasionally to churches in Brooklyn, N.Y., Washington, D.C., and Boston,
Mass. On one such pilgrimage, in the spring of 1995, I attended a "convention" at another Spiritual Baptist church in Toronto's suburban west end.
On other occasions, I attended pilgrimages with members of both churches
to other Toronto churches. The out-of-town trips were organized by church
leaders with the assistance of church mothers and the church secretary, in
particular. The price covered bus fare on a chartered bus. Pilgrimages were
sometimes made in conjunction with long-weekend holidays such as the
Labour Day holiday, which is held on the first Monday in September. During my research period, this was the occasion of a pilgrimage from a Toronto
church to a church in Brooklyn. Indeed, as I mentioned in the preface of
this study, my first interaction with the Spiritual Baptist community that I
would eventually enter as a participant/observer was when I took the bus
from Toronto to New York City in September 1987 at the start of my fourth
year as an undergraduate student. On that trip, I was not a pilgrim-traveller
but a vacationer bound to New York for a holiday.

Glazier surmises that three mitigating factors influence pilgrimage (1983:
317–24). Briefly, these include attitudes toward the land, i.e., whether it is
"sacred" or a commodity; the mobility of the gods (resident within the space
or mobile); and national sentiment ("inward" or "outward" looking). Of
these three, Glazier notes that it is the first, attitudes toward the land, that
is most salient in determining the nature of pilgrimages. The Trinidadian
view of land is that it is a commodity. This view is in contrast to the Haitian view of land as sacred. With regard to the second point, Spiritual Baptist gods are remarkably mobile, and the Caribbean's long colonial history
has cultivated a fundamentally outward-looking view that affords a higher
value to things outside of a Caribbean context.

The conditions of life in Toronto and experiences of belonging or alienation from the broad base of Canadian society, including citizenship status, have influenced the ways in which pilgrimage is conceptualized and
enacted by Toronto Spiritual Baptists. In other words, the wider conditions

of immigration to Canada and subsequent status vis-à-vis citizenship shapes the experiences of pilgrimage both within Toronto and to "external" sites in the province of Ontario, outside of the province but within Canada, and international sites involving travel to the United States, the Caribbean, and other countries. In many instances, it would not be stretching a metaphor to suggest that immigration to Canada be considered a pilgrimage in itself. As discussed in the first chapter, the historical positioning of Canada as "land of milk and honey" and "Canaan" in relation to the flight of the enslaved from the United States, as well as later twentieth-century Caribbean immigration, lends itself to this type of interpretation. On the latter point, I heard in 1999 of a Toronto Spiritual Baptist who travelled to England and planned to travel to the "Holy Land" in Israel as a religious pilgrimage. In order, for instance, for a church member to participate in a pilgrimage to the United States, because it is out of the country, his or her immigration status would have to be such that international travel is permissible. The terms and conditions of many domestic worker contracts do not allow international travel outside of Canada until landed immigrant status is achieved.

The annual Spiritual Baptist churches' pilgrimage to Sainte Anne de Beaupré Roman Catholic Church in Quebec is an example of a pilgrimage that combines both "journey to a sacred place" as well as "sacred journey" as outlined by Glazier (1983). I accompanied members from the two churches on their annual pilgrimage in the spring of 1994. The province of Quebec has had a long association with Roman Catholicism, dating back to earliest French colonial times in the seventeenth century. The Basilica of Sainte-Anne-de-Beaupré is renowned internationally as a sacred site, particularly associated with healing miracles. The basilica is located where the waters of the St. Lawrence River narrow, a spot long held by indigenous people as a "power spot" (Crowley 1995: 28). A sailors' chapel was first erected in 1658 in commemoration to Saint Anne for interceding in navigating the St. Lawrence River (ibid.). The first church followed two years later in 1660 (ibid.). The church's association with miraculous healing began shortly thereafter.

The pilgrimage is made primarily because Saint Anne is an important saint in the two Toronto churches where I did my fieldwork and the patron saint of one of them. This is an instance in which Toronto Spiritual Baptists have adapted a ritual practice from another tradition and made it their own. The sacredness of the church was established long before the immigration of Spiritual Baptists to Toronto. In 1665, for instance, Marie de l'Incarnation, a French-born Roman Catholic nun to the then French colonial possession, La Nouvelle France, noted miracles of healing (ibid.). The church members have adapted this practice and integrated it with their own sense of pilgrimage as a sacred journey. This was evidenced by the jubilant singing on the chartered bus to Quebec City and the fasting that church members and all who participated in the pilgrimage were encouraged to do. A Roman Catholic priest said a mass for the group of Spiritual Baptist pilgrim-travellers. It is significant to note that while the worship responses of the Spiritual Baptists gathered was noticeably subdued during the priest's homily, his pronouncements were met with verbal responses such as "hallelujah" and "amen." Here was yet another instance in which the ritual was adapted to meet the needs of Spiritual Baptists while there was an attempt to keep it ritually pure as a Roman Catholic, rather than Spiritual Baptist, church service.

Glazier also noted that pilgrimage takes place from the Caribbean to North America by Spiritual Baptists who travel to metropolitan countries as missionaries. It is one of the few instances in which missionaries travel from areas of the formerly colonized world, the "Third World," to industrialized, capitalist countries. Though not necessarily referred to expressly as missionaries, these senior leaders who travel from Trinidad to Canada are perceived as, and carry out, a missionary role by acting as mentors and teachers to Toronto-based leaders. During the time of my fieldwork in the Toronto churches, I met these individuals on a few occasions. Mother Sylvia whose comments appear at the beginning of the Introduction, in which she describes her meeting the same "zeal of di Spirit in America whey ah lef' in Trinidad" was such a person. She was a Trinidadian Spiritual Baptist Church mother whose pilgrim travels took her to several major North American cities. Mother Yvonne, a Toronto leader, has made similar travels to the United States.

West Indian Day

There are a large number of church social activities that serve a variety of purposes such as entertainment and fundraising. These include an annual church Christmas dinner and dance featuring a fashion show, tea parties, a "Christian" boat cruise and dinner in the Toronto harbour, and a "curry cue" (a shared meal consisting of curried dishes). The appropriateness of "Christians" participating in activities some consider worldly, though associated with church fundraising for basics such as covering the mortgage of the building, is not without controversy, however. Mother Pamela summarized the critique: "They feel that Christians really shouldn't have partying to hire to get the money to pay the mortgage." She holds an alternative viewpoint. In her estimation, "By serving God, or being a Christian, doesn't say that you cannot have friends, or have ... so it doesn't mean that you can't have fun or go to a party." In light of my earlier comments on acknowledging the social context of ritual, these events could be seen as ritual acts with religious significance in themselves. This is precisely the approach that I take in discussing one of the church's social events, West Indian Day.

As far as my review of the literature has determined, West Indian Day is specific to Toronto Spiritual Baptists. It is a social event held by the downtown church in a large park. My discussion of this ritual is based on my participation in this church social event on a summer day in 1994.

In this ritual, Toronto is recast as West Indian through the occupation of a small area of a large, popular urban park in the west end of the city. The activities, which recast this spot as specifically West Indian, as distinct from Torontonian or Canadian, are outdoor cooking on the public barbecue grills and the serving of West Indian cuisine, including boiled corn and desserts. Men, women, and children from the downtown church attended this event held on a summer Saturday afternoon. While "surveying" establishes the church's ground as sacred, it is the preparation and consumption of food; the relaxed atmosphere of people hanging out, "liming,"[8] and talking; and wearing casual clothing minus head covering for most of the women that establishes the spot as West Indian rather than Canadian.

West Indian Day is an important event because it was created in the context of migration to Toronto. It speaks to a nostalgic longing for home as well as a desire to transform Toronto public space into places that exhibit communitarian values affirmed by the community. Many of the Toronto Spiritual Baptists noted a marked contrast between the use of space in Toronto, especially public space, and worship. Most considered Toronto ordinances much more restrictive in the use of public spaces such as parks and streets for public worship, referred to as "open-air meetings." Queen Mother Pamela made this point in reflecting on her first learning about Spiritual Baptists as a child in St. Vincent. It was through the open-air meetings that she learned about the religion:

CBD: Did you ever go to any of their services then?

QMP: Hmhm. Like they uses to have a lot of open-air meetings. Here you can't because of the government here or the whatever, right? But back there it was free, you go and the police or whoever never bother you. So when sometimes when we going or coming from Sunday school you would meet the Baptist people having their services out—

[At this point, Queen Mother Pamela's grandson, Brian, brings some crackers for his younger cousin Malcolm. She interrupts her statement to taste the crackers to see if they are too salty for the child, then says to Brian: "Brian, this thing is salt. He not supposed to have this." Brian responds, "I don't know where the other crackers are." Miss Pamela replies, "Look underneath where the rice is on top that shelf there is a bag with crackers there." She turns to Malcolm and hands him the salty crackers saying, "Come, have this, come." She turns to me saying, "Salty."]

QMP: Yeah.

CBD: So you would pass the open meeting . . .

QMP: Yes we would stand—you know—you would stand around a little and—

[We are again interrupted by Malcolm and Brian regarding the crackers.]

QMP: —yeah, we would go. While passing you know you stand and you listen to—

[We are then interrupted a third time by Brian and Malcolm regarding the cracker.]

Yeah, so I knew about Spiritual Baptists before I came to Canada.

Mother Victoria also lamented what she considered the unusually stringent restrictions on the use of public space in Toronto and compared it to her growing up in the rural St. Vincent of the 1950s. She also notes the way in which this conception of public space affects community relationships, suggesting that the disconnectedness and alienation that many feel in Toronto may be due to the way in which space is fragmented by "ethnic" and other social divisions:

MV: Okay, um—like this thing now too, like Baptist back home, when you dead, right? Up here now, they carry you by this funeral place and sometimes you just two little thing in the church in the funeral parlour or whatsoever and they carry you to the cemetery and that's it. But back home now, if you—I going to church now there by bishop and I dead— is this church coming, is that church coming. You don't have place to hold people. Yeah. Funeral, where you doing down the road. You think you doing down the road in a coffin? In um horse rather? Is men holding you there! And according to your leader sometimes, woman fighting to hold on to the coffin to carry it. But you're walking, you see. And sometimes you get so mucha singing and rejoicing you feel you is in the church and is somebody alive they you talking to you know?

CBD: [laughter]

MV: Yeah. But over here, they don't—they don't do those stuff. They just—they just go in you know like in this so sorrowful way and—that's why I like home. And you having your third night, you're having your nine night, you having your forty days, you having your air night for the other people who living in the house. We keep prayers, we sing, we pray, we shout and kinda thing [hand clap]! And we make—you make your joke. But up here you can't do that. So it—

CBD: Why you feel it doesn't happen up here?

MV: Because you see, the country is one, the law is the next.

CBD: Could you—how you mean the country?

MV: Because, okay, now cemet'ry ain't nearby and as far as what I notice here, like, you have to be rich to get a ordinary a—a hole or whatsoever be nearby, right? Because it looking like if the Filipinos have they own cemet'ry. It look like if they Jamaican have their own cemet'ry. That's how it look to me, eh? Because like if somebody die, you have to go through so much things before you could get the body. Then when you done get the body now, you have to pay so much to—for a whole here. Back home, now. Especially in St. Vincent. In St. Vincent, when somebody dead, I ain't know well for the amount of years for the amount of years, I leave there, but before that, you have—you cut down breadfruit tree, because you burn coals and thing there, right?

When somebody die you know like if you up here and you father dead and you call out "Miss Victoria, you know Poppy die? Poppy dead, you know? Poppy dead last night!" I call and say, "Mammy, you hear what Carol say? She father dead, you know?" And you know, they going—they going and first thing they going and do look 'round because they always have board behind they house. Everybody. So going and look there. Now they going and get—her father and other people going around to see who coming to build the coffin. You get your coffin build, it ain't costing you a cent. You just have to buy little rum and you food, cook and carry for these people. The grave digger, you ain't have to ask he, he gone in the cemetry because it ain't have no black, no white. It ain't ha' no rich, it ha' no poor. It ain't ha' Catholic here and Baptist here. All [hand clap] is the same thing. You going in the one cemet'ry there. You understand? My father was a gravedigger you know? My father was a gravedigger. And sometime like, the person before that bury or you see a skull—he, my father—boy, I know that this thing here could come off here you know. [She points to the top of her head.] Because when he digging the grave and he take up that and he say, "You want this?" I was so scared start to run. And he say, "No" and he just wash it off, like a bone and drink water in it. I say, "Not me." From somebody dead skull?

CBD: [laughter]

MV: Not me, Sister Carol! Not, not—no, no, no!

CBD: What does it look like, like a cap or something?

MV: Yeah.

CBD: Mmmmhmmm.

MV: Mmmmhmmm. Yeah, just like the little piece in here [pointing to the top of her head]. Not me! And you seeing all these big bone! [She points to her legs and arms.] I say, "Lawd, what is this!" You seeing all where your knee join together here? All that. All yuh eye. Yuh bone inside here [points to her face] or your hole and—all these set a' things, man. MmmMmm. Because you see is a—I learn to do a little of everything back home, you know, Sister Carol. Because you know, muh father had so many lands, and he used to work up land. And back home people does um—like if you planting potato today, you just tell—anyone of the neighbour you want to tell, you tell, right? And before you tink and wink you done open dung di whole of Christie hey from Dupont to Christie subway yuh done work it dung already. And while them making the bank, it have people, youth or other chilren, you divide, they dropping. Or if is yam you planting or whatsoever, yuh see. So is a plenty, plenty different ting. And yeah, as I was saying though wid di funeral business, when you ahm—when somebody dead, you have people building the coffin, you have people cooking, you have people um, carrying the food, you have people by the cemet'ry. So, you—is no hard problem. And the onliest thing sometimes—sometimes, eh—is like if rain falling, it have people down there with the pickup van to put the coffin into to go [hand clap]. It not like up here—Canada is plenty—you have to pay so much money to bury somebody. [whisper] And I hear it is even cheaper to take the dead person back to wheresoever they come from insteada burying it in Canada, you know?

CBD: Because it's so expensive.

MV: But back home is not like that. It more plenty, plenty more cheaper. Plenty more. Then up here is everything you had to get a licence for. If you even building over your garage there, you have to get a licence. If you running a raffle, you had to get a licence. Too much, too much, man.

The perception of space that informs the West Indian Day ritual reflects the post-Shouters Prohibition Ordinance years in Trinidad after 1951. As Bishop Dickson's testimony regarding his early introduction to the religion in Trinidad and Tobago as a young man in the 1960s shows, by then, less than twenty years following the lifting of the ban, Spiritual Baptists had taken to the public spaces such as parks to hold their meetings.

One of the interesting aspects of West Indian Day is that, to observers, it probably appears as if church members are simply engaged in having an afternoon picnic on a summer's day while raising some funds for the church through the sale of various snacks and drinks. Without knowing that the people gathered are members of a Spiritual Baptist Church and that they are engaging in acts understood to be "West Indian," namely the food being cooked and the manner of its preparation, West Indian Day would not have any significance. However, it is the naming of the event and comments made to me by one church sister, that on West Indian Day it is like "back home," that highlighted its ritual significance. West Indian Day is internally significant to the group. That is to say, West Indian Day's demarcation of the park as "West Indian" through specific, cultural practices oriented primarily toward food preparation and consumption, does not require an audience or outside acknowledgment that the park space has been delineated in this manner. Indeed, as the "West Indian" events transpired, other park users shared the space, unaware, by all accounts, that they were witnessing "West Indian" events on transformed "West Indian" ground. The West Indian Day celebration contrasts sharply with prayers in public park spaces in which the distinctive clothing of Spiritual Baptist women signals their difference to non-practitioners. While West Indian Day and public prayers take place, ritual practices take place in privatized spaces and it is this distinction that marks Spiritual Baptist practice in Toronto from its Trinidadian counterpart.

Thanksgiving

In the above, I describe West Indian Day, one of the various communal meals (Zane 1999) that the church members shared. These ranged from meals that were specifically spiritual, such as the Eucharist or Communion that took place monthly in both churches, to the annual ritual feeding of the poor that took place in July, to the more secular annual Christmas church dinner and dance and picnics. Thanksgivings are a ritual that feature a service and a meal that is sponsored by someone in giving thanks to God (Zane 1999: 186). Thanksgivings are significant in that they are communal meals that bridge both the public and private, as well as sacred and secular because of the locations in which they are held, and in their interpretation by members of the church community.

I attended thanksgivings that took place both in church settings and in the homes of individual members. As communal meals, thanksgivings are a way in which the church as whole or individual members demonstrate their thanks to the Spirit. In one instance, I heard of a church mother who held a thanksgiving in her home in commemoration of her fiftieth birthday. In others, thanksgivings were held to celebrate the achievement of a specific goal or solution to a particular problem or issue that an individual might have encountered in their everyday lives.

As a church-based ritual, thanksgiving is related to church celebrations held by other Christian denominations such as Harvest as well as secular American and Canadian Thanksgiving holidays. However, the difference with Spiritual Baptist thanksgivings is their disconnection from the colonial history of conquest of indigenous people in North America on which the American and by extension, if not actual association, Canadian Thanksgivings are understood. In neither individual house-based nor church-located thanksgivings that I attended was this association ever mentioned, even though Canadian Thanksgiving was celebrated by individual members.

Thanksgivings are celebrated by the setting of the table with fruit, vegetables, cakes, candies, sweets, and other foods. Flowers and spirits (wines) adorn the table. Prayers are offered and hymns sung. These are festive occasions in which it is not uncommon for those present to "catch power" and "manifest the spirit."

After the prayers are offered and the formal part of the thanksgiving is brought to a close, a meal is shared and the food on the table is distributed to all in attendance. At the thanksgivings I attended in Toronto, in addition to the fruit, candy, and baked goods such as bread, buns, and cakes distributed, participants were often treated to a take-home meal such as roti. The thanksgivings I attended in Toronto, both church and home-based, had a festive atmosphere. They were eagerly anticipated by church members and provided an opportunity not only for giving thanks to God but also for meeting and greeting old friends and newer acquaintances.

Spiritual Readings

While thanksgivings whether held in a church or a private home are largely public affairs involving members of the Spiritual Baptist community and friends and family, spiritual readings tend to be private affairs conducted behind closed doors. Many of the leaders whom I met, both men and women, had well-developed reputations as healers within the Spiritual Baptist and wider Caribbean and black communities in the city of Toronto. Two even opened stores similar to the botanicas of New York City and other urban centres that supply candles, incense, statues, and other ritual paraphernalia related to Cuban *santería*. Healing, described by Brother Tee as the ability to "work," was widely regarded as a gift that enabled those who possessed it to help others within the Spiritual Baptist community and beyond. Regarding the latter, many members made reference to what they considered the "Nicodemus-like" behaviour of those who used the healing traditions secretly while disavowing any connections publicly to Spiritual Baptists or the larger African-based traditions from which they evolved.

Healing traditions included the prescription of cures for physical ailments to specific problems or troubles in life. What they held in common was a view of the body and disease that frequently located the cause of illness in life circumstances and the relationship of an individual to the spiritual world. In this way, healers in the Spiritual Baptist tradition extended their influence beyond their religious communities to the wider black and Caribbean communities. One woman healer also attracted clients from other ethno-cultural and racial groups in the city of Toronto. For some clients, seeking healing was the conduit to joining the religion.

JOINING THE SPIRITUAL BAPTIST CHURCH IN TORONTO

There are three major patterns of joining Spiritual Baptist Churches in Toronto. These patterns encompass people who are already "religious" or "spiritual"—i.e., engaged in some form of religious practice—and those who do not consider themselves to be "religious" people prior to becoming Spiritual Baptists. It is significant that among the latter group, many have been raised in households where their parents or other members of their extended family were regular churchgoers or participants in Caribbean traditions such as Trinidadian Orisha/Shango and the Spiritual Baptist religion itself.

First, there are members who were Spiritual Baptists in the Caribbean who then subsequently rejoined a congregation upon moving to Toronto. Differences in this group depend on the timing of their migration. For those who emigrated to Toronto before the establishment of prayer groups or churches, lapses may have been as long as two decades between their arrival in Canada and their participation in Spiritual Baptist forms of worship. In the meantime, they may have participated in more mainstream Christian denominations. In contrast, those who came to Canada after the late 1970s were able to more readily access Spiritual Baptist churches or prayer groups that had formed in the earlier period. Yet both groups often noted that they had assumed there would not be any Spiritual Baptist churches or Spiritual Baptists in Toronto beside themselves.

Brother James's joining experience typifies this first pattern. In his late thirties when I interviewed him in the late 1990s, Brother James had emigrated to Canada as young man in his twenties from St. Vincent. His mother was a Spiritual Baptist although she willingly encouraged Brother James and his siblings to attend a Methodist Church. Brother James, in his youth, endorsed this choice as he held a pejorative view of Baptists.

CBD: What kind of church you went to and ...?

BJ: Well actually when I was back home I didn't really like the Baptist Church because back there they look down upon Baptists. They go about in this white headtie and stuff and as you see the kind of commotion that they carry on with in church and stuff. Back there, jacket and tie and looking nice and stuff ... And the proud kind of attitude; they look down upon you who does not have the ability to dress, the good jobs ... Even if you work the lands and stuff, they still look down upon you and stuff. The Baptists ...

They seem to exalt those with the jacket and tie, those with the fancy job, the nice car, the good house and stuff like that. And unfortunately, most Baptists does not possess those things.[9] And I never really pay attention to the Baptists although I was brought up in a Baptist home. My mother was Baptist. She never take us to Baptist. I was Methodist. Most of my brothers is Methodist. She encourage us to go church. As a matter of fact, she would dress all of us and stand by the door and watch us go to church and stuff.

CBD: To the Methodist Church?

BJ: Yeah. She never take us to the Baptist. Don't ask me why.

Brother James became a Spiritual Baptist only after immigration to Canada. His wife and her family, who were already members of the downtown church, influenced him. He also noted that his memories of his mother's practice as a Spiritual Baptist also influenced his decision to join the religion in Toronto. In what follows, Brother James discusses the factors influencing his decisions to join the religion. Note the importance of the Bible for Brother James as the literal word of God in addition to the strong memories of his mother's religious life as a Spiritual Baptist woman in St. Vincent:

BJ: And I came to Canada here and [my wife] used to go to that church I went there for the first. Mind you because of the way my old lady used to pray and stuff, and the way things used to happen us, sometimes things doesn't work because of the constant prayer things began to work, work smoothly and stuff like that. I see these things. I see how my old lady lived and stuff like that. All these things have influence on me so I had a great belief in God.

I used to say my prayers and stuff and listen to all the preachers and stuff. I went to church and I remember all the [words are muffled]. I went to church one day and the bishop preach about repentance and he declare that it could be your last. And it kinda strike me. And I remember in the morning I going to work and because he declare I began to walk very carefully make sure that when I crossing the road no cars ain't coming I guess. Psychologically and stuff, I was kinda scared because of the attitude I had, maybe that was the revelation of the other part of me.

I become conscious about what is around me and what is happening. And I decide I going to be baptized. And since I baptize now ...

CBD: When was this?

BJ: I think it was in '70 ... '86, right. And I had done things according to my will and maybe continue to do things according to my will. That is you get into the Bible and see how far you are from God and how much you have to come up in order to get up to the standard and stuff. And you realize how weak you are. It only will come with constant communication and constant seeking to do His will but it's not easy.

It's not easy because guys always want to, people always want to use you and children get you mad and you still have to be cool, you still have to govern yourself because not only is people outside watching you but children is going to be watching to see how you react. And, like I said, the children cannot experience anything, it is what you give them that they take into life apart from what they have experienced through the times they've been growing up. If you set the right example notwithstanding their own motivation God put into them.

But in certain part of their life when they're confronted to the struggles of life, they will remember those true values and fall back on them. Not only that, they will also seek to keep solid all these that were happening throughout. When the struggles get great they know well, hey, this is where daddy and mommy used to go when these things happen. Because the Bible declare that I will be busy ... the generations simply because it's what you teach your child he's going to teach that child and stuff like that. So the doctrine begin with the granny. All the generations is going to go come down is going to have that doctrine. So you have to have sound doctrine ...

The second pattern of joining involves members who had never before heard of the Spiritual Baptist Church prior to coming to Canada. In most instances, these individuals were not from Trinidad and Tobago or St. Vincent, Caribbean countries in which the Spiritual Baptist Church is a well-known religious and cultural entity. These members were more often from other Windward islands such as Jamaica or Leeward islands such as Antigua. In one instance, a Spiritual Baptist leader from Jamaica, Mother Patricia, noted that her prior experience working on the "African side" and with "ancestors" had predisposed her toward Spiritual Baptist worship. She connected her earlier experiences as sharing a common ground of understanding, namely a cosmological view that was fundamentally "spiritual" in outlook. I return to an in-depth discussion of this woman's history in Chapter 7.

A middle-aged man in his fifties from Antigua, Brother Tee, had never heard of Spiritual Baptists prior to living in Toronto. In fact, he had lived in Toronto for nearly twenty years before hearing of them. His early religious experiences were in the Anglican Church, and he came to the Spiritual Baptist Church only when he was faced with a health crisis and he was referred by a friend to a Spiritual Baptist leader for a "spiritual reading." As I noted in the previous chapter, some high-ranking Spiritual Baptist leaders also conduct one-on-one spiritual counselling sessions through which they provide healing services for not only the Spiritual Baptist community but a cross-section of Toronto's Caribbean community as well. This practice continues a trend that has deep roots in Caribbean and other African Diasporic communities of "doctoring."

BT: I came into this particular area in 1985 when it was—use the word, luck. Because there were a lot of things that were happening to me and someone said to me, well, this is not natural, you know. This is not something that should happen naturally. Go and see somebody. And I used to as a young boy, my mother was very much into, like back in Antigua they call it, the obeah man, the obeah woman and I hated it. I never believed in that. So, reluctantly I went. I met Bishop. But [laughter]—as I look back on it [unclear word], he was not even the person I was supposed to meet. Because a friend told my wife that to go and see some man who is on … and they call and call and they never got to talk to this person.

So, eventually, someone gave my wife Bishop's number and say go down to the church. So, I say what the heck, go. And he were in his office and he was counselling me, you know, well I did gambles [unclear word], and you know, he was reading my life history. And he mentioned things that had happened to me and he's never [met] me. He never—he doesn't know—he knew who I was. And I—you know, it kinda struck me, how the hell did you know anything about me and you never even talk to me.

Well, I said to him, promptly, I don't believe in this thing, you know—hocus pocus story. But after that interview, I went back to him several times after and he said to me, okay, nothing is really wrong with me, do this and do that, you know, but I would like you to come to church. That was in '85 and I didn't go until about 1987.

The third pattern of joining involves those who, for a wide variety of reasons, were visitors to the church. In some cases, some visitors attended church services and participated with greater regularity than some members. In this instance, what distinguished them as visitors was that they were not baptized and had not yet declared themselves baptismal candidates. In other instances, they were visitors who were regular members of other Spiritual Baptist churches or other Christian denominations who would attend church services and other rituals on a fairly regular basis. Last, I encountered one man whose primary form of worship was not yet represented institutionally in Toronto. He belonged to a metaphysical order similar to the Masons or Rosicrucians. He found in the Spiritual Baptist Church a cosmology that approximated his worldview and beliefs. As the grandchild of a Spiritual Baptist woman who was raised Catholic in Trinidad prior to immigrating to Toronto in the 1970s as a teenager, he found community though not a perfect match for spiritual self-expression.

Many of the Toronto Spiritual Baptists whom I interviewed noted that they had found out about the churches by word of mouth. On street corners, at bus stops, in apartment hallways, the men and women told stories of hearing about Spiritual Baptist Churches from friends, friends of friends, or, in some cases, from "strangers."

CBD: How do people get introduced to the church or find out about it?

QMP: Ahm, like ahm, I know that the church is there and you and I have a conversation and ahm, and then I would invite you. Sometimes, you know, I met you on the street and you and I we get to talk and you come out of the blues and ask me, "What church does you go to?" you know? We talk and so and we might exchange invitations, you know and stuff like that, right? And then ahm, sometimes you put in, in the ahm, Contrast[10] or whatever you call it that they sells at the ahm, at the West Indian—they don't sell it, that they have at the West Indian stores ...

COMING TO CANADA

All of the Toronto Spiritual Baptists whom I interviewed were Caribbean-born adults who emigrated to Canada in their adolescence and early adulthood between the mid-1960s and the late 1980s, an approximately twenty-five-year span. There were some exceptions in which people had emigrated first to the United States and lived a portion of their lives there before moving on to Canada. These people tend to be older immigrants who arrived in their forties or even older. While younger members, primarily children and youth, were Canadian-born, the people whom I interviewed were, for the most part, with the exception of twenty-something Sisters Louise and Asha, adults in their late thirties and older. Besides this one common factor of having come to Canada and being born in the Caribbean, the stories of immigration had tremendous variations. Nevertheless, some broad commonalties in the "coming to Canada" experiences of the church members distinguish some stories as qualitatively different from others. Having said that, the experiences, in many ways, can be interpreted as a multiple-voiced utterance of late-twentieth-century Caribbean migration.

The distinguishing factors include the timing of their emigration—i.e., whether they arrived in the 1960s and early 1970s, the period of greatest migration from the Caribbean, or later in the late 1970s and 1980s; whether they had prior experiences of migration before coming to Canada, so-called double-lap migrants;[11] and their immigration status vis-à-vis Canadian immigration and citizenship laws. Cross-cutting these factors is yet another major distinction, the degree to which the church members' immigration experiences were mediated by the Spirit. Here I am referring especially to the influence of dreams, visions, and mourning experiences in either initiating or providing guidance for immigration.

The church members who arrived in the late 1960s and early 1970s tended to have achieved higher levels of education and economic gain than those who migrated later in the 1980s. There are several mitigating factors here, not the least of which is their having worked longer in the workforce and therefore having accrued greater financial assets, enabling the purchase of homes and automobiles. While all people described themselves as coming from working-class and lower-middle-class urban or rural backgrounds in the Caribbean, the timing of their arrival seems to have made a great deal of difference in their ability to increase their class position as measured by such criteria as home and automobile purchases, participation in post-secondary education, and professional certification. The booming post–Second World War economy of the 1960s and 1970s in Ontario gave way to a period of decline in the late 1980s. The employment experiences of women who came in the 1970s from those in the 1980s are markedly different. Those who came in the earlier decade were able to achieve greater economic and social mobility whereas those who came in the 1980s were more constrained by lack of availability of access to educational opportunities and significantly, by that period, the Second Domestic Work scheme, which offered the possibility of applying for landed immigrant status after one year of full-time work, was no longer in effect. In its stead, women were offered temporary employment visas with no assurance of access to landed immigrant status leading to Canadian citizenship.

WORK EXPERIENCES

As noted in the previous section, employment opportunities prompted most of the Spiritual Baptist church members to emigrate to Toronto. This strategy of outward migration from the Caribbean began in the post–Second World War II years. Facing financial hardship in the Caribbean, Caribbean people migrated first to the United Kingdom in the 1950s and then increasingly to Canada in the 1960s with the advent of the points system (Henry 1994).

The vast majority of the church members, well over 90 percent,[12] are female. Thus my account of the work experiences of Spiritual Baptists in many ways parallels those recounted in studies of employment areas in which there are concentrations of Caribbean women, namely paid domestic service (Silvera 1989; Calliste 1991) and health care, especially nursing (Flynn 1999). In Chapters 5 and 6, I return to a detailed discussion of Spiritual Baptist women's employment in paid domestic service and the contradictions between the high status that mothers of the church enjoy and the devaluation of paid domestic service.

The Spiritual Baptist men and women I interviewed worked in a variety of occupations ranging from skilled trades to telephone customer service representatives and food preparation, as well nursing and other health-care-related work such as nurses' aides and health-care aides. Most of the women, even if they had moved on to other types of work, had worked in some capacity as paid domestic service in private homes.

One persistent theme that emerged particularly in church talk such as sermons was the relationship between "paid work" and "spiritual work." For some, "equal time" had to be given to God just as it had been given on the job. What this particular occurrence signals is the divergence between "spiritual time" and "real world time"—a discussion to which I will return in greater detail in Chapter 6. Although church members took the time to arrange their daily lives to accommodate church ritual, there were moments when there was a clear tension between "spiritual time" and "real-world time," especially as it related to work. In each case, it would be resolved in ways that were highly creative and individualistic. For example, church members cooked Sunday dinners prior to church services; some who worked night shifts as health-care workers arrived at church with "work clothes" in a bag so that they could leave and go directly to their night shifts.

However, these accommodations were not always so readily available. A case in point is the experience of a church member who suffered from an illness for which doctors could find no conventional cure. She determined with the help of her other spiritual leaders that her illness was actually spiritual in nature and that it signalled a call to become a mother in the church and to take up her spiritual work. She was on a sick leave from her place of employment for what was considered a physical ailment. It was finally determined through consultation with her spiritual mother that the curative that was needed for this woman was for her to "mourn" with her spiritual mother in Trinidad serving as pointer:

> M: She said to me, "Can you come?" I said, "I'm on sick leave; I'm not supposed to leave the country." She said, "Nobody would know. Could you come?" I burst, I bust. That is what she felt. I said, "My husband is not working, we have to keep up with the mortgage …" She said to me, "Come."

After making financial arrangements with family members and friends, she travelled by plane to Trinidad within a few days. Interestingly, although she had been off for two months, at this point, her supervisor had never phoned her to check up on her status. The day she landed in Trinidad, the supervisor started phoning her Toronto home on a daily basis to try to reach her. She considered it a "trial."

> M: Watch the trial now. Carol, it was moving [snaps her fingers in a triple snap]. For two months, my boss never call me. [snaps her fingers in a triple snap] She start call. He [her husband] didn't know what to say [whispering]. He tell Mother but Mother don't want to tell me. Finally, he called. One day, when I was down, Mother came into the mourning room and in the meantime I was travelling. And Carol, I mourned. And I was getting so much.

The telephone calls from the supervisor became increasingly persistent. Her husband would then phone the spiritual mother in Trinidad who would relay the messages to the woman as she lay on the mourning ground. Her "solution" came from Spirit:

> M: Seeing all the trials, everything. But seeing it they [the Spirit and spirits] giving you the solution. Mother [her spiritual mother] came ... your boss has been calling ... He tell me to say this [whispering]. He said she call so much time, he don't know what to say. And without any hesitation, from under those bands and I said to Mother, "Tell her, you go upstairs and call [my husband] and tell [him] to call [my supervisor] and tell [her] I am fasting. And when I'm finished, I will call her. She doesn't have to know where I'm fasting." When [he] tell her that, she wants to know if she can talk to me where I am. He call back. Mother came back. I says, "Mother, tell [him] to tell her, I am in isolation, I'm in isolation and I cannot speak to her until I am finished." So she took disciplinary action against me.

With the initiation of disciplinary action by her supervisor, the woman decided to return to Canada to deal with the situation in person, cutting short her mourning from ten to seven days. Already, in that short time, after three months of excruciating illness, her health was greatly improved:

> M: She send the letter by courier. If I don't call her in so and so days ... Mother—I was going to spend the ten days down there. When I came out the Sunday she says, you know what, think. You wanna go home? Say yes and lemme see if I can change your flight. So, instead of going home the Friday, I went home the Wednesday. I was supposed to call my boss Thursday. I came back and when I went to Trinidad, this hand died. Not this one, but I couldn't carry. I was in so much pain. I couldn't, couldn't— ... Not even ... I went on the plane crawling and I came back bouncing.

Although she returned to Toronto via airplane to deal with her work situation, this woman still had one foot firmly planted in the world of spirit. Her liminality was symbolized by the fact that her spiritual mother had not removed the "bands"—the strips of cloth that are used to "seal" the pilgrim traveller. In effect, she was a pilgrim-traveller simultaneously walking both a spiritual and carnal path. "My spiritual mother didn't release me. Every band ... what she didn't put around me, it was on my head."

In confronting her supervisor, she noted that the period of fasting was necessary, as conventional medicine had failed her. She also noted that she was willing to pay the "price"—i.e., lose her job—if it meant that she would ultimately regain her health:

> And I said to her, "If this is the price that I have to pay for what I did, so be it." I said but you couldn't help me. And the doctors couldn't help me. I had to look for other help. And she was shocked, when I said that to her. But, if this is the price: If, I have to lose my job, for what I did, I says, "So be it."

The mother actually attended the company medical with her mourning bands still in place on her waist and her head:

> M: But the morning I got up, I didn't take off not one band. And I was going in … for a company medical.
>
> CBD: Mmmhmmm.
>
> M: Band on my waist, my head. It was the first time in history that I would walk into that company with my head tied.

The outcome, carnally, resulted in the company medical verifying that she was legitimately ill and on the mend, thus eradicating any threats regarding job stability. Spiritually, this journey marked her beginning of a new status as a "nation mother," a discussion to which I will return in greater detail in Chapter 5.

In summary, what is most significant here is the interaction between "work time" and "spiritual time," which formed the crux of this woman's crisis. She confronted a situation in which her spiritual life as well as her material life, represented by her job, were both on the line. The resolution lay in her ability to move between the spiritual and material worlds.

"IT HURT ME FEELINGS": NAMING RACISM

Racism, the systematic rank ordering of humanity on the basis of ascribed meanings to perceived physical differences, is one of the major challenges that non-white people in Canada have faced over past generations. Canada, like other metropolitan, white settler colonies, has had a history of using immigration, settlement, and employment policies that have effectively stratified the population on the basis of race. Race has been a central organizing principle in the formation of the imagination of Canada. So much so, for instance, that the notion of who is Canadian is almost always tied to an implied whiteness. The phrases "white Canadian" and a "real Canadian," which support common-sense understandings of Canadian identity, point to the importance of race in national identity even in the face of explicit federal policies of multiculturalism.

This implicit notion of whiteness as tied to being Canadian grew out of a history in which notions of race featured prominently in the trajectory of economic and political practices that shaped the formation of the Canadian nation-state. These included the subjugation and colonization of aboriginal populations; the participation in the Atlantic slave trade and slaveholding practices of Upper and Lower Canada during the colonial era; the structuring of subsequent waves of immigration on the basis of racial and cultural criteria that overwhelmingly favoured people from northwestern Europe as most suitable for settlement while effectively curtailing emigration to Canada from areas of the world such as Latin America, the Caribbean, Africa, and Asia populated largely by people of colour; the admission of people of colour from these areas to meet specific needs of the labour market such as the use of Chinese male labour to build the Canadian Pacific Railroad in the closing decades of the nineteenth century and black, Caribbean women's labour in domestic service in the twentieth century.

As noted in Chapter 1, life in Toronto was not the only context in which Spiritual Baptist men and women had encountered constructions of race and practices of racism. It is important to take into consideration the Caribbean region's history of race, colour, and class in situating Spiritual Baptists' experiences of race and racism in Toronto. In many instances, it is the interface between these past and present experiences of race and the similarities and differences between them that shape and nuance the experiences and solutions to racism proffered by them.

All the church members with whom I spoke told me about experiencing racism in their lives in Toronto. Most often these experiences revolved around relationships in their places of work as well as in public spaces such as Toronto streets and on the public transportation system. These experiences echo those reported by other Caribbean migrants to Toronto in earlier studies (Christiansen 1974: 70; Brand and Sri Bhaggiyadatta 1986; James 1990; Henry 1994). What characterizes the recounting of these experiences by the Spiritual Baptist men and women, a quality that is very difficult to reflect in a literary genre, is the mixed emotions of outrage, sadness, resignation, and determination to resist often present as a speaker recounts an episode.

This emotive quality, though difficult to capture in a textual form because it was often conveyed through subtle cues of communication such as tone of voice, wry, sarcastic laughter, facial expression, and hand gestures, is nevertheless important to take into consideration for it points to the very real pain of experiencing racism. This challenges what Painter (1995) refers to as the "super survivor" model of contemporary black experience that suggests that in overcoming and surviving racist attacks and hurts, somehow the recipients escape emotional pain. I will return to this topic at greater length later in this chapter in discussing participation in church services and rituals as a way of dealing with challenges faced in everyday life in Toronto among Spiritual Baptist men and women. It is in confronting this pain that the church attempts to provide for the spiritual, political, emotional, and psychological needs of its members.

Spiritual Baptist men and women report incidents of racism in relation to their workplaces, school, and movement in public spaces such as Toronto city streets and public transit. In both enclosed and public spaces they report being targets of racism both from white people they knew in work relationships and from anonymous strangers performing a drive-by verbal assault. This experience is akin to Frantz Fanon's assertion that the bodies of black people, their "fact of blackness" to use Fanon's term (1967), in racist societies make them targets for assault.

"It hurt me feelings," Brother John said. This simple statement poignantly expresses the psychological pain and trauma that racist assaults inflict on the dignity of black men and women living in Toronto. While Brother John went on to offer a cogent political, historical, and economic analysis for understanding manifestations of racism in present-day Toronto and by extension Canada, his assertion of psychological pain points to the visceral experiences of racism encountered by black people from the Caribbean experiencing racism in Canada for the first time.

As an eighteen-year-old, in 1977, Brother John was placed in Grade 12 in high school shortly after coming to Toronto from Trinidad where he was reunited with his mother who had left several years earlier. He felt alienated in his school environment and subsequently left school in a dramatic and bold move when he "walked out" and never returned. Brother John describes these feelings of alienation in high school that prompted his decision to leave school:

BJ: But it seemed I wasn't communicating with anybody. I wasn't talking. So ... there was no communications.

CBD: This is with the teachers or …

BJ: Well, nobody. I was just … in the back seat there sitting. There were um … If I fail in anything, you know, power of lack of communication. So, I went, I put everything together.

CBD: Mmmmhmmm.

BJ: But just … made up my mind was to leave. So … I got up one afternoon, I think it was half day—it was half day, and I just pack all of my stuff from di locker—

CBD: Mmmmhmmm.

BJ: —put it in a bag and I went home and I never went back.

CBD: Did anybody ever contact you?

BJ: They contact me but I never really go back. I never look back.

Brother John further reported that he was comfortable with his decision to leave school as he had not formed any friendships while at high school in Toronto and deeply missed his friends in Trinidad:

> Because um … I had no friends. The environment was different, it was strange. I didn't understand di people. … They didn't understand me— it was because America was different, Canada was different. It was thrown in that I wasn't brought up here. I was brought up … and having after left school from back home—you know? I tell meself well, I will enjoy meself now. But I had to fly out here. Flying out here kinda take way everything. So, all me friends was back home. I begin to miss them.

Following his leaving high school, Brother John sought employment in a variety of manual labour occupations such as shipping and receiving, which he described as very "hard work." His relegation to this segment of the labour market following school leaving and being subjected to a racial, verbal slur eventually led to Brother John's return to Trinidad at the age of twenty-two, four years after coming to Canada.

In the following description of a racial, verbal assault, Brother John describes the incident that effectively drove him from Canada, so shocking was the impact on his psyche. This incident, combined with the extreme hard labour of the job in shipping and receiving, confirmed his decision to leave Canada:

And you know? Is a funny thing. Even type a' people I know. You see, I just come from school in a environment where everybody know one another really as one ... What was strange for me was the environment. White people ... I never heard di word "nigger." I heard it one night when I was coming home. I went town and I was coming home maybe two in di morning and somebody call me that. ... It hurt me feelings. Dat was di first time ... I came to understand ... What—my way of understanding, I just walk out. I walk away. Da' was—da' was di reason for me going back home. ... I just by my will, pick meself up, walk outta school, begin to work, save some money and go back home. And when I reach home, there I began to grow. I begin to grow. I begin to understand.

After living in Trinidad for about four years, Brother John decided to return to Canada—ironically, given his departure from Canada due to experiences of discrimination based on race—because of class-based discrimination he received in Trinidad:

BJ: 'Cause is—they may be negative in a certain way, here. Back home, when I went back home certain—di tings I saw with people, dey own people of same colour, your colour, everyting. You know? I couldn't understand it, either. So, I end up running back to here, again.

CBD: What were some of those things? Could you tell me a bit more?

BJ: Publicly—they don't deal much with you know, public relations.

CBD: Mmmmhmmm.

BJ: They don't—is like, you go and you ask somebody a question, they answer you harsh and rough. They deal with—you know, they don't have that training. Whereas you ask di person a question here, they answer you polite. They are well trained. But, you know they mighten have that love for you. But this is they job. They take they job serious. In the Caribbean, people don't take they job serious.

CBD: Was there any one specific incident in Trinidad that you—?

BJ: Oh! Yeah, there's many, there's many! Because you see, I come from di lowest a' di classes in that a messenger—is how some people perceive a messenger to be. You know how some people perceive messenger work. I was a messenger back home. So—

In the following, Sister Asha, relays what she refers to as her "one experience" with racism since coming to Canada:

CBD: Um, how do you feel about issues of race and racism living in Toronto? Has racism impacted?

SA: Well I had just this, I think it was one experience with it and that was when I just came to Canada. I used to work at this um restaurant and um it was a really, really, really nice place to work. You know, I make a lot of money and actually was my first experience dealin' with white people, you know. Because you know in Trinidad you see them from a distance and you don't talk to them, right? You know you laugh at them because they look so different than, you know, the people that I'm used to. Anyways, um, I used to work at this restaurant and, you know, the people and myself we became very close because we work together on a daily basis. And we—I had this one run-in with this waiter and because I—lookin' at it now I understand where he was comin' from, because he couldn't get his order on time, no fault of my own, you know, he sweared and, you know, he called me "black." And I was so surprised! I goes, but this is the guy that you know usually come in "Oh hi! How are you?" you know, everything, you know. But with the change of atti- tude, you know. But you know, now I understand, you know, that's how he live, right? If he doesn't get his order to the customer on times—on time, then he don't get a tip, awright? And sometimes the tip—they get paid so little—the tip makes up their salary, right? So, I understand it now, you know, but, you know, that was just my, you know, my experience.

In recounting this incident Sister Asha moves from feeling personally rejected and hurt by her co-worker, with whom she had previously enjoyed cordial relations, to "understanding" how his use of a racial epithet was motivated within the context of the demands and stresses of his work. It is an instance in which Sister Asha moves from righteous indignation to a posture that, in attempting to find a reason for the basis of the racist behav- iour, exonerates the perpetrator and simultaneously reinstates his human- ity. It is as if Sister Asha *needs* to find a way of explicating the racism directed toward her in this experience that borders on the absurd. Her initial reac- tion is akin to Fanon's recollection of his first encounter of racism in France. A white child accompanied by his mother saw Fanon as monstrous and not as the middle class, French-speaking medical student but as a "negro" and exclaimed, "Look, a Negro!" and "Mama, see the Negro! I'm frightened!" (Fanon 1967: 111–12). Fanon's identity, as Stuart Hall suggests in Isaac Julien's meditative biographical film *Frantz Fanon: Black Skin, White Masks*, is shattered in the child's utterance. Sister Asha is similarly shattered but manages to recoup her sense of self through the provision of an excuse for her co-worker's racist expression.

Sister Louise employs a similar strategy but takes it a step further in actually denying racism as a part of her reality when I initially asked her if she had ever had any experiences with racism living in Toronto. Her denial of racism was also expressed in her search for alternative explanations to account for incidents that the young black children whom she cared for in one of her jobs as a domestic worker reported:

CBD: We hear a lot about racism in the media. Have you had any experiences with racism here, here in Toronto?

SL: Not really, I don't have any. Why I—normally when I used to babysit those two kids in Pickering, they were black, and when she come from school, she used to say, "Oh my teacher doesn't like us. Us the black one. She never like us. She would send us outside or she would not listen to our answers." But I would say to her, it's just your own imagination. Maybe you were just pushy and she didn't want you to answer yet or she want someone else to answer who … you know sometime kids are in the back and they don't answer the question when the teacher ask. And there's always the smart one to push their hand up first. So, sometime the teacher bypass that smart one and try asking the one who does not answer. So I told her maybe it's some case like that, that happen. But she's saying, no, there's racism here. But I've never experienced any.

However, Sister Louise explicitly names racism and class distinctions, as influencing her life as a black woman living in Toronto. In the following statements, she points to how her gendered and raced status shape her life expectations and opportunities in comparison to persons from other ethnocultural groups in Canada. Sister Louise also comments on the pressures she feels about contributing to the economic support of relatives "at home" in St. Vincent, especially her two children. What is especially telling in her testimony is the role reversal she feels as a young woman who, instead of depending on parents to support her, must act as the one on whom family members rely:

CBD: Mmmhmm. How do you feel as a black person—as a black woman living in Toronto.

SL: In terms … ?

CBD: Just in terms of your own sense of self.

SL: Well ... sometime I feel oh, they have us so low down from the beginning, you know, that we have to fight so hard to get something in this world. Even in Canada we have to fight hard. 'Cause—even though we—we are still working hard they don't recognize us as someone who have it and who can do their best what they want. They don't recognize us as that person. They just bypass us and look us over. I think so. But then, I wanna make the difference. I wanna dwell with them and do the same thing that they do. . . .

CBD: So who do you see as "they" and "them"?

SL: Well I look at the white people, the Chinese ... I look at all the other races that are making it, going to school, having their education and getting whatever professional ... I see all of them as different from me because of they getting what they want. They asking they parents for this and their parents are able to give them. Whereas our parents, the black ones, they don't have it give us, we have to go out there and fight for ourself. In the case where my mom is back home, I have to fight here for myself, work—try working, sending money for her, support her and my kids. So it's like the role of family and everything is on me. It's really hard. I take it—going to church and praying as come easy.

Mother Victoria, like Sister Louise, also expresses her feelings about her status as a black woman living in Toronto in terms of feelings of exclusion from access to resources and goals available to other Canadians. Unlike Sister Louise, Mother Victoria does not name specific socio-cultural groups in her notions of who "belongs" in Canada, but her comments imply that whiteness is an essential characteristic of being Canadian. Mother Victoria also expresses her longing for her daughter back in Trinidad, from whom she is separated:

CBD: So how do you feel as a black woman living in Toronto?

MV: Well—all kinda feelings does come to me sometime, you know? Because number one ah does say like maybe di Canadian people ain't waan nobody else in di country. Because so many crimes doing and di white people is who doing di crimes too, you know? But dey blaming di black people, too. And ahm, yuh up here and yuh have to be working for dis small set a money because you ain't have piece a paper nor notten, you know? Ah does feel real down and everything. But I does say as long as I ain't get meself in trouble. 'Cause I does go to work when I have to go to work and from work I come straight home and the onliest place I does go is over by [a friend]. If ah have to go in di store, well ah go to di store and home. If ah have to go to di grocery, well di grocery right dung here to me, so that is di nearest one. Sometime ah come in an then go dung or sometime ah take di bus, drop out and walk up. Yeah. It ain't no problem. But ah does only tink about my daughter, you know. While she dung dere, I up here and—

CBD: Do you write to her?

MV: Yeah.

CBD: Does she call sometimes?

MV: Yeah.

Mother Patricia also expresses a similar sentiment in reflecting on her experiences of being a black woman living in Canada:

CBD: How do you um? How do you know feel about being a black woman living in Canada?

MP: Oh.

CBD: I know is a big question but um … [laughter with MP]

MP: Yeah. [laughter with CBD] As a black woman living in Canada, I know we have reached some—we have pass over some pothole, some big ones, but we still—we haven't reach halfway yet. And we must always remember that we must never. What we already get, don't ever try to let go what we have else we never go forward. That's what I believe. You know, like if we have, ten holes, we have to cross. If we are in our faith, we can't come back and say, "Okay, I'm gonna give up this … to reach back to number three" because we wouldn't reach nowhere. We have … the struggle have to keep on. And, when people tells me then they're not racial, it's get me um, upset. I am a *black* because I am a black woman and I think my skin is very important.

The similarity lies in naming struggles, the so-called potholes, as Mother Patricia calls them, which black women have passed over, collectively, yet acknowledging that significant changes have to take place for the liberation of black people. Similar to most of the other Spiritual Baptist men and women with whom I spoke, the "struggles" were not named in explicit terms, initially. Only further in conversation were specifics named. In the

Conclusion, I return to this discussion of hope and aspirations for the black community.

"I Say You Can Call Me 'Damn Bitch' ... Just Don't Call Me 'Madam'!": Challenging Sexist Racism

Implicit in Mother Victoria's comments about racism in Toronto is the significance of stereotypical images of criminality among black people combined with the reality of working for low wages exacerbated by issues of immigrant status and family separation. Mother Victoria's analysis also points to a coping strategy that involves living life as quietly as possible without calling undue attention to oneself.

In spite of employing this particular strategy, Mother Victoria and other women such as Mother Patricia recount experiences in which they were pushed to limits they were not prepared to transgress and therefore engaged in dialogue and behaviour that, in fact, drew attention to themselves, by stepping outside of established, raced, classed, and gendered boundaries of conduct. bell hooks (1988: 5) referred to this behaviour, especially as it applies to female children in U.S. southern black contexts, as "talking back." "Back talk" has been noted as a strategy of resistance of female slaves in the Caribbean.

I grew up with the expression "back talk" or "back chat" in my Antiguan upbringing, which had a similar meaning to the Southern African-American expression. To "talk back" or to "back talk" in the Caribbean context was to engage someone in conversation who was in a position of authority in relationship to yourself such as parent, older family member, or teacher.

To "back talk" was often regarded as a dangerous, transgressive behaviour, especially in young female children. Females who "back talked" moved in ways—dangerous ways—that were outside of their culturally prescribed roles both in gendered and in raced hierarchies. There was an implied understanding that to "back talk" as a child was a sign of bad things to come in the future, such as "mad" (read "out of control,") behaviour that violated norms of femininity and "wayward" (read facety[13]/feisty, independent) behaviour often involving the emergent sexuality of a young woman. It was a sign that the young woman was on her way to becoming a "bitch." Bitch, in this sense, refers to another derogatory stereotype of black women as castrating, unloving, and unlovable—in other words, the quintessential Sapphire, the foil of Mammy and Aunt Jemima. As such, engaging in "back talk" often carried with it the price of a punishment that was severe and swift. As hooks noted in her growing-up experience, "To make yourself heard if you were a child was to invite punishment, the back-hand lick, the slap across the face that would catch you unaware, or the feel of switches stinging your arms and leg" (1988: 5).

For the individual woman, the adult equivalent of punishment for "talking back" publicly, particularly in work-related contexts, often results in the "back-hand lick" of economic reprisal in the form of job dismissal, negative, inharmonious work relations, ostracism, or some combination of all of the above. I have purposely focused on the women's experiences at this juncture because none of the men with whom I spoke recounted any experiences of "back talk." This is not to suggest, sweepingly, that black men do not "talk back." Individual black men have talked back, and continue to, in critiquing racial, class-based, and gender-based inequality. In fact, one can point to a long legacy of outspoken, critical, boundary-transgressing speech among black men in the African Diaspora from Frederick Douglass in the nineteenth century to Frantz Fanon's anti-colonial treatises, Malcolm X and Martin Luther King, Jr. in the 1960s to more recent examples such as the Reverend Jesse Jackson, filmmaker Marlon Riggs and scholar Cornel West in the contemporary United States. In the context of this study, black male Spiritual Baptists, such as Bishop Dickson, Brother John, and Brother Tee, all talk back to the status quo on issues of race and representation in Canada. What I am suggesting here, however, is that this speech, "back talk," is a black female phenomenon, given practices within black communities of not encouraging black female children, in particular, to speak their minds. As hooks noted, in her growing-up experience, similar behaviour in a male child might have been taken as a sign of a "calling" to speak, perhaps as a minister. Not so for a female child (1988: 6).

In the following, Mother Patricia comments on how her willingness to name racism, which can be characterized as a kind of "back talk" given the unspoken code of not naming racism, resulted in her being judged as "too sensitive":

MP: At my workplace they say I'm too sensitive. But I don't think so. I tell them nobody makes joke with my skin. You know? Because I tell them this is—in the summer, they have to go home to tan. I don't. This is natural. You don't have—I say, with all the sun, it's gonna be nice, black and beautiful. But some of them, like, they will not talk to you for the whole year but if it's a Christmas party, they like "Oh, I didn't know you look so beautiful." And they will, you know, and I call that hypocrite. Because, come on, you seeing me every day. You scarcely want to say "Hi," but then they never see you *dress*. So, of course, when they see you dress, then they see the way how you look. Now they play, they want to come to meet you and they want to come and say "Hi" and they wanna come. You know, they always "kissy, kissy" eh? And I—I could not stand them, so I say, "Don't go." And then they say, you know, they say different things. But that's the way I feel.

Mother Patricia's comments reveal that the labelling as "too sensitive" has occurred within the parameters of acceptable workplace speech that often fails to critique the power relations embedded in what may be considered neutral or proper business terms. In the following, Mother Patricia comments on her objection to using the terms "madam" and "sir" in her workplace because as she says, "it brings me back to slavery." In her analysis, she points to the significance of language as embodying historical relationships of power. In this instance the words "madam" and "sir" are seen by Mother Patricia as representative of master/slave relations, which she connects with her own personal family history vis-à-vis her enslaved ancestors referred to literally and symbolically as her great-grandparents.

CBD: So, have you had any problems with racism? Like on your job or ... ?

MP: It's there.

CBD: Yeah?

MP: Like, my boss very—he don't like black. But, they know ... one day, my supervisor said something to me. Um, "All-you black women, all-you husband—all-you men and dem beat up you all." And for me I find that rather racial. So, when I go in the office, they tell me I "misinterpretate" and this kinda thing. But yet they wanted to send me home for half day. And tell me, um, well if I did. I said, "I'm not going." Because, if I had gone then it would look like if I did, you know, you didn't hear what they say. So I told them, "Look here, I did not come here for all-you to like my skin. I did not come here for all-you to like my colour nor either [words unclear]. I came here 'cause of a job. And when we come, if we have to talk, here is what we talk about." 'Cause I don't sit with them—like, only when it's about we need to talk about the work. But you know, like to sit down and carry on conversation. No. Conversation pieces I don't want. Because the last thing between then, they go on double standards. Stab in your back. So, I don't. But it's there. And, make them to know, "Look—I don't—" My supervisor never used to come up there for he want me to tell him more. So I told him I doesn't work that way. And I stop telling him why. And then one day, my boss was in the kitchen and I came in and I tell him, why and I didn't tell him. And then we had a meeting and I—I said, well he didn't tell me. So, I am no—he's not bigger than me. And I'm not bigger than him. If he tell me, he didn't want in when I come in, and I come there before him. I'm gonna tell him, "Good morning." But you know, it's better now, you know. 'Cause I tells them that I'm not the one who's going to um—and I will tell them my fortune. I don't like somebody to say—um, what's your name, what they love to say to you. They like um, "sir" and um, "madam." I told them don't call me "madam." My great-grandparents had to be in slave where they beat them to be saying to the boss wife "Madam, madam this and madam that." Now, my great-grandparents have made for me that I don't have to call *nobody* and they don't have to call me. So, when—I don't care if you is the um, president, I tells them I don't want them to call me madam 'cause I will not calling anybody madam and sir. I don't call nobody sir and I don't call nobody madam.

CBD: Who do you call them?

MP: Uh?

CBD: What do you call them?

MP: I call them by they name. I don't like to use "sir" or "madam" period.

CBD: Yeah. I hear that.

MP: 'Cause to me it brings me back to slavery.

CBD: Mmmmhmmm.

MP: I know, like, sometimes, it's just a matter of speech, but some people you have to, you know, "madam." I say, no, no, no, that was when my great-grandparents have to was in slavery and everything, they had to say "Madam, could I go to the washroom? Madam, could I do this? Madam, could I do that? Madam, could I—?" No! And "Sir." And "Could I shine your shoes and could I help—?" Come on!

CBD: Yeah.

MP: No. It makes you feel like you're poor. I couldn't. I say you can call me "damn bitch," whatever you want to call me. Just don't call me "madam." But women, we still have a lot of ways to go.

CBD: In terms of sexism?

MP: Yeah. Yeah. And even our own black people. Because, if we are going to a like—I was going to say, my black brothers out there—If my black brother is going to wasten down his black sister, how can we go forward? You understand, me?

THE CHURCH AS COMMUNITY: SUPPORT NETWORKS IN THE SPIRITUAL BAPTIST CHURCH

At the outset of this chapter, it was established that ritual, often viewed solely as action, was not separate from the symbolic, conceptual thinking aspects of religion. This discussion proved to be particularly relevant for understanding Spiritual Baptist ritual as a form of "enacted thought" expressing the central theological concept of the religion, "so spiritually, so carnally." This chapter, subsequently, shifted focus to consider the significance of racism on the lives of Toronto Spiritual Baptists. From this discussion, it is evident that Spiritual Baptists' existence within the everyday world of Toronto is fraught with gendered, raced, and classed power dynamics that potentially threaten to fragment and consume church members so all-encompassing is their reach. Of particular concern in our discussion is the way in which these interlocking systems of power shape pivotal events in Toronto Spiritual Baptists' lives. Namely, coming to Canada—the immigration process itself—work experiences, and confronting institutional and individual, interpersonal acts of racism. Given that racism has proved to be so fractious and pervasive in the lives of Spiritual Baptists, and given also the relatively marginalized position of the churches vis-à-vis not only wider Toronto but also Toronto's black communities, what then is the basis of community building? The remainder of this chapter is devoted to this discussion, to which I will return when I discuss the experiences of the mothers of the church, for it is their work both in its spiritual and carnal contexts that forms a large part of the community's support networks.

If ritual is not conceptualized as solely action but as "enacted thought," that is situated within a wider context of social actions, then in many respects ritual constitutes a kind of social ethic. For Toronto Spiritual Baptists, "so spiritually, so carnally" discussed earlier as representing a worldview, a "seeing" and conceptualization of the complex relationships between humanity and Spirit, can also be understood as a social ethic of care that links Spirit with action in the everyday world. It is this ethic of care that informs the building of community through the informal support networks of the church.

From this perspective, Spiritual Baptist ritual activities serve multiple purposes. They foster community cohesion, provide entertainment, raise funds for the church, and provide healing for practitioners. In communal meals, especially the secular ones such as West Indian Day picnic and Christmas dinner and dance, the churches provide an important entertainment outlet within a value system that is acceptable to most of its members. With the Feeding of the Poor, in July, in which church members prepare meals for homeless people in Toronto, the church makes an outreach to the wider community in Toronto through the tradition of almsgiving. On that day, homeless men and women are transported by vehicles to the church and given a meal during the early afternoon hours, thus giving them enough time in the early evening to find shelter at the hospices and shelters in the city.[14]

The downtown church extends itself not only to the poor within Toronto but also to its own members through a food bank. Members are encouraged to donate non-perishable goods for the use of other members who may be in need of food. Financial loans for members were not generally available, as the church itself was not in a financially secure position. Monthly contributions, church socials such as dinners, as well as the collection plate at weekly church services provide the revenue for operating expenses.

Mothers of the church play a key role in organizing and carrying out these activities. I will return to this in Chapter 5 and discuss the role of the church mothers in more detail. Suffice it to say here that these women's roles are pivotal in providing support not only to church members but also to members of the black community who may not be affiliated with the Spiritual Baptist church in the context of worship. The work of the mothers is key in establishing the church as a kind of quasi-social welfare agency for its members and others in the black community.

CONCLUSION

This chapter has discussed the significance of Spiritual Baptist ritual as "enacted thought" that is significant in individual Spiritual Baptists' lives as well as the basis of community development. Throughout their experiences, the intersection of a "this worldly" and "other worldly" orientation was evident in the way in which Spiritual Baptists negotiated living in Toronto. However, as much as Spiritual Baptist worship is profoundly rooted in an engagement with material life, there is an important connection to places and spaces that lie beyond the everyday. One of the most significant of these places is Africa—both historical and imagined. While there may be varying theories concerning the question of origin of the religion, its connection to Africa is widely noted (Zane 1999; Glazier 1991; Houk 1995). In Chapter 4, I explore the multiple meanings of Africa in Toronto Spiritual Baptist experience.

NOTES

1 An excerpt of these comments appears in Henry (1994: 163).
2 Excerpts of this conversation appear in Henry (1994: 163).
3 An illustrative historical example is the case of *vodun* in colonial Saint Domingue and post-revolutionary Haiti. *Vodun* provided a basis of mobilization for the rebel forces of the enslaved. Under the leadership of Toussaint L'Ouverture, himself an enslaved African, the enslaved waged a war between 1791 and 1803 against the combined colonial forces of the British, French, and Spanish to emerge victorious. As a result of this twelve-year struggle, the Republic of Haiti, founded in 1803, became the second republic in the Americas following the United States of America in 1776. Significantly, it is the only instance in recorded history in which a slave revolt resulted in the founding of a republic (James 1963: ix).
4 In Chapter 4, "Africaland," I return to a discussion of this notion of "connectedness" and Diasporic African consciousness in discussing the significance of "Africa" in the Spiritual Baptist Church. The question that is raised here concerns the usefulness of claims of "connectedness" as expressed, in this case, in theological terms for critical analysis of black identities and cultures. Africadian (Acadian African-Canadian) poet and literary studies scholar George Elliott Clarke suggests that such analyses are problematic in their generalization about black identities, often making what he terms "mystical" claims that suggest accessibility of divergent black cultures on the basis of a shared, common "blackness" (1998).
5 Section Three of the Ordinance authored by the Clerk of the Council, Harry L. Knaggs, reads: "It shall be an offence against this Ordinance for any person to hold or to take part in or to attend any Shouters' meeting or for any Shouters' meeting to be held in any part of the Colony indoors or in the open air at any time of the day or night" (Jacobs, 1996: 137). The Ordinance also circumvented the establishment of home churches in Section Four: "It shall be an offence against this Ordinance to

erect or to maintain any Shouters' house or to shut up any person in any Shouters' house for the purpose of initiating such person into the ceremonies of the Shouters" (ibid.).

6 Roman Catholic Saints and Orisha "powers" are represented by flags in the four corners of the church. The "bounded centre," which contains an altar and centre pole extending from the floor to the ceiling, represents the place where all of the "powers" meet and manifest themselves into the material world.

7 The documentary *God's Gonna Trouble the Water* on Gullah culture in the Sea Islands off the coast of South Carolina features "seeking" in the "wilderness," a ritual that is strongly reminiscent of mourning except that the ritual space is not a secluded room or "ground" in a church, but outdoor space. Margaret Washington Creel describes "seeking" among the Gullah in *A Peculiar People*.

8 A Trinidadian and Caribbean Creole term that refers to an informal, relaxed, social gathering.

9 Excerpts of these comments appear in Henry (1994: 162).

10 *Contrast* is a now defunct black community newspaper that was circulated, free of charge, to consumers in West Indian–owned businesses such as specialty West Indian food stores, barbershops, and hair and beauty salons. *Contrast* was published during the 1970s. The costs of publication were covered through the sale of print ads to businesses and, as Queen Mother Pamela has noted, church and other social announcements. Black and Caribbean community publications such as *Share* and *Indo-Caribbean World* continue to provide news, both international, Caribbean region-specific, and Toronto-based to the black and Caribbean communities.

11 Henry (1994: 32–34) uses the term "double-lap migration" with reference to Caribbean immigrants in Toronto who migrated first to the United Kingdom in the years immediately following the Second World War and then to Canada in the 1960s and 1970s. Henry points out that these migrants are counted in the census as "British," obscuring their inclusion in statistics on the actual numbers of Caribbean people resident in Toronto (28). Drawing on the work of Simmons and Plaza (1991), Henry notes that referring to country of birth is perhaps the most accurate way of determining the size of the Caribbean population in Canada at any given point.

12 At one church service, a group of Spiritual Baptist women who had newly formed a church attended as visitors. By all accounts, the group was exclusively female. And indeed, in the two churches in which I did my fieldwork, there were occasions, especially Tuesday night services, in which there was near exclusive female attendance with the exception of a male leader and one man who attended regularly.

13 Pronounced "face-tee," this term is Jamaican patois for bold behaviour that transgresses social norms. Ford-Smith describes the term as meaning "rude, impertinent" (1987: 308).

14 I heard of only one instance in which someone joined the downtown church as a result of being a recipient of a meal through the Feeding of the Poor. During the period of my fieldwork this individual, a young black man, was not in regular attendance at church services. Since I completed the fieldwork for this book, homelessness has become an increasingly urgent problem in Toronto. Further study of the impact of the Feeding of the Poor on Toronto's rapidly growing homeless population and on the church itself is warranted.

CHAPTER FOUR

"Africaland"

"Africa" in Toronto Spiritual Baptist Experience

I wish you were all nearer to me. Anyway, that's life. Last night I dreamt I were travelling in a car with your g.father [grandfather]. Apparently, we were going some place over sea. It was so natural.

—MAMA'S (DOROTHY SEBASTIAN PRINCE) *letter, April 4, 1978*

All the way from Africalan,' comin' to hear dem pray
All the way from Africalan,' comin' to hear dem pray
'We're comin,' we're comin'
Comin' to hear dem pray-ay
We're comin,' comin'
Comin to hear dem pray

—*Spiritual Baptist song, as heard in Toronto Spiritual Baptist Church*

INTRODUCTION

The central existential predicament of all enslaved people is the quest for freedom. In the case of enslaved Africans in the Americas, escape home was equated with journeying to Africa. For their descendants, removed by both distance and time from Africa, the continent itself has become imbued with a variety of meanings. In the Jamaican Rastafari tradition, for example, Africa is equated with Zion and Eden while the West is symbolized as Babylon, the land of exile (Chevannes, 1994).[1] In this instance, geographical references of the Old Testament are appropriated to fashion an expression of exile, a critique of colonialism and capitalism, and a longing for return home.

I posit that for generations of Africans, especially those born following the British-initiated 1807 international banning of the transatlantic slave trade, connections to Africa were generated increasingly through the memory and myth-making of what Rex Nettleford, in the documentary film *Caribbean Crucible* (1984), calls "indigenous African-American" cultures. Nettleford makes this distinction between the nineteenth-century African cultures and those that preceded them because, for the most part, they were populated largely by Africans who were born in the Americas. This scenario is markedly distinct from the eighteenth century in which there were infusions of newly enslaved Africans along with American-born in slave communities.

During the period of slavery, longing and desire for home was expressed in myriad ways. These included large-scale slave revolts aimed at social transformation as well as personal acts of rebellion such as running away for short periods of time.[2] Another arena of expression was the symbolic. Here, images of home, heaven, and Africa merged in the formulation of nation. Homi Bhabha (1990: 291) observes the following in his discussion of nation and metaphor:

> The nation fills the void left in the uprooting of communities and kind, and turns that loss into the language of metaphor. Metaphor, as the etymology of the word suggests, transfers the meaning of home and belonging, across the 'middle passage,' or the central European steppes, across those distances, and cultural differences, that span the imagined community of the nation-people.

In this chapter, I discuss the significance of Africa as nation in Toronto Spiritual Baptist experiences. This discussion is couched in reference to this question: What does Africa mean to descendants of enslaved Africans who have emigrated to Canada from the Caribbean 500 years after Columbus's watershed voyages to the Caribbean that prompted Western European overseas colonial empires and the emergence of the Atlantic slave trade? Here I discuss the ways in which Africa is evoked as a historical homeland and imagined place of ancestral significance, and as a place of future possibilities. These ways include the mourning experiences and other symbolic reference points such as wearing "African clothes," eating "African food," speaking "African tongues," and the incorporation of symbols such as West

African fabrics that have their reference points in the cultural and aesthetic movement that accompanied the civil rights and Black Power movements of the United States and that also had an impact in Canada and the Caribbean through style in hair and clothing. The mourning experiences of Spiritual Baptists are particularly important here for it is in the context of this ritual practice that the practitioners travel to Africa. While one Spiritual Baptist woman whom I met in Trinidad had made a pilgrimage to Africa, none of the Toronto Spiritual Baptists had travelled there in their everyday life experiences. Significantly, however, of those who had mourned, all had either travelled to Africa or interacted with people whom they identified as African as revealed by their mourning tracts.

In interviews, sermons, mourning tracts, and song, Africa is as much an imagined place, space, and time as it is a historical homeland for Toronto Spiritual Baptists. Benedict Anderson's notion of "imagined community" (1996) is significant here for understanding the way in which a collective is constructed outside of the conventional notions of community that, in the contemporary capitalist world, is the nation. Africa, in other words, signifies a range of possibilities for individual Spiritual Baptists in Toronto and is represented by a multiplicity of symbols, some of which are commonly acknowledged while others appear to be highly personal for the individual church member.

My task here is to make sense of the multiple meanings of Africa for this particular group of people of African descent who have migrated from the Caribbean to Canada in the post–Second World War years. My research suggests that Africa for Toronto Spiritual Baptists represents both the past and the future as a terrain of possibilities. Here the temporal past is the arena in which imagined futures are grounded. It is the place to which people return in their mourning experiences, which are very important, for it is here that each individual mourner receives his or her spiritual gifts and future roles in the church. This viewpoint reflects a perspective on time that differs significantly from the conventional, linear approach with a clearly delineated past, present, and future. From a Spiritual Baptist perspective, there is a clear distinction between the time of the everyday and spiritual time and their experiences and conceptualizations of Africa exist in a tension between everyday and spiritual time.

To begin, it is necessary to revisit the discussion of sacred place, space, and time in the Spiritual Baptist religion, for it is within the temporal and spatial dimensions of the sacred that Africa is imagined. Following this, I will then discuss the various ways in which Africa is invented, imagined, and revisited. These ways can roughly be characterized as practices in which Spiritual Baptists travel to Africa (mourning) as distinguished from other practices through which Africa is invoked such as through dress, utterance, food, and the Spirit. Of course, this typology is artificial, as the actual enactment of accessing Africa can involve both forms.

AFRICALAND

In Chapters 2 and 3, the discussion pointed to the ways in which the Spiritual Baptist tradition in Toronto was simultaneously preserved and reinvented to meet the needs of its practitioners within the specific circumstances of their everyday lives as Caribbean immigrants. It was also noted that, while the Spiritual Baptist Church can be described as a form of Protestant Christianity symbolized by a direct and personal communication with God as represented by Jesus the Son and the Holy Spirit of the Holy Trinity, for some members this characterization does not adequately represent the full range of religious experiences. For some, the Orisha religion is especially relevant in representing a polytheistic conceptualization of deity that reflects the Caribbean region's multi-religious, multi-ethnic history. In this instance, some Spiritual Baptists refer to themselves as "belonging to Orisha" but worshiping the Spirit in a "Baptist way." As noted, there are various ways of characterizing the Spiritual Baptist religion. However, several researchers have noted its association as a particularly African phenomenon, which originated in African historical experiences in the Caribbean. The Rt. Rev. Eudora Thomas, a Spiritual Baptist leader in Trinidad and Tobago, characterized the religion as a response of "the Black African people" in which they "expressed a form of cultural and religious resistance to oppression" using the "excerpts of Christianity" (1987: 17).

My interviews with Spiritual Baptists in Toronto and in Trinidad confirmed this viewpoint:

BROTHER JOHN: If you sit in the Spiritual Baptist community, right? You sitting on di African people. Right? And dey may confuse you also. Because … because in di African community—right? You might come across some Muslim. And you might come across some Shango. Right? You might come across, you know, some Indians from some … right? So there's mergin'! Is a lot of mergin.'

ARCHBISHOP DICKSON: [O]ur religion is based strictly or mostly on the African culture. Most of the thing, or a lot of the things that we do is from the Eastern hemisphere and um from the way-back African culture. And what we are trying to do is to entertain our ancestors' way of worship which was our original way of worship which was taken away from us. And um, we deal a lot with African powers. So lot of the things that you see that is done in the church—the jumping, the moving—it's what was done in olden times in African culture. There is a way in African culture that we know when someone dies. If we have to beat a drum, the very sound of the drum could tell you that someone has passed. If someone has had a baby, a new child, the beating of the drum, the way the cymbal sounds can tell you that there is joy, 'cause there is a baby life that was given. So our religion is centred and circled a lot around the African culture.[3]

While there may be general agreement on the significance of Africa in the formation of the Spiritual Baptist Church, it bears examining which Africa and whose Africa is associated both with the religion's historical emergence and with its continued significance for contemporary practitioners. In this regard, Africa is both geographical place and invention.

As well, it should be noted that Africa is situated in a wider cosmological framework that Bishop Dickson identifies, above, as "the Eastern Hemisphere." Brother John points to the "mergin'" of the Spiritual Baptists, whom he sees as fundamentally African, with Shango/Orisha and Islamic influences. Here both Bishop Dickson and Brother John underscore what Glazier refers to as the "heterodoxy and orthodoxy" (1980) that characterizes Spiritual Baptists' incorporation of elements from a variety of religious traditions. In other words, while the Spiritual Baptist religion draws on a variety of reference points, the "syncretism" of the religion is characterized by a ritual separation. This is evident in ritual practices as well as the arrangement of items on Spiritual Baptist altars. My research suggests that this separation also extends to the spiritual landscape such that when a pilgrim travels to Africa and interacts with others there, this territorial basis of the spirit is yet another signal of the separation of cultures in the Spiritual Baptist worldview.

The excerpt from my grandmother Mama's letter with which this chapter begins may read, at first glance, as simply the desire of an elderly woman living at home in the Caribbean to see her relatives living in the Diaspora. However it is in her next statement that her expressed desire moves out of the ordinary everyday world and onto the terrain of the spirit. Here Mama notes that she had a realistic dream—"It seemed so natural"—in which she travelled by car with my grandfather to an "over sea" destination. What signals her expression as lying outside of the everyday realm of experience is the linking of "over sea" travel with an unlikely mode of transport, namely a car.

I have included this excerpt here because of its reference to travel to destinations "over sea" through dreaming, a state of altered consciousness. Though the dream experience differs significantly from mourning in that it did not take place in a ritually prescribed context, it nevertheless points to the concept of spiritual travel. While only a small section of the letter is quoted, what struck me on re-reading it many years after it was written was the way in which this idea of spiritual travel is incorporated into Mama's narrative as an integral part of her discussion of her longing to bridge the gap between herself and her loved ones. This excerpt served as a pivotal moment in understanding the continued resonance of the Middle Passage and other transatlantic voyages "over sea" of Caribbean people separated from family through various forms of migration. It also strongly resonated with songs of flight and freedom in the African-American sacred music tradition such as "I'm on My Way to Canaan's Land" and "Swing Low Sweet Chariot." In her letter, Mama expresses a longing for a connection that has links with earlier processes of migration and separation, namely the Middle Passage.

Zane in his recent study of the Converted in St. Vincent and Brooklyn, New York, notes that the Africaland song was sung to him as a welcoming song by a group of Converted when he attended his first service in St. Vincent (1999: 3). In the following, Zane recounts his welcome to a Converted church service in St. Vincent:

> I was a little nervous at my first Converted church service. I sat on the unpainted bench trying to adjust to the humid weight of the tropical air while the congregation said the opening prayers. Presently the pastor gestured to me and invited me to introduce myself to the church. As I stood, he stopped me and said, "Would one of the sisters …?" A song in polyphonous harmony sprang from the congregation, "All the Way from Africaland, Coming to Hear Them Singing, All the Way from Africaland, Coming to Hear Them Sing." The song continued for five minutes while two older women danced with me at the front of the church. I was later told, "That is a greeting song. We don't have one for America. So we give you that." (ibid.)

Though the words are slightly different in the Converted version Zane heard from the Spiritual Baptist version I heard in Toronto, it is recognizably virtually the same song. In the version sung by the Converted in St. Vincent, those gathered were "coming to hear them singing" while in the version I heard in Toronto it was the "praying" for which the community had gathered. The similarity lies in the fact that both singing and praying are very important ritual activities in Spiritual Baptist worship. The Converted church leader's words—"That is a greeting song. We don't have one for America. So we give you that"—point to Africaland as a malleable, or ambiguous, source of meaning and as a reference point for "over sea." In this instance, Zane, a white male American researcher, is greeted as a visitor from Africaland representing an "over sea" destination outside of St. Vincent. In the Toronto Spiritual Baptist church where I heard the song, it was used to welcome the Spirit and to welcome those gathered for worship.

Sacred Space and Place in the Spiritual Baptist Church

As noted earlier in Chapters 2 and 3, the sacred, in relation to space and place, is mobile, from Spiritual Baptist perspective and practice. In other words, sacredness is embodied within Spiritual Baptists themselves. Thus, from this perspective individuals make the space, "this spot of ground," sacred through their presence.

Individuals can travel to sacred places spiritually and carnally through mourning and pilgrimage, respectively, but they can also invoke the sacred through their inhabiting of a space and through ritual acts to invite the Spirit. The Spirit in Spiritual Baptist experience is remarkably mobile. It is in this regard that the centre pole, a feature of Spiritual Baptist churches, is significant as a conduit through which the spirit world and the material world are linked. The centre pole is a long staff from floor to ceiling that symbolizes the spiritual centre of the ritual space. Around this staff are placed offerings of grain, meal, milk, honey, and water, as well as flowers and other ritual items, including a ship's wheel. This last symbolizes the voyaging of the church as a ship as discussed earlier in Chapter 1.

In the following, Bishop Dickson describes the significance of the centre pole. In 1992 when I first visited his church, the centre pole had not yet been erected. By 1994, however, it was in place. Here in conversation with me, he comments on the organization of the ritual space of the church:

BD: The vessels, the things that you see in the church um, we call them vessels or instruments or tools that is used only for spiritual purposes. And um, we use them a lot if we are doing healing or dismissing of any evil forces which is in the world—there's evil forces. Um, the centre of our church—if like in the Caribbean, most of the churches have what you call a centre pole.

CBD: Yes?

BD: And it's erected. Okay, um I don't have one. But anyway, it would be something about the size of this [makes gesture with hands] or even bigger and it's from the base of the church right up to the roof which signifies the centre of the church and we claim that Christ is the centre of the church, the centre of our lives, the centre of our heart.

CBD: I understand.

BD: And um, the thing that is placed around it are just vessels that are used. If we had what you call a centre pole we would have had twelve flags on the top of the pole signifying the twelve tribes.

CBD: I understand.

BD: Signifying the twelve tribes because there are twelve tribes that comprise the spiritual realm but we do not all operate alike because um, there was the tribe of Levi, there was the tribe of Benjamin, there was the—and you know they scattered the world over. They operated differently but towards the same setting.

Um, there is certain times when depending on what entity enters the church we would use a lot of fruits. Fruits signifies life, prosperity. It signifies growth, okay? And um, fruits become a great blessing because if a tree, according to the Bible, is not fruitful, then it is going to be hewn down by God. [words are unclear] ... we term ourselves as the tree and the fruits are our children. The fruits represents the children of the church.

The grains—we use a lot of grains, we scatter the grains in a form of feeding the unseen powers and uh, you know for prosperity.

SACRED TIME IN THE SPIRITUAL BAPTIST CHURCH

In the Toronto Spiritual Baptist churches in which I did my research, there was a marked demarcation between the time of Spirit and all things "spiritual" and time in everyday life. It was apparent from their ritual practices that Spirit did not "use clock time" in the same way that other people in their everyday lives depended on time to order reality by making distinctions between past, present, and future. In fact, in some services, the length of time became a noted issue. In many cases, it was accepted that time flowed "as the Spirit moves," which implied that there could be instances in which time could be experienced in ways that were noticeably slower or faster in pace. In some instances, members reported incidents in which time was manipulated, seemingly by divine forces. Brother John, for example, related an incident in which he accredits mysterious time changes as the source of his escape from serious harm or death. This incident was taken by Brother John to be the first sign of his calling to become a "spiritual" person:

> But anyhow Ah begin to get interested, show interest in di Bible. And … so, Ah started to read and Ah couldn't understand anything. But anyhow, both di Bible and scripture and Ah saw dis name Jesus and di words in red was His sayings. So, I went to work with Jesus. Anyhow, when Ah come later and Ah find out who is dis Jesus ting dis Bible talkin' bout— 'cor like it talkin' about one man—you know? And, it was early in the morning, I left to go, to go to work and running. Ah saw di bus was coming, so I decide I would cross di road to catch di bus before I pass di stop. And when I run in front di bus—dis was di bus here—I run across and run in front dis bus. A next bus was coming here and I didn't see it. Right? Two buses meet and I was in di centre here. And, dis bus continue here and I keep running. And it was like if something hold me back in between because di bus was closer. It just have space enough for me to stand up there. But—like if something hold me back—held me back—from between these two buses. The bus pass so, and I ened up on the other side of the road. And I didn't see—I didn't see any way of my coming out there alive. So, that was me first conviction. And I tell meself—I was trying to reason it out. But then I realize I was beginning to understand this veil on my eyes[4] dey talk 'bout.

TRAVELLING TO AFRICALAND

One of the most important ways in which Africa is referenced by Spiritual Baptists is through the mourning ritual. When the pilgrims travel, one of their most frequent destinations is Africa. As I sat in a Toronto church in September 1992, attending a "bringing up" ceremony for a pilgrim, the church member next to me commented that the pilgrims "always go to Africa. They always go to Africa." Indeed, in subsequent "rising up" or "bringing up" services in which portions of the pilgrim's mourning tracts would be recited to the congregation gathered, Africa was frequently referenced. It is significant to note that for many pilgrims it was the first place they visited.

The following is an account, a bringing up service from the fall of 1992, as recorded in my research notes, of a Toronto Spiritual Baptist woman's whose spiritual travels took her to Africa.[5]

The pilgrim entered the church at 8:10 p.m. with bands around her eyes. She was supported by four Mothers of the church including the Queen Mother. They passed under two large staffs linked together over the entrance. Two young men dressed in long, white robes held these staffs. The entire congregation was singing "Roll Jordan, Roll." The pilgrim sang out "Oh-aah-oh-aah-oh" in greeting to the congregation. The entire congregation answered back, "Oh-aah-oh-aah-oh." She then chanted, "I'm coming, I'm coming" and proceeded up the church aisle to drumming and chanting based on the rhythm of her breathing. She was "pulling 'doption"—a kind of rhythmic "over-breathing" that often precedes spirit possession. The procession was dancing, not walking to the front of the church.

Spirits were entertained at the front of the church, near the centre pole. The pilgrim's breathing and that of her attendants, including the Queen Mother, provided the accompaniment. The pilgrim and the Mothers danced around the centre pole to the accompaniment of their "pulling 'doption." The members of the congregation sang hymns while accompanied by the "'doption" of the pilgrim and the Mothers. The pilgrim reached the front altar by 8:25 p.m. The pilgrim knelt at the altar. She was dressed in white satin, with a veil like a bride. She was barefoot and holding a candle in her right hand and three carnations of red, pink, and yellow in her left. She was still attended by the Mothers of the church. The water and the flowers are symbols of life—what it should be. The oldest member of the church, a woman who looked to be in her eighties, presented the pilgrim with flowers and candles as did the Queen Mother.

The pilgrim greeted ministers, members, Queen Mother, and visitors. She continued to march in place as she talked, supported by a Mother. On the first journey, the pilgrim saw the Canaan sea. She was walking and walking into the sea after seeing a lot of children. She took a child out of the sea.

The Bishop then asked: "How did you go to the sea? You just walk, so?" The pilgrim then demonstrated how she went down into the sea through a combination of dance and "pulling 'doption." The guitarist accompanied her as did the congregation. The congregation then stood and sang a hymn.

The pilgrim then continued her story. She said she saw a beautiful garden with flowers and birds singing in the air. She was not acknowledged at the garden and so she moved on. The pilgrim walked up the street and continued her travels. Then she saw a beautiful woman dressed in pink. The congregation stood and sang a song about Mary, Queen of Heaven. The pilgrim went up to the beautiful woman, who put her hand on her head and said she was a Mother.

The pilgrim continued her journey. She entered a church with lots of nuns who were singing. The nuns were all dressed in white. There was one nun who was dressed in brown, white, and beige. The women greet her. The pilgrim then remembered the child in the waters and picked her up and put her down on dry land. The pilgrim went up to the Mother Superior in the church. The nuns were singing a hymn that the pilgrim started to hum and eventually sang along with members of the congregation. I recognized the hymn as one commonly sung in the Anglican Church, "Lift Up Your Voice." The Mother Superior put a veil over the pilgrim and said, "You are one of us, a Mother of the first degree."

The pilgrim then left the church and went back to the water. There she picked up the child and put her on dry land. She then continued her journey. This time she was headed for Africa. The pilgrim described herself as a "pilgrim traveller seeking wisdom, knowledge, and understanding."

On her journey there were small people who peeped at her from bushes. She saw an old man in khaki pants who gave her water to drink from a calabash with a flower in it. People came out of the bushes and danced. The pilgrim saw a table with African foods. After eating, the man gave her a calabash and clothing. Someone in the congregation asked what chant and dance was shown to her. She then did the dance. The dance was very West African and was performed to a calypso rhythm. The Queen Mother and other Mothers then held her candles and flowers. I recognized the dance steps as being a variant of the basic calypso two-step. Some of the steps looked like *belé*[6] steps from Dominica.

As the pilgrim walked up the street, she had to go into a cave. She had to go deep and crawl on her belly into the cave. Other members of the congregation repeated the breathing pattern and chant with which the pilgrim had entered the church. The pilgrim saw tools with oil in the cave. The Bishop said they were spiritual tools. The pilgrim said she was told how to use them. When asked if she took them, she responded "Yes," and said she put them in her dress. The pilgrim then finished her testimony.

A Mother approached her to have a conversation about the garden. A second Mother approached the pilgrim and sang a song in which the rest of the congregation joined. She talked to the pilgrim about motherhood.

AFRICA AS EDEN

The above summary of a Spiritual Baptist woman's mourning tract raises the question: What is the significance of Africa for Toronto Spiritual Baptists who access this terrain through mourning? Glazier, in his study of Trinidad Spiritual Baptists, posits an interpretation of mourning rites and the interpretation of the pilgrim's tracts as intrinsically related to progression within the church's hierarchy of leadership. From this perspective, mourning tracts are viewed as formulaic and restricted in their ability to provide an avenue of self-expression for Spiritual Baptists. I have suggested, however, that in the context of the everyday lives of Toronto Spiritual Baptists, many of whom work in marginalized and largely devalued occupations, mourning provides an avenue for church members to experience empowering identities through their participation in the ritual and the resultant bestowal of spiritual gifts that are enacted as spiritual work within the church community. In this light, travel to Africa often represents an authoritative ground of meaning. Africa and Africans are acknowledged as ancestral land and ancestors as well as a source of meaning. In the above mourning tract, for instance, this Spiritual Baptist woman's status as "mother of the first degree," the highest rank of church mother, was bestowed upon her by none other than a Marian figure, if not Mary, mother of Jesus, herself. Her enactment of her motherly role, however, is linked to her status as healer. For knowledge of this role, she was given specific ritual items and tools in Africa by an African man.

Some visions of "Africa" present a vista that is Edenic and paradisiacal in its description. From this viewpoint, Africa is presented as a utopic paradise, as well as a landscape imbued with references to home. In the following, Mother Ruth's Africa is a lush jungle that can be visited in spiritual travel. This Africa can also be tonally invoked through the voice intoning drums, "to beat a drum with the mouth in spirit," to quote Mother Ruth. As important as the sounding of Africa is for Mother Ruth, she is critical of the use of drums in Toronto Spiritual Baptist churches because she perceives that while congregants jump and shout they do not necessarily travel spiritually. For Mother Ruth, the long-ago Baptist tradition of vocally representing the rhythms of drums is the most authentic aural and oral representation of Africa. The irony is that, historically, drums were banned in slave societies in the Americas because of their communicative potential for uniting Africans. Enslaved people replaced the drum, musically, with handclaps, foot stomping, and vocal patterns. In a late-twentieth-century context in which the drums can be literally brought back into the worship of African-Caribbean people without reprisal, they represent an inauthentic experience for Mother Ruth. It is also significant to note that, for Mother Ruth, access to the African landscape and "walking that African road" are not dependent on being a person of African descent. The salience of this statement is noted later in her admission that she "moves with a Chinee spirit. There's time when I get into the Chinese when I could talk Chinee, you know. And there's some I could get in the African spirit."[7] For Mother Ruth, then, Africa represents the ultimate ground of meaning, and the physical landscape of Africa can be invoked through sound.

> CBD: What about the place of Africa for you? What is—Is that significant for you? I know for some people, as I've heard, we've all been there in church, and you know, heard people sometimes [talk] about how significant it is to be a Spiritual Baptist, in terms of being a person of African descent or being a black person. Is that of significance for you?

MR: I don't think so. I think anybody could be a Spiritual Baptist and anybody can walk that African road, you know, or whatever. Ahm, because, I mean, some of us, we don't know nothing about Africa. You know, we never been to Africa. But spiritually, if you mourn and thing, and you travel in the spirit, you would reach Africa in the spiritual world, in a sense, you know. And, I mean everything would look real to you. You would catch yourself maybe going through the African jungle. You know, you may hear the African—the drums and so on. Because this is something I'm sortofa—kind of against in a way. Not that I'm really, really against it. But I—what I find how you go into these churches and all these churches have these drums and they beat, beat, beat these drums and sometime you hear the drum beating and they jumping up and it looks to me like Caribana[8] [laughter] downtown, you know? And, sometimes you spend hours in church and you now get this jumping up to this drum beating and everything, you know. And ahm, what know long ago, back home—I have to watch the time. It after eight. I have to leave here. I have at least nine-twenty to leave. [She is referring to the need to leave to go to work.]

Ahm, long-ago Baptist used to make beautiful—when I was growing up, I didn't know nothing 'bout drums in church. Baptist used to sing and clap and make beautiful music with their hands, their feet, and their mouth. But now you don't find that anymore. And if you're travelling and you find yourself travelling in Africa and you going through the jungle, you hear all the different beats o' drums, right? And it have all different sizes o' drums. It [have] drums start like from that [indicates a few inches off the table top] and rise and rise and rise and rise 'til it reach to the big drums, right? And every drum have a name—like you would know in music, it have the bass, it have the dis, it have the dat, whatever. And if you travellin' the African jungle and you hear the drums, some of them start like from this [indicates a few inches off the table top] goin' up and everyone have a different sound, right?

And long ago, I know when Spiritual Baptist get into the spirit and they enter into Africa—that African spirit and they start to beat a drum with their mouth in the spirit, you would think you in the African jungle. Because you would hear them start with the different sounds—pi-pi-peep bi-doom do-doom doom doom doom, you know. And it moves to all that. Just like how you would hear somebody beating a drum and every little one, you know, have a different sound. But now I don't hear that.

CBD: What you think happened?

MR: I don't hear that. I don't know.

CBD: What do you hear now?

MR: All I hear now is they have the natural drum in the church beating and they don't even go anywhere with it.

CBD: When you say, go anywhere, you mean—?

MR: They just beat there and they jump up. They just beat there and they jump and that's it. They beat pa-da-lung, pa-lung, pa-lung-bung and everybody jumpin' up and they shoutin' but they goin' nowhere. Even if you some of them get in the spirit, if you get into that real spirit, you going to start to speak in tongues, in the African tongues. And they beat the drum.

CBD: But with your voice.

MR: You in the spirit and you would be—you know?

CBD: So what does speaking in tongues mean then, that sense?

MR: Ahm, well, then as the Bible say, on the day of Pentecost, when Pentecost came and the Holy Spirit, you know, everybody spoke in the different tongues, right? And, I think, depending on the spirit you are walking on and what country or whatever, once you are in the spirit and you get into that, you would speak their language. 'Cause then the African have a lot of different tribes, right? And every tribe speak a different language. So, when you get into the African spirit, depending on what tribe you're in, you going to speak that language. Now is something you don't have no control of, you know. Because I sitting here talking to you now, I can speak in African tongues, I can speak in Chinee tongue. But if a spirit manifest upon me, then I would speak it, you know.

AFRICALAND AND THE AFRICAN DIASPORA

In addition to being accessed through mourning and utterance, Africa is also referenced in clothing, food, and serving spirits that are considered "African powers." In this sense, the *orisha*, the divinities of the Yoruba religion, play an important role in their identification as specifically African. Mother Ruth, once again, notes the importance of ritual separation in worship with reference to Orisha and Spiritual Baptist worship:

CBD: Sometimes people kind of mix in some Shango or some other stuff. How do you feel about that?

MR: I feel there is a time and a place of everything. Okay, um, last year, you were around when they had a three days feast, they Orisha thing? … That is something different than Spiritual Baptist, right? So you could be a Spiritual Baptist and you could have this Orisha thing. But there is a time when it's time for the Orisha thing, right? And there is time for when you spiritual, right?

One woman, Mother Patricia, went as far as saying that the Orisha should not be "condemned" because they were connected with the ancestors of black people in the Americas even if their connections were not accurately known. She saw this connection as being especially significant given the fact that most black people in the Americas cannot trace their ancestry to Africa because of the disruption of the transatlantic slave trade:

MP: But is something you can't condemn because it's like, if you condemn it today, down the road, it's like, the white from white people— I watch a program, what day it was, they condemn black and they now when they trace they heredity, they have black in they family and then they feel bad now because, you know. And they says their cousins, first cousin, and second cousin. So, what I am saying, on the Orisha side, you have to understand because this is our—this went back. I say if I had money I would have liked to move where my um, my true ancestors which tribe did they come from. But I—if I had money I would have liked that.

CBD: Me too.

MP: You know? Know which tribe. Because here we know we are from African descendant but we don't know what tribe.

CBD: Mmmmhmmm.

MP: Because we become Harry and John and … and these English but is not ours. So if—that is what I would like to know for sure. Okay, I— you from the Watusi tribe, you from the Zulu tribe, you from some of the different tribes.

CBD: Mmmmhmmm.

MP: I would have liked to know. I don't like the marking, but I would like to know. I don't like the marking in my face. I don't mind if is anywhere else but I don't like it in my face. To me at that time if you don't study that some people had bad skin?

CBD: Mmmmhmmm.

MP: But you see, some people, you don't even see they face—the other day, I saw a man, his face rake like this. And you could see it's a tribal. You know? Not in my generation. Probably in my grandchildren generation they might go and find out who are they. But is one thing if I have money, I would have go through um, history books and go back there and do research to find you know. You know, I know it's taking a—a needle in a haystack but it's something you—

CBD: Mmmmhmmm.

MP: —good to find out about.

Clearly for Mother Patricia, the *orisha* are important not only as divinities but as an ancestral presence that links her to an African past, however undefined and unclear that may be. She expresses this sentiment in her account of a live performance of African dance that she attended in Toronto:

MP: You find that when you see a certain dance and some—like in *Roots*[9] and the Orishas and you see a similar. And I went to a—[performance] and they were from Africa and they were doing this. They had about fifteen different dance troupe from there. And they were from different tribes and you can see a simulation just like when you—you in the Orisha and you get a different pause, you dance the same way.

CBD: So, you could see the similarities between the dance they were doing on—

MP: —on the stage.

CBD: —and the dance that the Orisha—

MP: Yes! Because the drumming were coming from four different angles. That day when I went to that, my head was like … it was like spinning. And I said anytime I go to that again, I'm gonna wrap my head. I didn't wrap my head but my head was spinning. Because it was so—it was such a communication. So, I believe the Orisha have a lot to do with our—with the ancestors. I think is like—is there it originate from. It's just to say that, um, in the years, some kill it out by some of us not carrying on the tradition, you know?

However, there were some men and women who did not share this belief in the significance of Africa as an ancestral home. Here one mother expresses her views on the syncretism of African spirits, in this case the Yoruban deities, the *orisha* with Catholic saints disavowing belief in either:

> I still ain't believe in them things. No! I ain't believe in nothing. I just figure that somebody—you go—every individual, right? have like the Indians, they say they from India. And the Chinese, they say from China, right? And I know right now as the war fighting between black and white some people saying a white woman shouldn't have a black child and a black woman shouldn't have a white child. And they fight against these things all the time. But those things are from creation, right? The white feel the white should be by theyself and the black feel the black should be by theyself. But they never [hand clap] come [hand clap] to the part [hand clap] where they [hand clap] ask [hand clap] theyself [hand clap] the question [hand clap], right? Where the first white or the first black came from? You understand?

This woman also did not believe in prayer to saints, professing instead a more conventional, Protestant Christian belief in the Trinity, particularly in God the Father:

> Now, God say I am God, right? And God made us, He form us and He fashion us. Then when some people come out and say, oh they have St. Anne say to pray—and mind you I don't believe in going by that St. Anne's they have there and kneel down to pray neither, you know. No.

Many of the Spiritual Baptist women whom I interviewed in Toronto spoke about how important wearing African clothes was to them in fostering a sense of African identity. This clothing afforded a special status and was worn at important church social functions such as the annual Christmas dinner. Some women also wore African clothes to church services. One of the churches held a fashion show in conjunction with the 1995 Christmas dinner featuring African clothes.

Here Mother Patricia discusses the importance of wearing African clothes in making connections to Africa:

> **MP:** Yeah. I like wearing African clothes. To me, I say the rich man has get a lot of my money.
>
> **CBD:** Mmmmhmmm.

MP: [laughter] So, if I can die with one or two dresses and I know it come from—in Africa, then I know I have contributed to one of my people. That is important.

CBD: Yeah.

MP: Yeah, I like—and when—when I wear spiritual clothes—not spiritual clothes, but when I wear African clothes, I feel good in them. I feel good.

Sister Louise also noted how "good" dressing in African clothes made her feel:

SL: Fashion! Before, I never used to look at fashion because—I look at it yes, but, in a sense that only look and cannot have it, because I didn't have the money to like, get it. But now that I have—like I can afford it for myself, I more like the African styles. That's what I like.

CBD: Okay, when you say the African styles, what kinda styles?

SL: Like styles … you know, the big clothing on you, the long skirt down to your ankle, the wrapping up of head, even the hat on.

CBD: What do you like about it?

SL: It just make me feel … I don't know, it feels different on me. It makes me feel good about myself. Just good.

Mother Victoria, however, pointed to the need to know the significance or meaning of African clothes worn by churchwomen. For her this significance was not specific to these clothes but emerged out of a framework in which spiritual clothes were gifts gained through mourning that became an important part of the wearer's spiritual identity:

MV: But then again, I had spoke to a Sister one Sunday about this … headtie she have. Now ahm, some people when you mourn, they says they goes to Africa, right? Some say they goes to China. Some say they go India. Now, these—if you notice how Indian people dress, right? Chinee have they favorite cloth and how they make the clothes. And Africans use this thing. Just the other day, myself and somebody was talking about all these set of African cloth you see Spiritual Baptist wearing now. But if you ask them, "Listen me ahm—wha' is the meaning of this dress. Uh, the way that you dress?" They can't tell you, right? All they know "Well my culture wear this!" And that is not good enough.

Because if you wear this thing, you must know why you wear it, right? It have pink. It have yellow. It have red. It have blue. It have green. Right? And all these colours have their meaning, right? Now, I have—I had a book that I write down because sometime my head—I don't remember, right? Is the colours meaning something, right? And this last time when I went back and mourn I had get brown, right? Most people wear brown just because they see the piece of cloth and they just feel to wear it. But when you get these colours—the brown is the earth, right? Because I had asked the question. I say, "What is the meaning of this brown?"

CBD: This is when you were in the spirit?

MV: Mmmhmm. I asked the question and the answer was "The earth is the Lord and the fullness thereof." Right?

In some instances, the significance of contemporary, post-civil rights, African-centred philosophy and aesthetics arguably formulated most influentially in notions of "afrocentricity" (Asante 1988) have also influenced Toronto Spiritual Baptists' images of Africa. Afrocentricity refers to perspectives that emerge from African historical and contemporary experiences. This philosophical and political approach emerged to counter "Eurocentrism," which places European experiences and history at the centre of critical theorizing and inquiry. I agree with Clarke (1998) who points to "négritude" (Fanon 1963) and "black nationalism" (Garveyism, for example) as older relatives of the "afrocentric idea" (Asante 1987). The term "afrocentric" has become a catch phrase, promoting not only a supposedly African-centred approach to politics and philosophy, but also a way of self-presentation. In this sense, forms of self-representation, including choice of hairstyle and clothing, have become identified with afrocentric ways of knowing and being.

In this light, twenty-something Sister Asha, one of the younger women in the church, discusses her choice in clothing as a part of her identity as a black woman that is specifically African-defined:

SA: Before, I, you know, I would have got—I was caught up in the European style and fashion and everything but now I tend to get more into my roots and cultural fashion because it's nice. It's beautiful and you know, you—you—I tend to see black, white, Indian, Chinese, everybody, you know, in the fashion, and it's good—makes me happy and proud. Yeah.

CBD: So what kind of fashions are you sportin' these days?

SA: As one friend told me, you know, although I have a lot of the African culture in me, I still have a little bit of European or whatever the word—European in me, that needs to be—you know, I should be more down to earth.

From the above, Sister Asha is clearly aware of her own hybridity vis-à-vis African and European frames of cultural reference. She sees personal style in fashion and hair as not only self-presentation but a mode by which she can work through her own contradictions as an African-identified woman who still struggled with "a little bit of European." Sister Asha acknowledges that commodification may be involved in current fashion trends toward "ethnic" and African clothing. However, even in light of this fact, wearing afrocentric fashions underscores some notion of an authentic, black identity:

SA: Yeah, because I think, um, whether it's black people or white people, you know, um producing the fashion, they're uh, most of the, as you say, afrocentric fashions, I think it's black people bein' portrayed in what they should have been from—or should have done from day one.
　　Because if you look at it, at the Indians right? from India or Bangladesh or whatever, you see them sticking to their native although they would wear, the everyday jeans, or in the winter, you know, all these heavy clothes. You know, ever, ever so often, you see them in their native outfits, awright? And that's—that's good. That means they didn't forget where they came from, right? But as black people we get so caught up in the European fashion and we forget our native, or our native clothes or African styles or what have you, you know? But I'm, I'm happy that it's comin' back in trend and you know, that they usin' it not only as style and fashion but, you know, also as a—a, cultural roots type of clothes. Like, you know, for instance, if you see a black person in a dashiki or whatever, you know that's representation of what she stands—or he or she stands for, you know, yeah. It's good.

CONCLUSION

In this chapter, it has been demonstrated that Africa has multiple meanings in the Toronto Spiritual Baptist experience. It is homeland, ancestral place, and ultimate ground of meaning. Africa is peopled by Africans as well as figures from the biblical holy lands such as Mary, mother of Jesus. Africa is accessed through the mourning ritual. As well, it is tonally invoked and can be represented through personal, stylistic practices in hair and clothing. While the discussion has primarily engaged the symbolic and metaphoric constructions of Africa as sacred place and time, it should also be noted that these meanings infuse everyday life. This issue is taken up in the next chapter, which discusses Spiritual Baptist women's experiences of motherhood.

George Elliott Clarke in his essay "Treason of the Black Intellectuals?" notes that black intellectuals' nationalist visions are either "domestic" or "otherworldly" (1998). Clarke notes that recognized forms of nationalisms in Canada emerge, primarily, from the federal government, the province of Quebec, and First Nations. Nationalist visions of black intellectuals are mostly externally oriented, or borrowed from the aforementioned, recognizably Canadian nationalisms. Clarke is especially critical of notions of a monolithic black culture to which all Africans have access, especially its tendency to position some African culture as more authentic than others, thereby erasing the others' experiences. In this light, he points to the erasure and subsuming of African-Canadian identities and realities under a monolithic black culture.

This chapter's discussion of Toronto Spiritual Baptists' conceptualizations of Africa engages the issues of authenticity and erasure of nation. While some Spiritual Baptists cultivated visions of African that seemed to reiterate primitivist, noble savage images of Africa, others talked about understandings of nation that had their basis in the pre–Second World War British colonial empire. Brother Tee, for instance, noted the importance of cricket as representing a place that he can call home:

> Before I came to Canada, I used to like to tell my wife—we weren't married then—that was the—the first time I wrote to her, that's the first thing I asked her, if she see them playing cricket in Canada. She say, don't worry because she used to live at Rosedale[10] … And they used to play cricket all day in a small park. She said, don't worry, right where I live there's a cricket pitch [laughs with CBD]. I said, okay, I'll come. [laughs with CBD] And I mean it, I would never come here if they didn't play cricket.

His views on the importance of cricket go back to his early childhood in Antigua when British Commonwealth cricket games were imitated down to the rituals of having tea and lunch:

BT: Yep from so high, we play with coconut barks and all this … And in school, I used to—in those days we used to play with tennis ball … I used to—we have the balls handicraft, we have, you know … I used to make cricket bats you know and score. And when I joined the village club, I was the youngest. For years and years, I was the only school boy that ever joined the club. I used to go and help them roll the pitch and um, bring water and everything. Score—the whole thing. Oh yes. When we were growing up we used to play test match. West Indies against England. A lot of guys, you know, we do it just like everything, tea time, lunch time.

CBD: [Laughs with BT]

BT: And you know wha' we eatin'? For lunch is sugar cane, for tea sugar cane [laughs with CBD]. 'Cause in [my village] we have three estates right nearby. We used to go and tief cane man, we come back. [laughs]

CBD: So, which side were you on?

BT: West Indies. [laughs with CBD]

CBD: And who won?

BT: [laughs with CBD] Well, it was—a lot of times the games up in a draw, you know, because we were really good!

In contrast to Brother Tee's boyhood memories of nation constructed in relationship to cricket, Spiritual Baptists looked not to England but to Africa as homeland. It may certainly seem the case with Toronto Spiritual Baptists that their visions of Africa as nation are highly essentialized and "cloaked in the mystical trappings" to which Clarke makes reference in his article. However, I suggest that this reading of Toronto Spiritual Baptists' relationship to Africa is both dismissive and narrow. While "Africaland" may suggest a subsuming of all African experience into one category, the highly personalized nature of the mourning experiences and the individual members' own life experiences mediate the totalizing tendency of "Africaland." Travels to Africa (or any other spiritual land for that matter) in one Toronto church, for example, are mediated by the hanging of a Canadian flag in the church. As noted earlier in Chapter 1, this flag symbolizes that the church-ship is on Canadian ground. It suggests a view of nation that is both rooted and transitory, not unlike the migratory experiences of the church members.

One of the most salient features of the imagining of Africa present in Toronto Spiritual Baptists' accounts is the way in which their constructions of Africa, in some cases, play on stereotypical representations of Africa as primitivist paradise. In the next two chapters, I focus on Spiritual Baptist women's experiences of motherhood in Canada. Here the use of imagery that has troublesome associations with stereotypical representations of black people is also apparent. Chapters 5 and 6 discuss the challenges that Spiritual Baptist women face in their roles as mothers of the church. The identity of church mother stands in sharp contrast to the sexist-racist image of Aunt Jemima that is related to stereotypical viewpoints on black women as mothers and workers in North America. In these chapters, I explore Spiritual Baptist women's construction of empowering identities for themselves out of a variety of sources, including autobiography, wider black community history, and subversive re-readings of a stereotypical image such as Aunt Jemima.

NOTES

1 One of the biblical scriptural references for this symbolism is Psalm 137, which forms the basis of the song "By the Rivers of Babylon" in the Revival tradition and popularized in reggae versions.
2 See, for example, Michael Craton's discussion (1982) of a continuum of resistance in which he discusses those acts that were personal, small-scale, and temporary, such as tool breaking, and those that were communal, collective, and transformative on a larger scale, such as the establishment of maroon communities and slave revolts.
3 A portion of this quotation appears in Henry (1994: 160).
4 The veil to which Brother John refers is commonly called a caul in African-Caribbean traditional medicine. Sociologist and writer Althea Prince defines a caul as "a piece of fatty tissue (water bag) which remains over the faces of some babies at birth. In rural Antigua, the caul used to be removed by the midwife and given to the mother or the women attending her at the time of the delivery. The mother would keep the caul and put pieces of it in the baby's porridge later on. Babies born with a caul are said to be able to communicate more easily with the spirit world and would not be called back to that world if pieces of the caul are included in their food" (author's note accompanying *How the East Pond Got Its Flowers*, 1991, back page).
5 This tract is also referenced in Chapter 5 in discussing the identities of church mothers.
6 One of a number of Creole dances in Dominica that emerged from a blending of French folk dances—in this case the *bellair*—with West African drumming movement patterns. The *belé* features women dancers in wide, long skirts. It is a "flirtatious" dance in which the dancer shows off her petticoats and dancing skill. In 1985, in Toronto, I met a Dominican woman who remarked that a woman who can dance the *belé* can "talk with her feet to the drum."
7 The talking in "Chinee" and "African" to which Mother Ruth refers is represented by atonal speech that approximates the sounds of Chinese and West African, especially Akan, languages. Out of a church context, the production of these sounds

could be read as based on stereotypes of African and Chinese speech especially as produced in mainstream Hollywood movies and television shows. However, taken in context with the Caribbean's multilingual, multicultural history and the church as an arena in which this history is constantly re-enacted, these atonal sounds are much more than stereotypic sounds. They represent a tonal invocation of the spirit world into present, material circumstances.

8 Caribana is a Caribbean cultural festival held annually in Toronto. Established in 1967, the festival runs for two weeks in summer and features a Trinidadian-style carnival.

9 *Roots* is the popular U.S. mini-series based on Alex Haley's book (1976) of the same name that aired in 1977. It chronicles Haley's family history dating back to an ancestor who came to the United States via the slave trade in the early years of the nineteenth century. Largely regarded as a record-setting television event, it also bore the distinction of presenting information about slavery in the United States for millions of viewers in a way, wrongly or not, that many considered to be authentic and real. Note that in Mother Y's reference, *Roots* is cited as a source of African culture.

10 A wealthy neighbourhood in downtown Toronto noted in the popular discourse of the city's history as the traditional home of the white, British-descent, Protestant, business, and cultural elite.

CHAPTER FIVE

"Dey Give Me a House to Gather in di Chil'ren"
Mothers and Daughters in the Spiritual Baptist Church

So ... dey give me a house to gather in di chil'ren. So ah mus' be a mother.   —MOTHER RUBY, *Movant, Trinidad*

INTRODUCTION

In African-American communities, women known as "mothers" have historically held powerful and influential roles in sacred and secular settings (Gilkes 1997: 368). The lives of these women, however, have rarely received critical attention and examination (368). Gilkes's discussion focuses on church mothers in the United States; however, similar leadership roles also exist in Caribbean communities in Toronto. In this chapter, I discuss the experiences of "mothers of the church" within a specific socio-historical context: the emigration of African-Caribbean women from the English-speaking Caribbean to post–Second World War Toronto whose paid work is primarily in domestic service in middle- and upper-middle-class Euro-Canadian households.

Makeda Silvera's groundbreaking work *Silenced* (1989) presented experiences of Caribbean domestic workers in their own words. This chapter adds to this discussion by analyzing how Spiritual Baptist women, who have worked, or continue to work, in domestic service, make sense of motherhood in sacred and secular contexts in their everyday lives. A crucial part of this analysis is a discussion of the ways in which the history of domestic work in Canada, stretching back to the colonial and slavery eras, has had an impact on contemporary African-Caribbean women's participation in the labour force. In this context, it is also necessary to consider the ways in which these women have reinterpreted icons of Christian womanhood such as St. Anne, mother of Mary, and Mary, mother of Jesus. On this last point, it should be noted that in many ways there are two trinities in Spiritual Baptist theology. In addition to deity conceptualized as the trinity of God the Father, Son, and Holy Spirit, there is also an alternative trinity of St. Anne, Mary, and the Christ child. This trinity mirrors extended black family forms and the central role that grandmothers and elder women have played in black community life.[1]

This is a situation that is fraught with contradictory images and notions of motherhood in the context of the women's work lives, their religious lives in the church, families left at home in the Caribbean, and new familial and interpersonal relations in Canada. A significant tension here is that on the one hand, mothering in the context of church life is highly valued and respected, while the mothering work performed for pay is largely devalued in the wider society. Another set of tensions focuses on the search for home in the face of immigration and obstacles such as isolation and discrimination based on gender, race, and class. In a very real sense, the church in black communities has become one of the "homeplaces" (hooks, 1990c) where church members can find a sense of fellowship and community and where church mothers play a crucial role in the creation of this home.

This chapter is concerned with the ways in which Spiritual Baptist women provide support for the church and wider communities and thereby create an empowering identity for themselves through their roles as mothers of the church. While the Spiritual Baptist Church hierarchy tends to be dominated by men in the very highest positions, as church mothers women nevertheless exert considerable influence on the life of the church and wider black communities. In the context of migration to Canada, these roles have taken on additional significance as many women are themselves separated from their own Caribbean-based support networks—their church mothers, their own children and other family members, and their friends. In many ways, this post–Second World War wave of migration strongly echoes prior historical circumstances of family and community separation, namely the experiences of dispersal and disconnection engendered by the Middle Passage and the experience of slavery itself in the Americas.

The mothers of the church, as a part of a church family, itself a form of community that has its origins in the slavery and colonial eras, have emerged as pivotal figures in the Toronto Spiritual Baptist Church. However, this most recent experience of migration of people in the African Diaspora differs in one very significant way from previous historical experience: while people are separated by distance and time, advances in communication and transportation technology go a long way in lessening distances. For instance, Mother Patricia, when I interviewed her in July 1995, was preparing to go home to Trinidad for a family reunion. Queen Mother Ruby in discussing her role as spiritual mother, noted with regard to her adopted children, "Ah come and adopt chil'ren and dey grown big man and ooman. Dey gone on dey own now. When dey ready, dey come and look for me and dat's dat." Nevertheless, there are many individuals who, because of financial and any number of other personal employment-related reasons including their immigration status, remain separated from their blood relatives at home for extended periods of time. These people may also be marginalized in accessing support from municipal social service providers. It is in this scenario that the influence of the mothers of the church will be discussed.

This chapter and the next grew out of my reflections on the experience of "othermothering" in my own life and in the lives of the Toronto Spiritual Baptist women with whom I interacted during the course of doing fieldwork. Many of the Spiritual Baptist women whom I met treated me as a sister or daughter. In some cases they referred to me as "daughter" and I referred to them as "mother." I initially understood this reference as drawing on the "churchtalk" of the Spiritual Baptist Church in which congregants are "brothers" and "sisters," signalling familial relationships of blood, spirit, and community. While this language was recognizable, the utterance of "father" and "mother" occasioned a pause. While the churchly "brother" and "sister"—often pronounced as "brotha/h" and "sista/h"—have crossed over into popular speech in contemporary African-Caribbean communities in Toronto as a reference to black men and women, generically[2] "father" and "mother," sometimes represented as "papa" and "mama," have not crossed over as easily as generic terms into contemporary usage among African-Caribbean and African-Canadian speakers. The historical and contemporary connections between the experiences of mothering in African Diasporic religious traditions and wider black community life deserves critical attention because there is a powerful link to contemporary black feminist consciousness and empowerment.

Being referred to either by name or in treatment as daughter by many of the women of the church was not the first experience that I had of being regarded as a daughter by women other than my own birth mother. Growing up in England, Antigua, and Canada, I was mothered not only by my birth mother but also by a variety of women, including my grandmother, Mama, older cousins, aunties, and teachers at school and most memorably at Sunday school. As I have grown into womanhood, I too have mothered my niece and nephews and the children of my friends.

My experience mirrors that of many other black women who are mothered by "othermothers"—women who are friends or relatives in addition to, or instead of, their birth mothers or "bloodmothers" (Collins 1991: 119–23). While Collins's analysis is grounded in African-American experience, the concept of othermothering is exemplified by African-Caribbean and African-Canadian women's experiences of mothering and being mothered in a variety of relationships.

Cheryl Townsend Gilkes (1997) points to the significance of mothers of the church, women who hold leadership roles in black churches that may extend into influence in other areas of black community life, as being important to the development of African-American church and wider community life. The mothers of the church can be regarded as a form of othermothering.

One of the central aims of this chapter is to extend Collins's and Gilkes's analysis of "othermothers" and "churchmothers" by exploring these ideas in the context of Spiritual Baptist women's experiences of immigration to Toronto. Following from my earlier discussion, it is necessary to investigate experiences of blackness that situate black identities within a particular socio-cultural context rather than as a component of a monolithic black history. In this instance, the monolithic identity that is being interrogated is that of the black mother.

The chapter is organized as follows. First, I discuss the wider socio-political context in which some women members of the Spiritual Baptist Church perform their work as paid domestic workers through a review of the history of domestic service in Canada. Following this, I discuss the tradition of mothers of the church. I then present excerpts from conversational interviews I have had with Spiritual Baptist women in which they discuss different aspects of church mothering. These include ancestral mothers, often connected to biblical figures such as St. Anne, who transcend barriers of time and space to connect with contemporary women. I also discuss the process of becoming a spiritual mother and its relationship to "carnal" motherhood and the church as a home. Last, I present the perspective of

Sister Asha, who is in her twenties, on the value of church mothers. Sister Asha is separated from the mother figures with whom she grew up in Trinidad and greatly values the church mothers in her life. This discussion addresses the ways in which Spiritual Baptist women negotiate meanings of motherhood and daughterhood in their everyday lives and in the process construct empowered identities for themselves. However, before discussing these specific stories, I will present an overview of domestic service in Canada as a way of contextualizing one of the most significant arenas in which wider public perceptions on black women as mothers in Canada are shaped.

AN OVERVIEW OF DOMESTIC SERVICE IN CANADA

The demand for paid domestic service in Canada has traditionally been fulfilled, not by lower class women within the locality that the service is needed, but by women from outside the region (Lacelle 1987). The low value and accordingly low status that domestic work is afforded is acknowledged by all classes in Canadian society. Thus the domestic workers are usually recruited from outside the locality.

During the early 1800s, domestic workers were recruited form surrounding rural communities as well as from among urban dwellers, to work in the homes of the urban middle class in Canadian cities such as Toronto, Halifax, Montreal, and Quebec City (Lacelle 1987: 21). Most domestic servants were from a working-class background, and the majority, two-thirds, were between the ages of sixteen and twenty-five (56). At this time, both men and women were employed in almost equal numbers as domestic servants. Widows and widowers were also employed as domestic servants. Children whose families could not provide for them were sometimes entered in domestic-service arrangements with better-off families who would provide subsistence and sometimes even some educational arrangements for them.

The massive influx of British immigrants after 1820 had a significant impact on subsequent social, economic, and political developments in Canadian society and domestic service was an area influenced by this immigration. Whereas during the first two decades of the nineteenth century, domestic servants came from surrounding areas, by the 1870s, many domestic servants were either immigrants themselves or the children of immigrants.

With the growth of industry in Canada during the first two decades of the twentieth century and the accompanying availability of industrial work, by 1920, the proportion of Canadian women doing paid domestic work declined as factory work was a relatively more lucrative alternative (Turritin 1981: 94). The need, however, for paid domestic service for middle- and upper-class households had not declined, and the Canadian government, despite an exclusionist immigration policy, allowed the immigration to Canada of women, including some from the Caribbean who would have otherwise been declared "undesirable," to work exclusively as domestic workers.

The Immigration Act of 1927, which was in effect until 1962, prohibited entry to those who were deemed unsuited for the Canadian "climate." It is no coincidence that those who were seen as most unsuitable were non-white people such as blacks and Chinese. This policy was implemented specifically to restrict non-white immigration into Canada. By basing qualification for immigration to Canada on climatic criteria, the policy facilitated and encouraged emigration from the favoured climatic areas of the British Isles and northwestern Europe. Despite this policy, from 1925 to 1964 between three and four thousand West Indians women entered Canada and were subsequently employed as domestic workers (Turritin 1981: 96).

The demand for domestic service grew during the post–Second World War period when Canadian women's participation in paid labour reached new heights. The recruitment of domestic workers under the West Indian Domestic Workers Scheme, starting in 1955, was enacted as the solution to the problem of increased demand. However, this solution proved to be problematic for the domestic workers, the employers, and the Canadian government under whose directive the scheme was implemented.

The Canadian West Indian Female Domestic Work Scheme was implemented in 1955 when 100 women from the English-speaking Caribbean were brought into Canada to work as domestics in middle- and upper-middle-class households. Those affected the most were applicants from Trinidad and Barbados. Eligibility for the Work Scheme was based on the following criteria. The applicant had to be single, have the equivalent of Grade 8 education, be in good health, be between the ages of eighteen and thirty-five, and agree to work in Canada as domestics for one year before moving into other occupations. As a result of the scheme, over 3,000 West Indian women came to Canada as domestic workers from 1955 to the late 1960s (Turritin 1981: 97).

The women who came to Canada as domestics were primarily working-class Caribbean women, although some had held professional positions in nursing, teaching, and secretarial fields and had left these jobs to pursue what they perceived as better opportunities in Canada. Many came with the objective of remitting money home to dependants in the Caribbean as well as obtaining landed immigrant status, which they had a chance to apply for once their year of servitude was completed (Silvera 1989: 11). However, they faced the unforeseen difficulties of sexual harassment, long eighteen-hour workdays, cramped living quarters, lack of food, inadequate pay, culture shock, homesickness, and racism (1989).

The Domestic Scheme had a built-in flaw as far as meeting the demands for paid domestic service on a permanent basis: domestic service was limited to one year only after which the worker could apply for landed immigrant status and was free to pursue employment in other sectors. Considering the low status and low pay associated with domestic work, the vast majority left domestic service after completing their one-year contract. The situation was once again one in which there was a shortage of domestic workers.

To remedy the situation, the Canadian government took two measures. First, in 1973, a change in the Immigration Act prohibited the practice of coming to Canada on a visitor's permit, securing employment, and then applying for landed immigrant status from within the country. Second, a temporary employment visa program was implemented during the 1970s. This category of visa was created to meet the demand for labour in certain specific job categories. These included "domestic labour, seasonal farm-work and other non-union jobs, where the wages are rock-bottom and the working conditions reminiscent of the nineteenth century" (Silvera 1989: 14). The temporary employment visa is specific with regard to job, the employer, and the duration of employment. A change in any of these three criteria required the visa holder to report to the Employment and Immigration Commission. Failure to do so could result in deportation.

Between July 1973 and June 1976, the period in which a number of the Spiritual Baptist women I met came to Canada, holders of temporary employment visas were primarily from the West Indies, the United Kingdom, and Western Europe (Employment and Immigration Task Force on Immigration Practices and Procedures 1981: 51). During the same time period, however, 4,269 or 40.7 percent of the 10,482 workers who came to Canada on temporary employment visas as live-in domestic workers were from the West Indies (Arnopolous 1979: 62 as cited in Turritin 1981: 98).

Beginning in the 1980s, an increasing number of women from the Philippines have also come to Canada as live-in domestics (Employment and Immigration Task Force on Immigration Practices and Procedures 1981: 51), once again altering the ethnic composition of the sector of paid domestic services. Their recruitment is yet another instance of the implementation of the Canadian state's strategy of recruiting women from the Third World to work in domestic-service occupations.

The temporary employment visa solution to the problem of domestic-service shortage resulted in a situation in which domestic workers were exploited not only at the hands of their employers but of the Canadian state. Although the Employment and Immigration Commission stipulates minimum standards of work, pay, and living conditions, there was a wide variance in the living conditions of live-in domestic workers. The majority of domestic workers lived in poor, deplorable conditions that would be unacceptable to most other workers. However, the threat of deportation and of losing the source of money, which in many cases is the sole support of dependent families in the West Indies, accounts for the tolerance of many domestic workers.

Following a protest led by seven Jamaican women against deportation by Canadian immigration officials, changes were made to recruitment practices that attempted to provide greater job stability than the temporary work visas (Macklin, 1994: 17–18). The seven women were targeted for deportation by immigration officials even though they had been admitted as immigrants years earlier under the Caribbean Domestic Scheme. The banner of their cause, "good enough to work, good enough to stay," focused on securing the same rights for domestic workers as other categories of workers who were also in high demand (18). As a result, the Foreign Domestic Movement (FDM) program was put into effect (18). It was a federal policy that allowed foreign domestic workers to apply for landed-immigrant status within Canada (18).

The scheme was updated once again on April 27, 1992, by the Minister of Employment and Immigration following a moratorium announced on January 30, 1992, for all domestic workers who had not gained prior approval for landed immigrant status (26). The new scheme was called the Live-in Caregiver Program (LCP). It introduced "stricter criteria" (29) for applicants, such as having the equivalent of a Grade 12 Canadian education and a full-time, six-month-long program of formal training related to the type of caregiving position for which the applicant was applying (26).

Most of the women whom I interviewed came to Canada during the years of the temporary employment visa scheme in the 1970s. Some came after, in the 1980s under the auspices of the Foreign Domestic Movement scheme. Those who continue to work in domestic service have tended to move on to paid domestic work in commercial settings rather than in private homes or childcare in daycare settings. Some, however, remain employed in private homes.

In the following, Mother Patricia describes the conditions of her employment in paid domestic service between 1977 and 1982, shortly after coming to Canada:

MP: I started babysitting. And the guy was from Trinidad and he was— the wife was white and he was black. But I think that was the mistake there, huh [laughter—indicating that she thought that this man being a black person from the Caribbean would have had an impact, a positive one, on the way in which she was treated and lessened the likelihood of exploitation]. Because at that time he wanted you to work for uh—you was just working for seventy dollars a week. But he—but when you say now working for fifty-five dollars but he said, um, he asked me to cook. And I said, well if I have to cook it's going to be seventy-five dollars. And he said, he can't pay. So he was gonna give me fifty-five. But what he used to do, every day, he and di wife will take down di meat ... from the freezer to the fridge and then will call me around two o'clock and they will say, um, "Could you um, put this in the oven for us? Could you peel four potato and put it around the roast?" So what you endin' doing? Not cooking?

CBD: Mmmmhmmm.

MP: You were cooking. So then I started to realize that.

Clearly, Mother Patricia was exploited by her employers who exacted more work from her at the same time that they reduced her wages. After several months she left her job with this family. This job was followed by work as a "home-care worker," in which she provided domestic work to individuals who were recuperating from illness. Mother Patricia noted that some of the white people whom she met in this line of work were "very nice" while others were "very prejudiced" in their interactions with her:

MP: Worked with homes and that was hard. You meet some nice—nice white people. They were very nice. And it have some they were very prejudiced.

CBD: Mmmmhmmm.

MP: I met one. Now, I believe that don't matter if you already reach your age and then your—she wanted me to press her panties. So, I think that was a little too much for me.

CBD: Mmmmhmmm.

MP: So, I said, I wash it and when it come up from the laundry, I fold it. What you need your panties pressed for? I don't know. But I had one where she was ninety-eight ... and that woman was as beautiful as anything. Her house, when you go there, you will think—her husband died forty years before—but you will think her husband is there. The way she talks is like if he just gone out. So, you could she had a good living ... and she had a—she was very nice to me, you know.

CBD: Mmmmhmmm.

MP: She was very nice. But you met some was *very* prejudiced.

Mother Patricia recounted one case in which the children of the white family for whom she worked became so attached to her that when asked by their parents if they wanted to visit their grandparents or stay with Mother Patricia, they would choose Mother Patricia:

MP: [laughter] So that weekend I would stay with them. But they were—they were good kids. The big girl had to take a little while for she to settle in because like she would say, "I'm going across the street." And I said, "No, you're not going there. You'll wait until—I coming out there to cross you"—because they were living [at a busy downtown intersection in an upscale section of Toronto] ...

CBD: Mmmmhmmm.

MP: ... and that is a busy place. I tell you I ain't want no police coming here to ask me any questions. It was hard in that time. And then I got married in 1982. Um ... when I went home, I got married there in '82—'81.

Mother Patricia continues to work in paid domestic service although in a commercial rather than private residential setting. Some women managed to move away from paid domestic service but continue to work in so-called nurturing professions such as teaching and nursing. This was the case with Sister Maria, a Vincentian woman. She emigrated to Canada in 1982 after living for a brief time in the Dutch Caribbean islands of Aruba and Curaçao. In Toronto, Sister Maria worked as a live-in domestic worker with two families for several years before she was able to work her way out of domestic service. She did so through upgrading her education by attending night school and through supplementing her wages earned as a domestic worker by taking a telemarketing job as well as working part-time at a hotel:

> SM: I used to do telemarketing in the morning when the kids gone to school. I get dressed, drop them off—there was ways—and I gone and do telemarketing half day. Come back. Pick them up for lunch. You know do my laundry, clean my house and get my dinner ready. And then weekends, I had a job at a hotel. That's how I met my husband. And I was going to school at nights.

> CBD: Wow.

> SM: Okay? And um ... after that, I dropped telemarketing. That was a headache! Just really, really had it. And then I went into the daycare, okay? 'Cause B went into daycare, so then Mrs. C, this lady, she really likes me and she offered me the half-day position. So I go and then when I drop B off to daycare, I stayed there and do my work until um, four-thirty until eight-thirty. And I came home and get dinner ready. And then I go to school at nights. Then weekends I do my hotel stuff.

Sister Maria eventually became an early childhood educator for which she trained by completing a university degree. While Sister Maria represents a "success story" of sorts in the way she worked her way out of domestic service, many more women seem trapped in an endless cycle of working in domestic-service jobs. Long hours, low pay, and job instability make it difficult to upgrade educational and job skills necessary to move into other employment sectors. Combined with the need to remit earnings to family members at home in the Caribbean as well as providing for their own subsistence, many women continue to work as domestic workers.

Exploitation at the hands of the Canadian state is evident in many ways. First, although domestic workers pay unemployment benefits and Canada Pension premiums, they are ineligible to collect these benefits. Special forms are available to claim back the premiums paid but not many domestic workers have been informed or are known to have utilized this refund. Second, until recently, many domestic workers were not protected by the four major pieces of labour legislation in Ontario: the Employment Standards Act, the Human Rights Code, the Labour Relations Act, and the Workers' Compensation Act. Third, the state, in issuing temporary employment visas to immigrant Caribbean women, explicitly acted to limit the accessibility of landed immigrant status to these women. These women were not wanted in Canada as citizens or permanent residents, but only for their labour power in the household.

It was not until 1984, after publicity in the media and the pressure of interest groups[3] concerned about the welfare of domestic workers, that the Canadian government formally changed its policy on foreign domestic workers' accessibility to landed immigrant status. This revision allowed women who were recruited as domestic workers to apply for landed immigrant status provided they had been working in Canada for three years and an immigration officer deemed them to be self-sufficient or to possess the capacity for self-sufficiency. The latter criterion for eligibility still places within the hands of the state tremendous power in deciding the success of an applicant. And so it remains today, that despite legislative changes, domestic workers in Canada are still vulnerable to extreme exploitation at the hands of their employers and, implicitly, from the agents of the government. It should be noted that in an effort to economize and cut costs in the household, the paid domestic workers' wage and living and work conditions may be adversely affected. For as Armstrong and Armstrong noted in the late 1980s, a time period in which many of the women whom I interviewed worked as domestic workers:

> Falling wages and rising unemployment change expenditure patterns in the household. The most flexible items in domestic budgets are children's extra-curricular activities such as drama and art lessons, leisure activities, child-care, food, clothes, *and paid domestic workers*. (1987: 241; emphasis added)

It was within the conditions outlined above that many of the women of the church have worked and continue to work as domestic workers in private homes. Even if they do not work in domestic service, as I will discuss in the following chapter, the ideological justification, based on notions of black women workers as inferior and destined to servitude, nevertheless affects their lives. I will now turn to a discussion of mothers of the church, an almost diametrically opposed identity to the domestic worker as low-status and devalued as that produced by Canadian state legislation and employment practices.

THE MOTHERS OF THE CHURCH

The mothers of the church occupy a crucial space in the history of black communities. These women are leaders who are valued and respected for their leadership and nurturing in both church-related and wider community matters. I suggest that the mothers of the church are linked to women's leadership roles in religions such as the *mambo* in Haitian *vodun*, and political leadership figures such as Nanny or Ni, leader of the Maroons in Jamaica. The link is the legacy of women in powerful and respected leadership roles in West African societies such as Ashanti Queen Mother Yaa Asantewaa, who led a military and political struggle against British colonialism in what is now contemporary Ghana. In fact, the term "queen mother," which is West African in origin (Gilkes 1997: 372) and denotes a woman leader, is used in the Spiritual Baptist Church in reference to the "mother of the home," the head mother of the church.

Gilkes notes that black women's church work "generally encompasses active membership in local churches, clubs, and religious auxiliaries, as well as teaching Sunday school" (369). This work could also include pastoring and the founding of churches and regional or national associations of churchwomen (369). Toronto Spiritual Baptist women's experiences mirror Gilkes's description. The first Spiritual Churches Convention held in Toronto in 1994 involved the participation of Spiritual Baptist Church women from Toronto as well as New York and Boston. This convention was significant in linking North American Spiritual Baptist churches as well as fostering ties with other Caribbean-based churches such as those in the Jamaican Revivalist tradition that exist in the Toronto area.

In the Spiritual Baptist Church, women's leadership roles include mother, nurse, warrior, evangelist, prophetess, and deaconess. Revealed "in the spirit" through mourning, these leadership roles are important ways in which churchwomen nurture the spiritual children of their community.

Very few women hold the highest-ranking offices of bishop, archbishop, or abbot. Those who do are sometimes referred to as Mother Bishop, a term that straddles both the feminine and the masculine. It was remarked by two high-ranking church women that while they were women carnally, they were men spiritually. This explanation was offered with regard to their being given spiritual gifts that included traditionally male roles such as administering communion. This too shows the malleability of the Spirit from a Spiritual Baptist perspective.

It is also an interesting case in which gendered identities, when constructed in a way that references both the carnal and the spiritual, transcend the body as a marker of social difference even in a situation in which gender roles appear to be fairly rigid and supported by biblical scriptures. Some women offered their own interpretation of biblical scriptures that had been used conventionally to support an inferior status of women within the church hierarchy and within worship services. One mother noted that biblical passages excluding women from preaching at the pulpit were purposely misinterpreted to silence women. In her estimation, the prohibition against women speaking in church was aimed only at women who did not have anything of worth to share with the church community. Women have a valuable role to play on equal footing with men in leadership roles in the Spiritual Baptist religion:

M: Yeah! You know? Because, you know, Carol … look where Paul says, women should be quiet in the church, when Paul spoke to the Corinthians women. And the reason why he spoke to them is because they were miserable. They make confusion. They … you know, they had the church in an uproar. And—and that was for me I feel strong that Paul did not mean, we should sit back and not administer the church.

CBD: Mmmmhmmm.

M: He was speaking basically to women who were mischief-makers.

CBD: Mmmmhmmm.

M: Don't … when you come to church, be quiet, because you are not doing anything to a divided church. What you're doing—

CBD: Mmmmhmmm.

M: —is to pull the church down.

CBD: Mmmmhmmm.

M: But when God calls us as shepherds, you know?

CBD: Mmmmhmmm.

M: And I know that he called me. I—I have no question about that. He has spoken that over and over to me.

CBD: Mmmmhmmm.

M: In a strong way. Because, my trials and tribulations coming into the spiritual faith, it was not easy and if I wasn't called I'd be gone. I—nobody—you wouldn't even know me in this faith.

CBD: Mmmmhmmm.

M: Because I wasn't even going to be a Baptist, you know? Because you do go through a lot of trials—you testing period is very, very heavy.

CBD: Mmmmhmmm.

M: You know? And if you don't have that strength and that faith to continue, I mean you just run.

CBD: Mmmmhmmm.

M: You run away and hide, right?

CBD: Mmmmhmmm.

This same mother went on to note that if women are ordained as ministers, they should be allowed to administer fully rather than to be given the role but have its authority and effectiveness undercut by notions of the appropriate place for church women that effectively place them as helpmates and supporters for men who go on to have "all the glory":

M: So—but, you see there's a chauvinistic way about these men in the spiritual faith. The women—they feel women has to do all the work, you know? And—and—and they has to have all the glory.

CBD: Mmmmhmmm.

M: No! If you are going to ordain us as ministers, we're working, we are the mothers, we are bringing in the children into the fold. We are doing all this work and then you don't want us to do anything else. We should just sit there and be quiet. Be a mother in the little choir. That's not what this is all about. The spirit of Almighty God knew I was a woman!

CBD: Mmmmhmmm.

M: When he called me to be a shepherdess! You understand what I am saying?

CBD: Mmmmhmmm.

M: So, because He knew I was a woman, He knows my function as a woman.

CBD: Mmmmhmmm.

M: You understand?

CBD: Mmmmhmmmm.

M: And I don't feel that we have to be quiet. I feel that we should be able to do all the things and administer exactly the way the men have been administering. 'Cause when you really think about it, you know we're—we're stronger anyway ... We are!

CBD: Mmmmhmmm.

She later noted that her position was not one of gender separation but of gender, if not equity, then parity:

M: You know? We need the men, eh! [laughter] We really do! [laughter] We need them! I told one Sunday, in my preaching, he's this little chauvinistic, I said to him, "Have you ever heard about the beehive? The queen bee's who controls the show?" [laughter with CBD]

CBD: Yeah! My goodness!

M: I said, "You know, the queen bee is who controls everything! Everybody has to do what the queen says! You know?" And I says, "She does nothing! She just—you know?" And he told me he was gonna get me for that when he got up to speak. He says, he knew of a garden that God placed a certain person in there, a man. You know? And um, he was very lonely and he took a rib off to create the woman and—and the answer to him was that and he was so stupid, the woman still outsmarted him 'cause she got him to eat the apple. [laughter]

CBD: Yeah.

M: You know? So, I says, "Listen, we need the men for the fertilization, but the women have their place in it!" You know?

CBD: Mmmmhmmm.

In another instance, this same mother remarked that while communion was a sacrament that should be administered only by a male leader, she felt entitled to give her congregation communion on the basis that she held a role that was on par with that of a male leader. For this church mother, ritual performance was tied to leadership role rather than to gender as determined by maleness or femaleness as defined by the body as a marker of difference. She noted that women as leaders of churches were not always accepted in those roles by male leaders:

... [A]s a woman head of the church, as a woman pointer—it's very hard to deal with these men. They don't wanna accept you as reverend and things like that. They're doing but … you could understand the fight that we have to put up with them. And they [can't] do without us. Cause we keep the church them … And we're their backbone.

In the following, this mother describes a mourning experience in which she was given the task of performing communion as she was recognized as a "man in the spirit" by four other "bishops in the spirit" during a mourning experience. The role of bishop is a high-ranking male leader within the church's hierarchy of leadership:

M: I was relevated as a shepherdess. A shepherdess in the spirit too. I said bishop [the pointer] … and when I gave bishop that tract, there was another bishop in the church, he told me he was gonna call the bishop to listen. And when the bishop came he said, "Number One [the bishop] is here." [words unclear] He just told me and I told him where I was, the church I was in, how I was escorted into the church by three more bishops. That was not the reverend role. That is elevation. Pure elevation. I was in the centre, there was a bishop here, there was a bishop here and another bishop here. And I was going up to their altar. And when I go up to the altar, my bishop was standing there with a shepherd rod. Not the one that I have but the one that was given to me. He had his shepherd rod.

CBD: Mmmmhmmm.

M: And he took his shepherd rod and the other three bishop came at my back, one at my back and two at my side, and blessed me with it. "The Lord is your shepherd." And while he was doing that, I don't know why, I started to sing because the cantata was wild. Huge. And I said to him, "I remember the choir sound like there were twelve choirs."

CBD: Mmmmhmmm.

M: It was so beautiful. They started to sing the Twenty-third Psalm in a way I never heard it. When I go deep, deep into that realm it comes back to me. I thought about it. [she sings the following] "The Lord is my shepherd, I shall not want. He maketh me to lie down in green pasture." And you should have heard that sound. And when they hit that "greeeeen" oh my, it was like the organ. It was just like, you know. And I was—I found myself walking up to the altar for the Eucharist. And the chestibul I was wearing I had it wrapped—the Eucharist— and I went straight up into the high altar with it and I took part into

the communion service and then I was made to administer communion. My spiritual father does not believe that women could give communion. But what he had asked the church is … I don't believe that
women—people put it in the wrong way to give communion. But who
is the pilgrim? The answer was the pilgrim is a man in the spirit.

CBD: Mmmmhmmm.

M: But people took it, "Oh he said, she can't give communion." But if
he—it isn't that. But he was trying to recognize who I am in the spirit.
In that role I was a man in the spirit. And [the other bishop] said to me,
"Mother Number One, do you realize that the spirit has just elevate
you from one stage to the next? You cannot be a bishop if you're not the
reverend. You're a priest in the spirit. You're a high priest. But carnally,
you must take ordination." And my spiritual father says to [the bishop's]
face, "When I ordain her you're gonna have a lot to say so I wanted you
to hear this tract."

In this mourning experience, this mother was welcomed by other bishops both spiritually and carnally as represented by her spiritual father and
another bishop who was present at the church. Yet another high-ranking
Spiritual Baptist mother, who was also a bishop, noted that she was a "man
in the spirit" in describing having to "prove herself" as a leader:

> … is like—I had to prove myself [laughs]. I had to preach like a man. I
> had to walk like a man—not that I wasn't a man in the spirit. I had to
> do everything.

These women's explanation of gender roles and their inversion is reminiscent of the scenario discussed by Wallace Best in his study of black religion in Chicago in the 1930s and the role of women leaders in black churches
(2005: 153). In describing the roles of black women pastors in the period of
mass migration of African-Americans from the south to northern cities,
Best notes that women pastors such as Mary Evans and Lucy Smith were
able to subvert gender norms by assuming traditionally masculine roles in
their churches. As Best notes: "Like many African American Chicago women
preachers of the time, Smith and Evans were free to construct religious
institutions, practices, and theologies to their liking. More importantly, they
were free to ignore those that weren't" (153). I suggest that similar impulses
were at play in the emergence of Spiritual Baptist churches in Toronto in
the late twentieth century in light of the flux and change presented by the

massive migration of Caribbean people in the post-1967 points system of immigration.

However, not all Spiritual Baptist mothers challenged existing gendered roles within the church on theological and ritual bases. There are those who uphold more conventional notions of men's and women's roles, particularly in relation to church rituals such as baptism and communion. In the following, Queen Mother Pamela describes the Protestant church in which she was reared as a child in St. Vincent. She notes that her views against women administering baptism and communion, in spite of recent changes in other Christian denominations to the contrary, stem from her early church experiences and biblical scriptural interpretation:

QMP: Gospel Hall. It's something like, evangelistic, you know? They don't say, "Praise God" and stuff, they operate different. It's like if you ever have been to a Methodist church ... is something like that, you know. The preacher would preach, you know. But then, it's men, right. Now in the Methodist Church now they have ... women. Long ago when I was growing, they didn't have—they had deaconesses. But then, they never uses to preach. But now, you know? In the Catholic churches now, I understand that women gives communion and stuff like that.[4] But then I wasn't—you know, I still don't believe in women giving communion.

CBD: And why is that, may I ask?

QMP: Because, just like women is not supposed to baptize, right. When you say baptize not like when you have a baby and you take it to the church and you christen that child—baptism. That is a form of baptism. Another form of baptism is water baptism where the pool, or the sea, or the river—they baptize you in the name of the Father, the Son, and the Holy Spirit, okay? In the Bible you never read of any women. All you read about that John did baptize Jesus, right? And other men in that ... biblical men in the Bible. You never hear they talk about women baptizing. So I—that is the reason why I don't believe. I am not chauvinist, but I, you know, I don't believe in that women should give communion or baptize souls or whatever.

Some women interviewed upheld the prohibitions against women speaking in the church from the pulpit. However, these women participated in worship services through giving testimony, praying, and singing from "the floor." They also spoke from the front of the church but not at the pulpit. Here Queen Mother Pamela in noting her seating in the church (in which she corrected my stating that she was seated "on the altar") points to the way in which she observes the practice of women not standing at the pulpit:

> So, I am not supposed to be sitting up on the altar, number one. Number two, women not supposed to be really sitting up on altar. But Catholic people they does that now, right? Well, we don't. So there is where I sit. At the front, in front the altar, there, right? So, I was chosen to be a mother, right? So that is the reason why you know, some would say "Queen Mother" and some will say "Mother," right? The mother of the home.

However, it should be noted that while Queen Mother Pamela is not at the pulpit she is a notable presence, nevertheless, in her positioning at the front of the church. It is indicative of how Spiritual Baptist women are able to negotiate positions of influence for themselves within the religion's prescriptions on men's and women's gendered roles that appear to conform to conservative gender ideology that positions women as subordinate to men.

An examination of family forms and mothering practices that Africans and their descendants developed during slavery and colonialism reveals some of the ways in which dominant cultural forms, institutional practices, ideologies, and discursive modes of representation were subverted. The prevailing dominant culture beliefs during and after slavery asserted that black family forms were either non-existent or deviant because of the harshness of the slave and colonial regimes, including the sale and subsequent separation of black families. Also important here were notions of bad parenting, expressed especially through a purported "black matriarchy" and sexual lasciviousness of black people. In actuality, black family forms emerged in innovative ways that drew on the West African traditions of extended families in negotiating the harsh economic and psychic realities of slavery and colonialism.

Experiences and representations of motherhood in North America are differentially shaped by images and practices based on race, class, gender, sexuality, age, ability, and other aspects of social difference. The image of the good wife and mother, embodied in the "cult of true womanhood," was a representation of the feminine ideal in Euro-American cultures in the nineteenth century (hooks 1981). This ideal, which was raced, classed, and gendered, presented idealized images of white, Christian, heterosexual, and middle- and upper-class women as real women. Enslaved black women, poor and working-class white women, lesbians, and women of colour were represented as the foil of this image—effectively non-women. Stereotypes such as the subhuman brood mare with her ever-increasing fecundity, the closely related contemporary image of the welfare mother, the emasculating black matriarch, the genial mammy, and the superwoman are distorted images of black women as mothers. Representations of motherhood that emerge from black women's experiences and that are self- and community-defined simultaneously challenge these stereotypes as well as position black women as historically located, critical, and analytical subjects.

As Patricia Hill Collins notes (1991: 119–23), through othermothering, which is the practice of women nurturing children along with, or in some instances in place of, their bloodmothers or birth mothers, individual black families and communities nurture and define themselves. The mothers of the church in the Spiritual Baptist tradition, in addition to their powerful leadership roles, are an example of othermothers who bridge sacred and secular roles.

The experience of mothering from a Spiritual Baptist worldview is shaped by both spiritual and carnal circumstances. The carnal encompasses sexuality and the birthing process as well as the material circumstances such as the economic, political, and socio-cultural context of birth and nurturing. The spiritual refers to both the individual's relationship with Spirit as well as an ontological reality that co-exists with the material, tangible world. As we have thus far discussed, this distinction between the spiritual and carnal is not a reiteration of dualism in the sense of opposing pairs, but the positing of complex, interconnected sets of relationships that encompass the whole. Thus the experience of mothering is informed by this interrelationship of the carnal and spiritual in a woman's life. A spiritual child, for example, is someone with whom the spiritual mother has a relationship in which she provides guidance and nurturing in both spiritual and (often) secular matters as well. The relationship between spiritual mother and spiritual child is grounded in an extended family of the spirit.

FAMILY IN THE SPIRIT: EXTENDED FAMILY
IN THE SPIRITUAL BAPTIST CHURCH

The terms "spiritual mother," "spiritual father," "spiritual child," "spiritual son," and "spiritual daughter" are used in the Spiritual Baptist Church to refer to relationships of care, nurturing, and sponsorship within the church community. Frequently, these ties extend beyond church settings to encompass other areas of daily life such as work and the wider community. Spiritual parents, be they spiritual mother or spiritual father, are responsible for nurturing their spiritual children. These relationships are often initiated as sponsorship for, or performance of, the rite of baptism. However, their significance is such that they often encompass guidance and nurturing in secular matters involving their spiritual children, as well. Given the worldview of the Spiritual Baptist Church, expressed succinctly in the phrase "so carnally, so spiritually," it is not surprising that a spiritual parent would also be concerned with the carnal as the carnal and spiritual are intrinsically linked. In the following, Mother Yvonne, a high-ranking spiritual mother in Toronto, comments on the significance of spiritual parents:

> A lot of love from my spiritual parents because there is that bond that we feel with them even if you not around. They—they—there's the real bond. I don't know. I know I feel it very much. And judging from how I feel about my spiritual parents and how my spiritual children feel about me, I know there is this bond ...

The notion of a spiritual family has its basis in the family forms of the enslaved and their descendants. The church, as a home, became the focal point of community activity. I suggest that the spiritual family formed initially during the period of plantation slavery and the colonial period has evolved to reflect the needs of its members. Henry's discussion of Toronto Spiritual Baptists notes the tradition of churches being formed around family groups "both fictive and blood, immigration, nationality and worship" (1994: 158). I wish to extend this analysis by suggesting that the notion of the spiritual family must be taken into consideration in the characterization of the family forms of the members of the Spiritual Baptist Church in Toronto. The spiritual family pushes the boundaries of extended family forms to include relationships that transcend conventional barriers of time and space. From this perspective, the ancestral is included within the notion of family. The ancestors as the "community of divine intermediaries standing before God" (Hood 1990: 217) link the temporal and historical community through the continuance of cultural values and community moral codes.

While spiritual parents are valued highly by their spiritual children and enjoy a high status within the church community, criticisms and cautions were echoed by many, including spiritual mothers themselves, about the need to "humble yourself" as a spiritual mother:

> ... if you're a parent in your home, right, and set down certain rules for you children. You expect your children to follow that rule, right? So you as a parent, you has to lead that rule. You have to do the good things that you want your children to do, you know, in order for them to follow you. You don't say, "I don't want you to go to party. I don't want you comin' in late. I don't want you do this." But you doing the things you tellin' your kids not to do you not doing do it. Because when they seein' you doin' it, "Why is Mom doin' this and she's sayin' to me it is wrong to do and she's doin' it?" You know? Right. And what I find about a lot of mothers up here, spiritual parents they are there in a way to guide you. God put them as a leader to guide you.
>
> And what I ... notice about up here [Canada], about a lot of spiritual mothers, some of them even making themselves, if they stand up behind you—you notice baptism and mourning up here, someone is standing behind you ... —and if they stand up behind you and they nurse you in baptism, or mourning or something, they want you to call them mother. They not a mother, they might be a mother in the spirit, but they're not your mother, you know. They're a bit higher than you; they're a mother in the church in whatever. A notable person like a Queen Mother, she's a mother carnally, she's a mother spiritually. So somebody like that you look to, you know. A mother is a person you go to them with something confidential. You tell them, they supposed to keep it to themselves ...
>
> The way I notice some of them want to talk to you, it's not right because ... okay, you have your children, you know, those are your children, you bring them into the world, you mind them, you do whatever for them and you talk to them in certain ways. And in this country when you ... you can't even talk to them. 'Cause ... now abuse. But when you come into the house of God, these are adults you are dealing with. And you have to know how far to go even if they are doing something

wrong, you have to know how to speak to them. You have to know how to come across to them, you know in order for them to respect you. Sometimes when you want to treat them worse than you, like a little child, I don't think that is right, you know. And if you're a spiritual person, you have to learn to be humble. You have to humble yourself, you know.

Clearly, church mothers are expected to carry out their roles in accordance with a certain moral code of humility and confidentiality.

In summary, then, for Spiritual Baptist women in contemporary Canada, their experiences of mothering are informed by the legacies of West African extended family traditions and leadership roles for women, the histories of colonialism and enslavement, contemporary Caribbean experiences, and immigration to Canada. Many of these women work in paid domestic service, which involves providing child care for the children of other women, primarily, though not exclusively, white middle- and upper-middle-class women. In many cases, these women have also been separated from their own children and mothers through migrations. This situation mirrors the experiences, during the slavery and colonial periods, of family separation due to incorporation into the labour force. An examination of mothering in the lives of Spiritual Baptist women points to the contradiction of the high value placed on motherhood within the church in contrast to the devaluation of mothering in the paid work that the women engage in, such as health care and domestic service.

In the following, I present the experiences of different types of mothers: "ancestral," "spiritual," and "nation," as well as those of a "daughter." Reflecting the hierarchical arrangement of Spiritual Baptist Church leadership, the mothers of the church are distinguished both by role and function as well as by the "degree" of their motherhood. They can be mothers of the first, second, third degree, and so on. These degrees of the spirit are akin to carnal degrees such as those granted by colleges and universities. They denote the seniority of the mother and the height of her spiritual gift. Rather than a solely prestige-generating status, the mothers of high degree all pointed to their spiritual work both as a gift and a responsibility in serving the Spirit.

For example, Mother Yvonne noted that when in her adolescence, her spiritual gifts as a healer manifested when she "fell" following her baptism in a Spiritual Baptist ceremony under the power of St. Michael (the orisha

Ogun) on a Friday morning, her mother lamented the responsibility that came with these gifts falling on the shoulders of one so young:

> And I recall they said that my mother cried that Friday morning. Cried when I fell under those powers. My mother bawled. She *cried*. And I thought, "Why are you crying?" I'm just a little kid who get the "power," you know? You know? We're in the faith. And, I remember she keep saying, to me, "You don't know, child. You don't know."

Mother Yvonne was taken out of school for a three-month period during which time she used her "gifts" to heal others:

> But within that time, I was doing a lot of healing. Sixteen years of age. The powers stayed with me for three months. I couldn't go to school.... Out of school, healing people. People would come ... I had a very strong African-English accent. My whole accent was changed. Very, very strong. And my mother used to look at me. I would go in and out of the powers. And she would cry, when everyone gone. And she says, "You don't know the responsibility, you don't know, you don't know.... Is a lot of responsibility to carry."

Over time, however, her family decided that the "powers" were too much for a school-aged girl to handle. Through a ritual process, the "powers" were made dormant rather than active in Mother Yvonne:

> And whatever conversation was with the family, my aunt decide I was too young.... And whatever they did, they cut ... she decided I was too young. And just have to finish school. So, they cut. So, the powers was there but was dormant ... because they had to beg off. You understand. This is how I'm understanding, how they had to beg off. Or they would go and beg the powers and all different things and they had to beg.... So, whatever was done, I know they had a very big prayers on Friday.... And then, I know the next week I was fine. [laughter with C] You know?

The "powers" resurfaced decades later after she emigrated to Toronto initiated by her "call" to do her spiritual work as a nation mother by an ancestral mother.

"IF YOU DON'T COME TO ME, I'M COMING TO YOU": ANCESTRAL MOTHER

Conventional notions of linear time and space are challenged by some Spiritual Baptist women's experiences of being mothered by women who visit them in dreams and visions. Sometimes the identity of these women is revealed to be religious figures such as St. Anne, the grandmother of Jesus. St. Anne is especially significant, given the importance of grandmothers as teachers, elders, and wise women in African-Caribbean cultures. It is significant that this saint is associated with female deities in the Orisha religious tradition such as Yemaya, a mother goddess who is "mistress of the seas."

The following account points to experiences of mothering in which West African notions of cyclical time are invoked. These ancestral mothers, who cross barriers of time and space, appear at moments of crisis to give guidance. They issue the summons for the woman to enter another phase of her spiritual life either through baptism or to become a mother herself. They are akin to Great-Aunt Cuney, Avatara "Avey" Johnson's ancestor in Paule Marshall's novel *Praisesong for the Widow*, whose appearance in a vivid dream precipitated the events that led to Avey's acceptance of her role as a spiritual reincarnation of Great-Aunt Cuney and teller of the story of the Ibo who walked across the water to Africa:

> And then three nights ago the old habit returned. Tired after a long day spent ashore on Martinique, during which she and her companions had traveled overland for hours to visit the volcano, Mount Pelée, she had gone to bed early that evening, only to find herself confronted the moment she dropped off to sleep by her great-aunt Cuney. (Marshall 1983: 31)

Mother Yvonne's story of her call by the *orisha* as an adolescent was recounted above. She received a spiritual call to "take up the work" of her great-aunt decades later, after immigrating to Toronto. Her story uncannily echoes Paule Marshall's protagonist Avey Johnson. And it is no wonder as Marshall's novel, while consciously structured to reflect a variety of religious experiences in the African Diaspora, among them Orisha and Haitian *vodun,* is rooted in the African-American Southern Shouter Baptist tradition. Here Mother Yvonne relays the dream that indicated she was the one to whom "the work" had "passed on" following her aunt's death:

MY: And I was working on a novena to St. Jude and I knelt at my bed at night and I say my prayers and I just put my head down to sleep and

I went right off in a trance.

CBD: Mmmmhmmm.

MY: And I saw all my dead family.

CBD: Mmmmhmmm.

MY: They all came. My aunt, my mother [words unclear]. I haven't dreamt about my mother for a long time. And when I saw her I was so happy! Oh Mom, I'm so happy to see you, I'm happy to see you! You know? And she said to me, "You're happy to see me ..." And when I looked, I saw my aunt, all the family I knew that was dead, they were there [words unclear]. It was a dream but it was so real!

CBD: Mmmmhmmm.

MY: And my aunt, I was very close to her.

CBD: Mmmmhmmm.

MY: It seems like there's a bond with she and I. She said to me, [whispering] "You're suffering. You're suffering and suffering." And Carol, in the vision, I said to Aunty, "You're suffering? I love you too much." "I don't want you suffering. Tell me what to do." And she says, "Take up your work." And I says, "I will." [words unclear] Carol I came out of that trance pouring! I was pouring! I was screaming at the top of my voice! Everything was so real! And then I called my sister. I said, "It was a dream but it was so real." And she said, "Come here, come here." I says, "I had a dream about Mom and Aunty and everybody." And she said to me, "You nevah had that dream." Oh no. And I told her. And she paused for a minute and she said, "Yvonne, you have just promised Aunty you're going to do her feast." I said, "I did?" She said, "Yes! You told her you're going to feed her." But my sister had more experience in that than me. And then she started to talk to me. I asked her to get a Bible 'cause I had to calm down now. And she said, "Remember that last feast that Aunty had before you went away." I said, "Yes." She said, "She said remember right after you had to get baptized." And I said, "Yes." She says, "Remember you fell into manifestation the Friday morning under the powers of St. Michael?" I said, "Who could forget that? It was three months. I couldn't even go to school." And she says, "So the more I hear, the work, it pass to you."

CBD: Mmmm.

MY: And I said, "Yeah." And she says, "Well, Aunty dead now, somebody has to take it up so I guess they find you."

CBD: How did you feel when she said that?

MY: I didn't know how I felt at that time because—

CBD: Yeah.

MY: —I didn't know the full responsibility of what was gonna happen.

CBD: Mmmmhmmm.

In the following, Sister Maria, recounts an experience of meeting St. Anne, mother of Mary, which heralded her baptism, the initiatory rite of passage of becoming a Spiritual Baptist. As she spoke, she held her own granddaughter:

And as it goes on, I used to get verses from the Bible and I didn't even know. Just in my dreams. Just in dreams. And I believe in dreams because I've seen things happen outright in dreams. And, one day, I had— I wasn't sleeping but I was lying on my bed reading that same Bible and with my son and my daughter and this woman came up to me, her house was like on the hill and you have to walk down from the main part of the hill. And I saw this woman in my dream coming up and she's walking so brisk and she's coming up and she came right up—we had glass door like this. And in my dream, the drapes weren't long enough to reach to the bottom. And I can see this woman out there. But she found me crying, okay? I never forget the position that I was in, I was like this. She found me like this. And she called me and I said to her, "Um, wait I'm praying." And she called me again. I said, "Wait! Can't you see that I'm praying!" And she called me the third time and she said, "If you don't come to me, I'm coming to you." And I could see her from out there. She's dressed. Everything was brown. Brown head-tie. Her dress was brown. Her sandals was brown. She had the Bible in her hand. She had the bell in her hand. Okay? And she came in and she give me the Bible in my left hand and the bell in my right hand and she shake. She said to me, "Continue to pray." … And I find well, this was strange, you know?

So, I went back to the country and I told my grandmother. And she said to me that you have to be baptized. And I said to her, "But Mommy, I baptize, already." You know? Baptism which mean I've been dedicated as a baby. Because we call it baptism, back home, but it's not really baptism. So she said to me I have to baptize. I said, "But I baptize already." Eh man, you can't and you know and stuff like that.

And then I came here. That was like maybe a year after or the year and a half after I came here.... And I used to go all the way to Albion and Martin Grove [streets] with a friend of mine to church. And I still didn't feel ... I felt something was wrong, was missing, spiritually. And then I start going to the Anglican church down on St. Clair. And still I felt, it wasn't right. 'Cause I'm accustomed hearing the words from the Bible, not how it takes and history and those stuff, right? And I still feel that it wasn't right. And um, then I start going to um, Cross Cultural—Domestic Cross Cultures of Canada on Spadina Hall. It's a community centre. And I start finding myself there, going and listening to their problem. Babysitter, a lot of babysitter. And I meet more women. A lot of them sit there and they tell you, you know. And then I—I joined the organization, I became a member. I wrote newsletters and stuff like that. And then one day I met [a friend] and she invited me to church. I felt really good in church. At that time church was a packed church. It was a full church. Swinging. And, you know, I used to work from Steeles [Avenue] and Don Mills [Road] babysitting and then I used to come down on weekends at my cousin's and then go the meeting at Cecil [Community Centre] and then from Cecil I go to church and doing the whole circle around.

And, I was a—Monday morning I got up, you know, doing my vacuum and stuff like that and girl, one piece of manifestation took me! I had to drop the vacuum, go to my room and pray.... I'm so glad that these people weren't home, eh? 'Cause they might have said that I was crazy. 'Cause they're Canadian. And I called Uncle. I remember I called him and I spoke to him. I call my aunt and I talk to her. And she said to me, "Don't you see the Lord wants you for his own." "Mmmmhmmm! Yes." ... But then, as I baptize, and this woman keep coming to me all the time. She keep—she never leaves. She keep coming to me and then later on ... I discover this woman is St. Anne's, the mother of Mary ... and she's the woman, the brown, and the brown represent Mother's Earth. I never knew that! I didn't even know that there was a mother St. Anne's. I know there was Mary and Mary brought Jesus but who was Mother St. Anne's? I never knew that.

Ancestral mothers, whether they are direct bloodmother ancestors of the women or spiritual ancestors play an important role in the issuing the "call" to Spiritual Baptist women that it is time for them to "take up the work."

"DEY GIVE ME A HOUSE TO GATHER IN DI CHIL'REN": SPIRITUAL MOTHER/CARNAL MOTHER

Sister Maria and Mother Yvonne relate their experiences of being led by an ancestral mother who issued a spiritual call. Some women become church mothers as an extension of their mothering capacity in their carnal lives. In the following conversation with me, Mother Ruby, a Queen Mother in Trinidad, relates her experience of becoming a spiritual mother. Though not a carnal mother herself, she notes that her identity and spiritual work as a spiritual mother was intimately linked to her long-time work as an othermother and child-care provider in her community:

> QMR: All right, I grow up. Ah come woman too, no chil'ren. Ah come and adopt chil'ren and dey grown big man and ooman. Dey gone on dey own now. When dey ready, dey come and look for me and dat's dat. Ah come here, I used to mind chil'ren. In those days was two dollar a week ... to mind chil'ren.

> CBD: Dey didn't sleep or anything?

> QMR: Some a'dem used to sleep, yes. Because some a' di parents workin' ... Ah does tell dem, "Well you see afta six o' clock? Don' come in my house at-all. Leave di chil'ren and all-yuh could do wha' all-yuh want." So dat is how you see, I come and dey-so everybody is Mother Ruby, Mother Ruby. All di chil'ren and dem dey come big and some a'dem dey still remember me! You see? So when I—when I baptize and mourn ... I didn't realize really what was my ... position.

> CBD: Yeah.

> QMR: Dat is after years. Dey give me a—ah used to make med'cine. Cure people. Right? Well, dat was good enough for me. But after everybody was ... when di people started to get good and dey wanted to settle demselves somewhere to hear di word of God ... is so dey come and dey give me di church. So ... dey give me a house to gather in di chil'ren. So ah mus' be a mother.

> CBD: Mmmm.

> QMR: You understan'?

> CBD: Mmmhmmm.

> QMR: Right? And from dere, how much years, ah still gatherin.' Dey comin,' dey baptizing; dey mournin,' dey stop in and dey ... who gone away, gone away. But yet still dey don' forget you.

CBD: I see.

QMR: But it isn't a easy situation.

CBD: Mmmhmmm.

QMR: It ain't a situation—it isn't easy, for sometimes chil'ren come, dey ain' have nuttin. Da' is where di mother part is, you know?

CBD: Yeah.

QMR: Dey have not nutting. And dey come to me. You can't turn dem down. Why? Because my deceased leader always tell me, when you could refuse somebody from mourning them, you cannot some—refuse nobody when dey come to baptize. Dey must do dat. 'Cor dat is di—dat is important in dey life. Well, God is good, man. I does survive. You see?

"GOD HAS WORK FOR YOU TO DO": NATION MOTHER

A nation mother is described by Spiritual Baptist women in interviews and also in ritual church services as a "mother of all nations." This identity is the basis on which community mothering, that is to say, mothering that then ventures into community activism, is founded. There has long been an association with the gendering, racing, and classing of land masses in particular in association with colonial rule. Examples here include colonial Britain as the "mother country" while Africa was cast as the ultimate, feminized dark Other, as the "Dark Continent."[5] The nation mother exists beyond this narrowly defined trajectory to represent a strong basis for leadership in a variety of secular and spiritual contexts.

Already referred to earlier in Chapter 1, the nation mother's positioning draws a powerful reference point to ancient Jewish history by pointing to the "twelve tribes." In that instance, Mother Yvonne referred to the twelve cords of different colours that she carried over her shoulder symbolizing the twelve tribes. The nation mother is also represented by multicoloured striped fabric: "And this is our nation flag ... the stripey one ... this represents the nation. The Indian, the African, the Chinese." Here, however, the flag as a symbol that is usually associated with patriarchal power is recast as an empowering basis of female leadership and authority within the church that extends, also, into the wider community. "Nation" here can be read as a metaphor for community. In mothering the "tribes," the nation mother represents othermothering that extends not only beyond bloodlines but across race, nationality, and ethnicity. Her children are potentially any and everyone. The nation mother is an othermother who reflects the Caribbean's multi-ethnic, multi-racial, multi-religious, and multinational history.

In the following, Mother Yvonne shares her story of her call to become a nation mother. After the death of her "original" spiritual parents in Trinidad who had sponsored her baptism many years prior to her emigration to Canada, Mother Yvonne prayed for a spiritual father and mother. In time, she was introduced to new spiritual parents. Her spiritual father was based in Canada while her spiritual mother was based in Trinidad. It was this spiritual mother who pointed out that Mother Yvonne's destiny was to be a nation mother in Canada.

MY: … And I prayed after I was given a spiritual father—

CBD: Mmmmhmmm.

MY: —I prayed for a mother.

CBD: Mmmmhmmm.

MY: I wanted a spiritual mother and I was sent to Mother Ruby in Trinidad to mourn.

CBD: Oh yes.

MY: You know, I cannot ask for anything more. That woman has been a—a—a pillar in my life. When I was going through all—and I was gonna *run* away from the faith, I was going right back into the Catholic Church.

CBD: Mmmmhmmm.

MY: The trials was too much.

CBD: Mmmmhmmm.

MY: The pain was too much. And I took the two weeks and I went down [to Trinidad] to her and we sat on the gallery for two weeks—I didn't go anywhere—and she *taught* me. And she say to me, "You *cannot* run away from this. You *cannot* go back into the Catholic Church." There's no room in the Catholic Church for you. And I'm saying, "It's a *big* church, what you mean there's no room?" "Not you." And these was her *words* to me, Carol: "Let me tell you something, Mother Yvonne, do you know who you are? Spiritually?" And I says, "I'm a mother." And she says "No, you don't. She says you are a *nation mother*! And not just any nation mother, and she says, God has—has work for you to do.

And if you don't go back to Toronto, and do what God bidding for you, you would be worse than a beggar on the street!" My spiritual mother told me that.

CBD: Mmmmhmmm.

MY: She says, "You would be *worse* than a beggar on the street." Part of the thing is I do spiritual reading but I just said to her, "I'm not doing it. I'm too young for that!" And she said, "Eh, you too young to die? Tell me?" I says, "Mom, I have my mortgage to pay, people who do these things are old people." [laughter with C] "Is not for me!"

CBD: Mmmmhmmm.

After enduring a period of "trial and tribulation," Mother Yvonne took up her spiritual work as a nation mother in Toronto. This work includes being the leader and pastor of a church as well as a spiritual reader. She was also the proprietor of a spiritual store that she says was "given to [her] as a medicine house" when she mourned. Through both spiritual counselling work and church leadership, Mother Yvonne lives her identity as a nation mother through ministering to her spiritual children in the church and to others, including non–Spiritual Baptists.

The mothers of the church also perform a variety of support services for the congregation members, including hospital visits and provision of emotional support during times of personal crisis. In the following, Queen Mother Pamela describes the work of her church although it is financially poor:

Now the church is very poor. But then we gives out, you know? We have give to the poor. Like it have a certain time of year, in July, that the bishop of the church and the other ministers would go to the byways and highways and whatever and bring in. That is in the Bible, relieve the blind, right? So we go out to the unfortunate people, we don't call them poor people, we just say very unfortunate people, bring them to the church, feed them, we bath them, we give them clean clothes to put on. But we only do that once. The church promise or we the members of the church promise that we should do it a little more often, no?[6]

Very powerful sometimes when we are there on Tuesday evening service, somebody from out the street will pass wondering why the doors are open and ask if we have any food or if we have any money for them to give coffee and stuff like that. But not housing, cause we really doesn't have homes to put them, you know?

The church has a women's group that is organized around the provision of support services for members:

QMP: Now, we ahm, we have its—we call them … The first group we had it was Women's Auxillary and then we change it to Women's League. We wear a certain uniform in order to identify who we are in the church and sometimes we go to visit different churches and if we know of anyone who is in the hospital, the Women's Auxiliary will go to the hospital …

CBD: This is a church member?

QMP: Yes, it have to be 'cause we cannot just go to the hospital, it's against the rules or the laws of the hospital. But if you and I belonging to the same order, right? And I hear that you're sick and you call me and say, well "Sister Pamela or Mother Pamela" or whatever you want to call me, I am going to the hospital on Monday or I am in the hospital, then I will get in contact with other members. I might announce it in the church that Sister Carol is in the hospital and need our prayers so we could pray for you right in the hospital—in the church there. But then we the Women's League would come and visit you in the hospital where you at. And go and visit shut-ins, those ones who cannot come out to church. You know you go and give words of consolation or stuff like that. And they live alone you offer your help if they need you to go to do some groceries for them or take them to the doctor and stuff like that, that's what we really does.

Church members also support each other through social activities and friendships:

CBD: What are some of your other activities, outside of helping to support people in that way? How else do you help to support people?

QMP: Well, out of church, we, like I would—if I, like if I feel not bored, because I don't feel bored in my home, I always find something to do.

CBD: Yeah.

QMP: Yes, but then if I feel like visiting, I could call your mother and say "Ahm, you going out later?" And stuff like that, you know. And ahm, in truth, if she not going out she say ahm, what to say to her, whatever, whatever. And say well, "Gyul I in the house here and I want you to come over to visit" and then I go and visit. By serving God, or being a

Christian, doesn't say that you cannot have friends, or have ... so it doesn't mean that you can't have fun or go to a party.

Another church mother, Mother Patricia, emphasized this last point on the importance of social networks in response to my queries about her social life. I had implied in my question that I was asking about her social life *outside* of church. However, her response clearly indicated that her social life and her spiritual lives revolved around church:

CBD: So what do you do for fun? Social?

MP: Social?

CBD: Yeah.

MP: You would not believe my social life involve again along that—[laughter with C]. It is the truth.

CBD: Yes.

MP: Because, in the week I go to work and come home. Sometime I go to sleep on my couch [laughs]. But I get up and I do something and then I go to bed. I go to work again. So, on the weekend is a—um, the church have something. It will have either spiritual or carnal. We back and we back again. So it—you life is a circle around.

"IT MAKES YOU FEEL LIKE HOME": SPIRITUAL DAUGHTER

For women who are spiritual daughters, spiritual mothers provide guidance in many areas of their lives. In the following interview excerpt, a young woman in her late twenties, Sister Asha, who is separated from her own mother through immigration, reflects on the role of the church and elders in her life. Sister Asha's mothers and elder immediate family remain in Trinidad while she lives in Canada with her older siblings. For Sister Asha, as noted earlier, church provides a feeling of being at home:

SA: And when I came to Canada, I realize it was the closest thing to home. It make you feel like—you're in Canada, but you're back in Trinidad because of how they worship in the Baptist. It's similar in most ways but you know, you find, you know, one or two things different, you know. Yeah.

CBD: So, could you tell me more about that feeling for you in terms of you're in Canada but you feel as if you're back home?

SA: The singin,' the people, you know. Because, ahm, you know, the Baptist that, you know, that I am going to right now, you know, it's the only place that I see besides Caribana, a lot black people, you know, associating all at once together. You know, and there I find myself at home. Because they were talkin' my language. You know, like, you know, the church where I go to there it's a mix-up of Trinidadians, Vincentians, Jamaicans, you know. And you get to meet people not necessarily from your same area but, you know, from the same country. And, you know, you could talk about the good old days, you know, like back in Trinidad. And it makes you feel like home. Yeah, it does.

Sister Asha goes on to describe the church setting as a school in which she is taught by her elders and in which she wrestles with self-definition in the face of community-defined expectations:

SA: But then as I say, I'm a babe, I'm growin' up, right? In the church. I see the church as a school, right? And I'm there to be taught, right? And if the elders not setting the right example, not doin' the right things, how could I do it, right?

CONCLUSION

The mothers of the church are a living bridge between an African-Caribbean past and an African-Canadian present and future in the lives of the Spiritual Baptist churchwomen. Church mothers encompass ancestral figures like Mother St. Anne as well as women who are related to contemporary Spiritual Baptist women by blood. These relationships move backwards and forwards in time and space and are witnessed and experienced in visions and dreams. They encompass family separation and reunification through multiple migrations. The experiences recounted here point to one of the ways in which empowering identities are forged in the context of a history of black womanhood in which domestic service has played a large role.

Nevertheless, troubling images of black motherhood that have their basis in the racial iconography of the U.S. Old South and Caribbean slave regimes—images that have influenced contemporary images of black women in Canada—persist. How do Spiritual Baptist women reconcile their self-defined and empowering images as church mothers with disempowering images of servility, acquiescence, and inferiority associated with black women as domestic workers in the figure of Mammy and Aunt Jemima? This question is especially salient given that many of the Spiritual Baptist women themselves perform domestic work in either private homes or in institutional settings. The next chapter addresses this question in relation to the figure of Aunt Jemima in Toronto Spiritual Baptist experiences.

NOTES

1   In the documentary *Mi'k Maq Family* (1994), members of the Mi'k Maq First Nation in Atlantic Canada, in discussing the significance of St. Anne, mother of Mary, as the patron saint of their nation, point to their reverence for this saint as an "elder." In this sense, the Mi'k Maq First Nation have incorporated St. Anne as a symbol of elderhood in accord with cultural values that predate their introduction to Roman Catholicism through missionary contact in the eighteenth century. In this last regard, Crowley (1996: 39) notes that it was Roman Catholic priest Pierre Maillard who was instrumental in performing missionary work among the Mi'k Maq. Maillard arrived in Île Royale (Cape Breton today) in 1735 from France (39). His headquarters were relocated to Île de la Sainte-Famille (Chapel Island today) (39). The Mi'k Maq continue to gather annually at Chapel Island to celebrate St. Anne's Day on July 26 (39).

2   While research on this particular point of etymology should be pursued in greater depth, I will comment here briefly from my own subjective experience as a member of several Toronto black communities. The use of the terms "brotha" and "sista" to refer to black men and women, generically (Smitherman 1994: 70; 207), has several reference points. African-American everyday use of "brotha" and "sista" communicated through mass media such as television and film, and popular musical genres such as hip hop and R 'n' B have been an important source. Another is the use of the term in Jamaican patois where it is pronounced as "bredda" (Ford-Smith, 1987: 305) and "sistah." Yet another source is Jamaican Rastafari dreadtalk—the language developed out of Jamaican patois by the Rastafari that expresses their worldview that sees all black people as exiles in the land of Babylon (Jamaica and the West) seeking repatriation to Zion (Africa) (Chevannes 1994). In dreadtalk, brothers and sisters become "bredren" and "sistren."

3   In the chapter on ancestral mothers that follows, note Sister Maria's mentioning of her involvement in domestic worker activism in the 1980s.

4   Women are not ordained in the Roman Catholic Church, at present. It seems as if Queen Mother Pamela makes reference to the Roman Catholic Church as a representation of mainstreamed, Christian denominations. Ironically, the Roman Catholic Church's views on the ordination of women are on par with Queen Mother Pamela's.

5   Patrick Brantlinger (1986) in "Victorians and Africans," discusses the "genealogy of the myth of the Dark Continent." Brantlinger notes that this "myth of the Dark continent" emerged in the latter half of the nineteenth century as a "Victorian invention" that was a part of the "discourse of empire" (1986: 217). It provided

ideological justification not only for colonization of Africa and Christian mission- ary work but also excused the ravages of the slave trade that had been formally abol- ished earlier in the century in 1807. From this viewpoint, Africa as "Dark" continent represented the apex of "evil" and was therefore in need of "civilizing" both through colonial economic and political arrangements as well as the spread of an "enlight- ening" Christianity. In this scenario, the "darkness" was being illuminated by the "light" of European civilization.

6 An excerpt of these comments appears in Henry (1994: 165).

CHAPTER SIX

Aunt(y) Jemima in Toronto Spiritual Baptist Experiences
Spiritual Mother or Servile Woman?

One day, I see dis woman, black like jet, girl. And she has her head tie like Aunty Jemima. And her apron—only her head tie-up I coulda see. And her eyes and her apron. And she calling me up this hill and she said to me, "You're ready. Come out. It's time for you to learn these things."

—SISTER MARIA, *Toronto*

And he called the name of the first, Jemima ... —JOB 42:14

INTRODUCTION

In the previous chapter, the significant role of the mothers of the church in Toronto Spiritual Baptist churches was discussed. It was apparent that church mothers as spiritual mothers contributed much to the development and nurturing of church communities. This empowering image of black motherhood was forged even while many of the Spiritual Baptist women engaged in paid domestic service, a devalued and lowly paid occupation in Canadian society. As Zane notes in his study of the Converted in Brooklyn and St. Vincent, "[D]espite the generally higher spiritual status of Converted in Brooklyn, once in America, whether as home attendants, as nannies, or as housekeepers, they are often servants to Whites [cf. Silvera 1989]" (1999: 166). Thus, while on the one hand church mothers are afforded a high status within the church community, many of the women perform labour in

215

their working lives in North America that is largely devalued. Even if the women are not employed in domestic service, as this chapter discusses, it is more than likely they would encounter, in one form or another, one of the most pervasive images of black women as mothers and workers, Aunt Jemima.

This chapter examines the ways in which Spiritual Baptist women in Toronto have resisted, subverted, and re-interpreted the stereotypic image of Aunt Jemima in their religious and secular lives. Aunt Jemima, an extension of the Mammy stereotype, has emerged from the history of slavery and colonialism in North America as one of the most pervasive images of black womanhood and black motherhood. Though clearly an "invention"[1]— scholarly examination and personal narratives and biographies of black women in historical and contemporary times fail to find women who conform to this image of servility—the stereotype is nevertheless powerful in its impact on hegemonic images *and* public policy concerning contemporary black women (Jewell 1993).

In this chapter, I explore the ways in which Spiritual Baptist women who have emigrated from the Caribbean have encountered and grappled in their everyday lives with this image, which has its basis in Southern U.S. iconography of slavery. While analysis and strategies that emerge from anti-racist, anti-sexist, and anti-colonialist discourses have tended to focus on ways in which stereotypical images are debunked and subsequently erased, a consideration of processes in which these images are re-appropriated by the stereotyped group, through a so-called reclamation and implied transformation, is also important. These processes, which explore a potentially contradictory and explosive cultural, psychic, and political terrain, are crucial in understanding the construction and reconstruction of gendered, sexed, classed, and raced categories as historically based and dynamic power relations.

As a girl-child in the 1970s, I met Aunt Jemima in a number of linked and related contexts of my schoolgirl existence: at the breakfast table, in television commercials, in supermarket store aisles as the name of a mass-marketed pancake mix, as an iconic stereotypic image in the form of shiny ceramic cookie jars, and in racial taunts in classroom spaces and on school playgrounds.

Yet it became apparent to me, through in-depth interviews with women in the church and through my critical ethnographic research on church services and other rituals, that symbolic physical, psychological, and emotional characteristics often associated with negative images of black motherhood, such as Aunt Jemima and Mammy, not only had an impact on these women's everyday working lives as domestic workers in Toronto but also that these same characteristics had been reworked and re-invented in the religious symbols of the church and in individual women's religious lives to provide an empowering image of black motherhood contrary to the servility implied by the stereotype. These characteristics, which include attire such as the wearing of a head-tie, long skirts and dresses, and an ethic of maternal care that extends beyond biological children, described by Patricia Hill Collins as a practice of "othermothering" (Collins 1991), serve as the basis of a self-defined and affirming image of black motherhood even in the face of continued economic exploitation justified, in part, by stereotypic images of black motherhood.

In my interviews with black Caribbean women in the Spiritual Baptist Church in Toronto, as well as in conversations with other non-Spiritual Baptist black Caribbean women who work in a variety of occupations, most recounted an experience of one sort or another with Aunt Jemima, either by name, or more commonly through an externally defined association with her stereotypical physical and emotional-affective characteristics. Most of the women I interviewed in the Spiritual Baptist Church in Toronto had had experiences as domestic workers, and many continue to be employed as domestic workers. They had stories to tell of co-workers and supervisors who expected them to be all-nurturing, servile, caring, and non-complaining under the most arduous and poorly paid of work situations. These emotional and affective characteristics match those of Aunt Jemima (Jewell 1993).

More telling still were their stories of how they recognized Aunt Jemima's presence in their work relationships and her continuing effect on images of black women as workers in a variety of locales. Not only was she present in kitchens in private homes and commercial settings, but she also affected images of black women as workers on factory floors, in hospitals, in retail stores, in classrooms, and offices. "Mavis Beacon" software, which teaches basic typing skills to computer users, comes in a package that features a mature, black, African-American female as the image of the instructor.[2] While Mavis Beacon's image as a no-nonsense teacher stands in stark contrast to Aunt Jemima's usual occupation as a low-status domestic worker, her visual image as a dark-skinned, middle-aged African-American female places her within the range of stereotypical visual representations of African-American women.

This chapter has three objectives. It explores the ways in which the symbolic reinvention of Aunt Jemima within the Spiritual Baptist Church strips away the veneer of sameness and subsequent voiceless anonymity imposed by stereotyping to reveal the varied textures of African-Caribbean women's lives that have been obscured by this image. Second, in discussing a reinvented Aunt Jemima and her symbolic connection to the role of the mothers of the church, the chapter points to one of the sources of what can be characterized as an indigenous African Diasporic feminist consciousness forged in the crucible of Spiritual Baptist women's everyday lives. Last, while there has been much scholarship concerning the syncretic nature of African Diasporic religions historically, this chapter locates the discussion of cultural and religious hybridity and symbolic reinterpretation within the everyday lives of contemporary immigrant African-Caribbean women in Toronto. In so doing, the discussion and analysis point to the role of individual Spiritual Baptist women's cultural imaginations in meeting spiritual and emotional needs, as well as to the continued dynamism of African-Caribbean religious traditions in the Diaspora.

"Seeing" Aunt Jemima

Please put the Aunt Jemima in that corner. I had noticed the Aunt Jemima statuette in the church several times before a service one afternoon in the summer of 1994. I had noticed and noted her in my journal on my very first visit to a Spiritual Baptist church in Toronto nearly two years earlier:

September 27, 1992
There are six altars in the church. Four mini altars. One in each corner; a centre pole at which water, flowers, libations, meal, flour and peas are kept in calabashes; a main altar at the front of the church. The altar in the back left corner of the church had a statue of a black woman in headdress and skirts like the women of the church.

I had noticed her and refused to "see" her until that summer afternoon in 1994 when she was called her name by the bishop, the male leader of the church. *Please put the Aunt Jemima in that corner,* he said. Aunt Jemima was the *black woman in headdress and skirts like the women of the church.*

"The eye," as Dionne Brand notes in her essay "Seeing," "is a curious thing: it is not passive, not merely a piece of physiology, practical and utilitarian; it is not just a hunk of living matter, gristle, tendon, blood. It *sees*" (1994: 169; emphasis added). In seeing, the eye uses its recollected memories and history to situate and conceptualize. As Brand continues in her analysis: "The eye has purpose and goes where it wants to in order to clarify itself. Or to repeat. It has fancies. Or to regulate. It is very precise as to how it wants to see the world" (1994: 171).

After my schooldays' experiences with Aunt Jemima, I had decided not to see her as a person. I would note her presence with the explicit intention of challenging stereotypical assumptions, but I would not see her. And until that day in church, I did not see that there could be people, including myself, behind that image in a way that belied and subverted the stereotypic associations.

I had left Aunt Jemima behind all those years ago. And yet, here she was in the church—"homeplace" (hooks 1990c), a supposedly safe space for black folks and occupying her own place within this sacred space. What was she doing here? *Who* had invited *her* in here in a church filled predominantly with black women? Aunt Jemima had come to represent all that many a girl-child I knew in the 1970s desired to flee as we grew into womanhood: servility, acquiescence, and undesirability. In spite of our collective desire for escape, we knew that she continued to shape societal definitions of black women not only as mothers but as workers. In my nascent feminist consciousness, in the summer of 1994, I saw Aunt Jemima as a woman who participated, actively, in her own oppression. In my mind, Aunt Jemima was not a feminist and she was definitely not *my* mother!

Aunt Jemima was ceramic. Shiny. Her billowing skirt, red head kerchief and not-people-coloured black skin gleamed from the fire. Cast in a mould and fired in a kiln, Aunt Jemima had not had any parents or family. She was a "ready-made"[3] woman.

The bishop's words cut a swath through my thoughts when he said, *Please put the Aunt Jemima in that corner*, as part of the preparation of the church for a service on that summer afternoon. She was being called by name and placed in one of the corners of the church. Aunt Jemima had been brought home.

Initially, before the bishop's naming, I had seen Aunt Jemima as a stand-in, a substitution for someone else "more important," surely, to black, Caribbean people in our sacred lives. I had rationalized her presence as the use of a figurine in the absence of finances to commission a religious artefact. She was another example of the syncretic use of symbols within religions of the African Diaspora. Surely, her name would start with "Saint" or "Mother" but not "Aunt."

In analyzing the location of Aunt Jemima within a Toronto Spiritual Baptist Church, two explanatory modes were pursued. On the one hand, I wondered whether the use of Aunt Jemima was an inadvertent re-inscription of racist iconography fostered through the use of the symbol as a substitution for another figure. The inadvertent re-inscription would come about through the sheer historical weight of the image, which would make it difficult for other meanings to be read. On the other hand, Aunt Jemima in the church can be considered a reclaimed figure, representing black motherhood with regard to the church member's own experiences. Indeed, based on the reverence held for the figure symbolized by her placement within the geography of the church, the latter explanation is relevant. However, it is necessary to place the church within its larger socio-cultural context of contemporary Toronto where stereotypes of black women as Mammy and Aunt Jemima not only affect everyday personal experiences of racism but have also shaped public policy (Silvera 1989).

To understand the ambivalence (for me) of Aunt Jemima's place within the church, it is necessary to revisit the "seen" as "scene," the physical location, of that initial encounter with Aunt Jemima at church. The outside world is demarcated as separate from the church environs. This demarcation is symbolized through the ritual of surveying the church in which the female members, usually the mothers of the church, ritually purify the four corners and centre pole of the church through prayers and offerings of grain, honey, milk, and water.

Within this purified space, "this spot of ground" in the spiritual nation language of the church, Aunt Jemima is something other than the racial stereotype of the Mammy that she represents in the everyday world outside of the church. Yet by her very naming as Aunt Jemima, that outside world is evoked.

Kenneth W. Goings in discussing the continued symbolic importance of racial collectibles notes that it is the emotional content of the words "Aunt" and "Uncle," even when used in the context of racial stereotypes that "symbolizes the power of these collectibles" (1994: xiii). As I will discuss later, the addition of the "y" by Sister Maria, a Spiritual Baptist woman in Toronto, signifies a shift in this emotional connection to an Aunt(y) Jemima imbued with meaning other than the stereotypic assumptions based in American Old South mythology.

Especially significant for this discussion is what Goings calls the "personification" (1994: xxiv) of the collectibles. By personifying these objects, Goings points to his personal relationship to them in light of his placement of them as subjects within the context of the struggles of African-Americans for dignity, equality, and justice in the United States. He describes seeing Aunt Jemima and Uncle Mose, her male counterpart, as dignified people beyond the stereotypes who are actively engaged in the movement for social justice in the United States. Goings's imaginary transgression of the boundaries of the stereotypes are countered by his realization that in the America of the 1990s, "Aunt Jemima would probably still be cooking and Uncle Mose serving—living their lives, as we all do, with dignity and self-respect" (1994: xxiv). Nevertheless, Goings pleads the following to explain his "personification" of the objects:

> *I hope the reader will not think that I have completely lost my sense of reality when I personify the collectibles in the way I have.* After all, I have been studying these objects for the last seven years, and they do now seem like people, like friends. Moreover, I am not the only one who feels this way. When two collectors were asked recently why they are preserving and studying black memorabilia, they replied, "If we don't portray it, people won't know how far we've come." They continued, "Precisely by possessing these objects, black people rob them of their power. *Silly and crude these things may have been, but ... generations of black people lived in their shadow. The souls of millions of black people were trapped in these heaps of mass-produced junk. Now at last they are being set free.*" (1994: xxiv; emphasis added)[4]

Goings's and the other collectors' observations are significant here for they point to the subversively imaginative engagement of Aunt Jemima and Uncle Mose as figures that encompass the hidden (from the stereotypic vantage point) dimension of the actual lives and possible lives of black men and women who laboured in domestic service. The gaze of these collectors subverts the hegemonic positioning of Aunt Jemima and her male counterpart, Uncle Mose, as a representation of inferiority and servility.

The presence of Aunt Jemima in a Toronto Spiritual Baptist Church is similarly subversive. Through her presence in the church, Aunt Jemima, this most profane and devalued of stereotypic representations of black womanhood, is made sacred and brought home. This is achieved via her imagined possibilities, based on the lives of both historical and contemporary black women who performed the work of mothering not only in domestic service but also in a variety of black community contexts.

(Re)Turning the Gaze on Aunt(y) Jemima

The image of Aunt Jemima is an ambivalent symbolic entry point for a discussion of black Caribbean women's experiences in Canada. Its ambivalence lies in the fact that while it is the symbolic image of black women's presence as workers in Canada through immigration, at the same time, in that particular Spiritual Baptist Church in Toronto, a subversive re-reading of the image became the symbolic point of entry for another status, mother of the home: one that is valued and cherished within the church community.

One way of understanding Aunt Jemima in the context of the church is as a representation of a historical, archetypal black mother: the mother who endured through the period of slavery[5] and who lives on to encourage and console in dreams and through the spiritual journeying of mourning. In the following, Sister Maria, a Vincentian Spiritual Baptist woman who emigrated to Toronto to work as a domestic worker, discusses her meeting with Aunty Jemima and its significance in helping her to decide to participate in the ritual of mourning:

> SM: Yeah. And um ... again before I went and mourn again, I used to be always in a valley. Always down there. And this woman used to come to me and she—I used to wash clothes and hang clothes out. You know, she used to tell me the clothes them dry, time to pick them up. Right? And then, I used to really go in deep manifestation and that will tell me that yes, Maria, I'm ready to pass, you're ready to mourn, okay. They're calling you, come, let's go.
>
> One day, I see dis woman, black like jet, girl. And she has her head tie like Aunty Jemima. And her apron—only her head tie-up I coulda see and her eyes and her apron and she calling me up this hill and she said to me, "You're ready. Come out. It''s time for you to learn these things." Okay? And these things that happen all of a sudden. They just happen, girl. And I strongly believe that if you're in Christ, your light is going to shine. You have to come out of darkness. Okay? Sometimes I used to start to go places and I went out to go to parties and stuff like that ... Carol and it just not me. It's just that I don't feel that I should be there, eh? You know if you don't feel right, you know this is not for you, get out?
>
> CBD: Mmmhmm.

Sister Maria's meeting with the woman in the valley, whom she identified in reference to Aunt Jemima, is indicative of the way in which this

racial signifier has been subverted. The same features, which are the quintessential signs of Mammy and Aunt Jemima—the skin "black like jet," her
"head tie-up" and her "apron"—are symbolic of Sister Maria's Aunty Jemima.
However, the addition of the "y" shifts Aunt to a personalized term of
endearment—Aunty—a shift that signals a transformation of Aunt Jemima
from the realm of racial iconography as a static, immovable figure, to an
active and engaging subject in Sister Maria's spiritual life. Aunty Jemima's
position in the valley "signifies" (Gates 1988) on Psalm 23 where the valley
is symbolic of a place of despair and the low points in a person's life.

The King James Version of Psalm 23 is a significant part of the oral tra-
dition of the Spiritual Baptist Church. Along with the Lord's Prayer, the
King James Version of Psalm 23 is one of the most widely used in Spiritual
Baptist worship:

> The Lord is my shepherd; I shall not want
>
> He maketh me to lie down in green pastures: he leadeth me beside the
> still waters
>
> He restoreth my soul: he leadeth me in the paths of righteousness for
> his name's sake.
>
> Yea, though I walk through the valley of the shadow of death, I will fear
> no evil: for thou are with me; thy rod and thy staff they comfort me.
>
> Thou preparest a table before me in the presence of mine enemies: thou
> anointest my head with oil; my cup runneth over.
>
> Surely goodness and mercy shall follow me all the days of my life: and
> I will dwell in the house of the Lord forever.

Sister Maria's encounter with Aunty Jemima in the valley suggests a
radical intervention in the interpretation of this psalm. In "signifyin'"
(Gates 1988) on Psalm 23, Sister Maria interjects a black, female, ancestral
presence in the valley along with the presence of God. An even more radical interpretation would be that Aunty Jemima, herself, represents a divine
presence. Sister Maria's signification also suggests that the text is alive in
her interpretative approach to the Bible. Her reading of the Bible inhab-
its the text as a lived experience imbued with personalized meanings from
her own biography as well as black women's collective historical experience in the Americas. It suggests that her relationship to the Bible, as text,
is one in which the book is not only a "talking book" as Gates (ibid.) suggests in pointing to the significance of the oral tradition in influencing

African-American literature, but that the text can be entered and transformed through mourning, a ritual of prayer and fasting in which the
mourner or "pilgrim" travels in the spirit. New Testament studies scholar
Allen Callahan in his study *The Talking Book* discusses the significance of the
Bible in shaping African-American religiosity, literature, music, culture,
and politics (2006).

Related to this form of biblical interpretation, Sister Maria relayed
another visionary experience, a dream in which she met her father, before
he died, and he showed her the scriptural source for biblical passages that
she had heard in church but had not realized their source:

SM: Okay? And then before my father died, he came to me in my
sleep and he said to me, "Come, come . . ." I could remember he took
me inside and he sit me down in the chair with my grandmother and
this time my grandmother already died, eh? My father was still alive.
But he took me into the house in my dream and he said, "Read this."
Um ... no, no, no. He bring the scripture, right? He bring the scripture to me and what was saying John, chapter one, okay? St. Luke,
chapter one. And I did not have a Bible to read but I wrote it in my
hand in my dream and when he finish reading that, he said to me,
why didn't I read with him. And I said to him, "Poppy, I don't have—
I didn't have a Bible, but see I write it in my hand and when I go home
I'll read it." Okay?

Stop that tape. [she goes and gets her Bible]

She's[6] been with me from since then, okay? And um when I open my
Bible, I got up the same night, okay? And when I open my Bible, okay?
St. um—St. Luke, chapter one.

CBD: Mmmmhmmm.

SM: [searches through her Bible] Okay ... reading from verse 23 ...
[turns the pages of her Bible] ... St. John, chapter one ... I'm getting
mixed up with my ... stop the tape. Are you taping now?

CBD: Mmmmhmmm.

SM: Okay, so it was St. Luke ... was it St. Luke or St. John, chapter
one ...

CBD: Mmmmhmmm.

SM: Let me try to get this ...

CBD: It's okay [coughs].

SM: Yes … okay. St. Luke … it's St. Luke, chapter one. Listen to this. And I was in [church] all this time and hear them saying this, okay, and I did not know that it was in the Bible …

CBD: Mmmmhmmm.

SM: … until my—before my dad died … he took me into that—my grandmother's house and he read this—brought this scripture and I read it[7] and it says, "To a virgin espoused to a man whose name was Joseph, to the house of David; and the virgin name was Mary. And the angel came unto her and said, 'Hail, thou art the high favour, the Lord is with me, *blessed* amongst *women.*' And when she saw him, she was troubled at this saying and cast in her mind what manner of salutation this should be, okay? And the angel said unto her, 'Fret not Mary for thou shall hast found favour with God and behold thou shall conceive in thy womb and shall bring forth his son and shall call his name, Jesus. He shall great and shall be called the son of the highest and the Lord God shall give unto him the throne of his father David and he shall reign over the house of David forever and his kingdom shall have—shall be no end. Then Mary said unto an angel—then said Mary unto the angel, How shall this be seeing I'm not known a man. And the angel answer and said unto her, 'The holy ghost shall come up on thee and the power of the highest shall overshadow thee, therefore also, the Holy thing which had been born shall be called the Son of God.' And behold her cousin Elizabeth she had also conceived a son in her old age and this is the sixth month with her who was called barren. For with God nothing shall be impossible. And Mary said, 'Behold the handmaid of the Lord, be it unto me according to the word' and the angels departed from her and Mary rose in those days and went into the hills concerning the countryside. And it spake unto her again and came to pass over and Elizabeth heard the salutation."
You hear the salutation in church, right?

CBD: Mmmhmm.

SM: "And of Mary the babe leaped in her womb and Elizabeth was filled with the Holy Ghost and she spaked unto him in a loud voice and said, '*Blessed* art thou amongst women and blessed is the fruit of thy womb. And when is this to me that the mother of my Lord should come to me.' For lo as soon as the voice of salutation sounded in her ears, the babe leaped in her womb for joy. And blessed is that, that believeth for they shall be performers of things which were told from her."
And the salutation goes on, okay?

CBD: Mmmmhmmm.

SM: The salutation that we sing in church all the time. "Blessed . . ." you know? And uh . . . and it goes on and Mary says, "My soul doth magnify the Lord and my spirit had rejoice in God my saviour. For he hath regard the low estate of his handmaid. For behold from henceforth *all* generations shall call me *blessed*! For he that is mighty had done me great things and holy is his name. And he and his mercy is on them that fear him from generation to generation. He has shown strength in his arms, he has scattered the proud in the imagination of their hearts. He had put down from the mighty from their seats and exalted them of low degree. He had filled the hungry with good things and the rich he had sent them empty away. He had helped his servant Israel in remembrance of his mercy. As he spake to our father, to Abraham and to his seeds forever."[8]

This is how I learnt that this is in the Bible. This was my thing from my [father]—and all this time I was going to [church], I never knew it was in here. And that's why you see in my little book here I have it written down. You know how long I have it written this here? [shows me her book] It's this here . . .

CBD: Luke, one . . .

SM: Luke, chapter one . . .

CBD: Mmmmhmmm.

SM: Okay? And that's how . . . my first time that I preached [in church], it was the book of John. The first time I went up to that pulpit to preach, it was John, chapter one. And that was my thing, it tells you ah . . . about the coming of Christ . . . ahm, when John went out crying, you know, telling the people, change from their heart, there's a messiah coming, who's gonna be—who's gonna be on the cross and crucify for you and uh keep you-all heart to receive him. That's was a great—that was a very touching, very touching thing to me, okay? And I still remember this. I even still have my . . . transcript from that—my manuscript from that first, first one. Okay? So that what goes back again, that I believe that I am being fed spiritually and there's from the spirit.

The significance of Sister Maria's experiences lies in the fact that prior to these visionary experiences with her father, these biblical passages existed solely as a part of the oral culture of the church. It was in her dreams and through a process of transcription (writing on her hand), that they were literally made known as "texts" to Sister Maria. Sister Maria credits the source of her knowledge as "inspiration":

> And my thing's inspiration; I don't *see*; I don't *hear*; but I'm inspired. I touch and I'm inspired. And again, I don't know everything in that religion but I know I have gone through a stage where I can go down in prayer, I pray and receive. I do not know if it's because of my spiritual background or maybe who knows there's a purpose for each and every one of us here on the earth, okay? Again, I've seen so much things in my dream and like when I say my dream grow, I'm not sleeping. When you're at peace with yourself and when I mean peace, not the material things around you, but a inner peace, peace that give you a feeling of joy, okay? These things were happening. You see things, you feel things, you smell things. These happen. And um, there's a lot that I didn't know.

RE-READING AUNT(Y) JEMIMA AND THE CREOLE WOMAN

Aunt Jemima's attire, including her head-tie, neck scarf, apron, and long skirt, as well as her large body size, receive an entirely different interpretation than the dominant one of servility and inferiority when they are positioned as signs of black feminine power. From the perspective of the Spiritual Baptist experiences in Toronto and the symbolic culture of African-Caribbean communities of the enslaved and their descendants, Aunt Jemima's clothing is representative of ancestral black women whose attire included both European and African elements. In Puerto Rico, this figure is known as La Madama. From Europe, the long full skirt, petticoats, and apron and from Africa the neckscarf or *fula* and the head-tie. We also see this image in the Creole woman attire in a Caribbean context.

The Honourable Louise Bennett Coverleigh, affectionately known as Miss Lou to her legions of fans in Jamaica, the Caribbean, and the Diaspora, successfully uses the visual image of the long-time Creole woman in presenting her poetry and monologues in Jamaica language or patois. A pioneer in the use and valorizing of patois as a legitimate language of critical reflection and significant creation of Jamaican culture, Miss Lou has appeared before Jamaican national and international audiences wearing the costume of the Caribbean Creole woman complete with head-tie, long, full overskirt, and petticoats. She used this image, which is so often regarded as a figure of comedy, to issue cogent critiques and reflections on various aspects of Jamaican culture, politics, and society in her role as a media figure on radio and in her publications and live performances.[9]

While many of Miss Lou's presentations are in a humorous and entertaining vein, the seriousness of her critique has registered within Jamaica and the Caribbean Diaspora abroad. In her presentations and her writings, Miss Lou employs the narrative strategy in which she *teck bad sinting meck laugh*.[10] The impact of her contributions to the legacy of Jamaican nation language and, by extension, the creative expressions of African-Caribbean people have bestowed upon Bennett the authorial stance of mother in the sense of community mother. As such, her wearing of the attire signals this authorial power and subverts the dominant gaze that would relegate Miss Lou and her Aunty Roachy[11] to a marginal status.

Aunt Jemima's attire, including her full long skirt, apron, neckscarf or *fula*, and head-tie are identical to the clothing worn by some Spiritual Baptist women as a sign of their church role as mother or nurse, for example, as well as a sign of their spiritual gifts. These clothes are not only a symbolic representation of these women's positions within the church's leadership, but also serve as a visible sign of their identity as Spiritual Baptist women within the wider framework of Toronto's diverse black and Caribbean communities.

Mother Victoria's introduction to the Baptist Church in Toronto was facilitated through a Trinidadian friend's identification of another Spiritual Baptist woman by virtue of her dress on a Toronto street in the late 1980s. Here is the story as told by Mother Victoria in conversation with me:

CBD: How did you come to go to this church?

MV: Well um, when I come up here—because I wondering back from home [Trinidad] if it ha' Baptist Church in Canada! [laughter] So I didn't really bring no—say well set a' clothes dat I does wear to church. I just bring up ahm—is only one? Think is only two dress I did walk with, right? But one day, di same guy, I ask him if he ain't know about no Baptist church. And I ask his sister and she say, "No." So one day, he was riding a bicycle going by a garage over to G Street by a friend. So when he come back he say, "Well, well, well. Ah find a church fuh you now." So ah say, "Go about yuh business, man! Which part yuh see di church?"

He say, "Ah meet a lady dress just like how does dress back home."
[laughter] So ah say, "Suppose di woman just feel to dress like that!"
He say, "No man. I talk to di lady and she tell me—look di number
here. She say call she and she going tell yuh where di church is." Well
da was Mother Y.

CBD: Ohh.

MV: So I call but she wasn't home and I call back di evening and ah talk
wid she and ting. And tell she well ah from Trinidad and so on and so
on. And ah want to go in a church. Ah tell she Spiritual Baptist. So she
say, "Well, I am a Spiritual Baptist too and I go to a church so if you
want to go with me is fine." So di Sunday, ah get up and go early and we
had one joke di Sunday now. Now she say meet her quarter to six, right
in—right in my street where I live. Yuh just go across di next street an
come up to di bus stop.

... So I hustling up di road now, because she say quarter to six di bus
passing. So I hurry up di road to reach to di bus stop. When I reach
there now, I see di bus coming. As soon as di bus coming now, di bus
break down. So I wait, I wait, I wait. Ah looking to see if ah see anybody
in head-tie. Ah ain't seeing nobody in no tie head coming from nowhey!
So it had a friend was by me dat same Sunday so I went back home, but
ah did ask her for di address, eh. And she tell me ...

Well I know now back home yuh does upon yuh church door. [hand
clap] I go back home and ask di guy if he could drop me because I say,
ah ain't see di lady, ah ain't know if she pass because it done six o'clock
now and she tell me quarter to six. So, he decide to drop me. Come
down di road here and ah looking and ah looking for di number. So ah
say, look at [it] here. But like dey wasn't singing because ah didn't hear
no singing. So, ah say, it ha' to be here. But no door ain't open. Because
I say now, how dey could be keeping a service in a church with the
church door close. [laughter]

So I open upstairs now where A— living up there—I open di door.
I in front and di man behind me. [laughter] When we nearly reach up
in di people bedroom den I hear di bell ring! [belly laughter with
CBD] Oh my gawd is downstairs! We had one joke dat Sunday. Ah
say—and people was in di house yuh know and dey don't even see we!
[belly laughter with CBD] Ah does always remember da' joke. When—
I nearly reach in di people bedroom, yuh know and I hear di bell ring.
So what dat doing so—is downstairs. [laughter] And then we go back

downstairs, ah say, "Ah wonder if is here?" So ah say lemme pull di door and see. So ah pull di door, di door was open. So is Y dat really invite me dere by dat church, yuh know?

In the following, Mother Victoria describes her relationship to her "spiritual clothes" as empowering symbols and, in so doing, points to a re-reading and re-inscription of the attire that, from the perspective of the dominant culture in North America, is synonymous with servility and by extension, inferiority. Mother Victoria's comments also respond to the interpretation of the head-tie and "Baptist clothes" by other Caribbean people in public spaces in Toronto as signs of suspicion of doing "devil work" or "obeah"— a reading that has its basis in a Caribbean context. For Mother Victoria, her church clothes signify her role as a mother and convey a special feeling of celebration and connection with the Spirit.

CBD: How you feel—I remember earlier when you were talking how some people does look at Baptist in a certain way, you know? And say "Oh they tie their head." You know, "They dealing with the devil" and stuff like that. How do you feel about that? How other people look at Baptists?

MV: Well sometimes, at first I used to get angry. But I don't get angry anymore because I only figure more or less looking at people me of me own self and seeing that di behaviour of dese people sometimes, especially when you dress, going to church. That's what make di difference. So I don't really—it don't really matter me again. Up to now, it still have people like they going to church and they don't tie they head from home. Like—you know—they just dress like ordinary and when they reach in church you see they go and tie they head. I don't do that.

CBD: You think people should tie they head from home?

MV: I figure, you leaving your home and you going to church, you leave from your house with your head-tie, you go to di church. Don't walk through di street or yuh ride di train, yuh ride di bus bare head and yuh dress up and when you reach in church your head-tie high up in the air. Don't care where I living, and you see me, I like—you see like when— I don't know—when Sunday time come like I does feel a special, special joy in my heart. You know why? Just to put on me clothes to go to church here.

CBD: [laughter]

MV: Just to put on my clothes to go to church, Sister Carol. Because you see I don't like my clothes short for church. I may go anywhere else in a short ting, but you see when I going to church, I always like my clothes long down there!

CBD: Why is that?

MV: I don't know. But I just like it to wear long and sometime I does say, the fact I don't wear all my clothes long, I like long clothes. [hand clap] Yeah. I love long clothes. Dat's di way I like to dress! My dress long and my head-tie tie nice!

CBD: And yuh feel good!

MV: Yeah! I going to church!

CBD: [laughter]

MV: minding more dan reach di church di church close! [belly laughter with CBD].

Yeah, ah feel good going to church! Because you know some people like you going to church, yuh put up di apron, yuh put di belt, yuh put all in a bag and they head-tie. And they gone bare head! And then when they reach in church now you see they come back upstairs. [hand clap] Ah say, well if God was to meet yuh on di road, yuh in di bare head. So I—if I live—where di place name, Alberta—ah coming to church and ah ain't coming without my head-tie tie, you know?

CBD: [laughter]

MV: I don't care who want to watch me on di train. I ain't want to know who want to watch me on di bus. But ah comin' just as from out di bus, into di church. Right in my seat. I ain't want to go downstairs. Di time it take to go downstairs, wha' happen?

CBD: So would you ever wear some of the clothes you wear to church, would you ever wear them somewhere else?

MV: No.

CBD: Just spiritually?

MV: —to church.

CBD: And why is that?

MV: Mmmhmm. Well because you see, you're going to church and that come as your spiritual garment, right? Well other things you wearing all about, it ain't worthwhile that you wearing it to—to church, you know? You church clothes, must be your church clothes. Because I don't wash my church clothes neither with my working clothes.

CBD: Oh, I see.

MV: Mmmhmm. Me nah work wid it neither.

CBD: You keep them separate.

MV: Yes. I wash them separately.

CBD: You keep them separately.

MV: Well, sometimes—because the guy that I mourn and ting with, he tell me, he say, "Sometimes when you go home from church you must sleep in yuh clothes, you know?" When your blessing—if di service was nice to you and you feel you enjoy di service, sleep in yuh clothes, leh di blessing stay wid you. So sometime I does sleep. [laughter]

CBD: [laughter] So you sleep in your clothes sometimes? Your head-tie too, Mother Victoria?

MV: Yes. And I does wake up just like how you see yuh coming church? Is so I does wake up, yuh now. Just like if I lie dung here and sleep, yuh wouldn't believe somebody sleep here, you know? Yeah, I get up. Sometime I does say, "Lord" and does go by people and see dey sheet do, dey bed so, you know? Anywhere I lie down and somebody call me hurry and just do so "ssshhhh" and gone!

CBD: [laughter]

CBD: Yeah!

CBD: Mmmhmm, so yuh ready!

TIE-HEAD WOMAN

In conducting research on Spiritual Baptists in Toronto, I revisited my relationship to clothing and my perception of spiritual clothes. These had been dually shaped by my internalizing of racial stereotypes that denigrated the head-tie and long skirts as symbols of inferiority and "mammification" of black women. They had also been shaped by deeply held feelings of respect for elder women, rasta women, and church women whom I knew who tied their heads and who frequently wore, if not "long" clothes, then clothes with hemlines well below the knee. As I went to church services, my head-tie visibly marked me as different in public spaces such as Toronto buses and subways. Indeed, there were numerous occasions in which I carried my head-tie in my bag, then quickly went down to the church's basement when I arrived and transformed myself by putting it on, as Mother Victoria astutely observed in the previous comments. On the public transit system, I was acutely aware of its signification, marking me as a "tie-head woman," a "churchwoman," a "Baptist," a "Christian," a "rasta woman," in the meanings imbued by these terms in the Caribbean community, and as culturally different and "exotic" within the wider North American discourse of fashion and self-presentation, femininity, and race.

Attending Spiritual Baptist church services in Toronto was not the first time I had worn a head-tie. I associated the head-tie with life inside the home because I had spent almost every night of my life since girlhood wearing a head-tie. Like many black, Caribbean girls I grew up tying my head at night as a bedtime ritual. With the busy work lives of our mothers and othermothers, many young girls' hair was braided in small corn-rows or "plain plaits" with the expectation that the hairstyle would last a couple of days if it were tied at night so as to prevent the mussing of the hair. I also associated the head-tie as a sign of elderhood in African-Caribbean women, as my own grandmother tied her head during her elder years. In conducting research on the Spiritual Baptist Church, I was afforded the opportunity to re-examine the head-tie in both my own personal practices of appearance as well as its wider significance within the Spiritual Baptist Church and within a variety of North American popular cultural contexts.

Black people's hair has been one of the sites of the construction of racial difference in the Americas. Racial stereotyping of black people has focused on hair as much as skin colour as evidence of racial difference. Mercer notes that the focus on hair as a site of racialized devaluation is second only to skin "as the most visible stigmata of blackness" (1994: 101). Talk about "good hair" and "bad hair" in the colour/caste systems of black communities in the Caribbean and North America is linked to the salience of hair as a sign of "race" or "colour." "Good hair" is associated with whiteness and the stereotype of white hair as straight and smooth-feeling in texture, while "bad" hair occupies the inferior half of this dualistic pair as stereotypically "black," kinky "nigger hair" (ibid.). In this dichotomy, black people with "good hair" possess a hair texture that approximates that of whites and is not too kinky or "rough" (ibid.). "Bad hair" is hair that is "tough," tightly curled, and kinky (ibid.).

As an extension of this signification on hair as racial difference, dominant cultural readings also position the head-tie as a sign of racial difference, which in this case is usually gender-specific to black women. The headkerchief became one of the quintessential signs of the Old South mammy, along with her large breasts, which positioned her not as sexual object but as a maternal figure (Goings 1994: 65). This association of the head-tie with servility is indeed "ironic," since the head-tie initially signified a connection with an African past for the enslaved where the wearing of a head covering originated (Goings 1994: 66).

Upon arrival in America, enslaved women were provided with a few items of clothing (Wish as cited by Jewel 1993: 39). These included two striped cotton dresses, three shifts, two pairs of shoes, and handkerchiefs. The handkerchiefs were worn by some men and nearly all women (ibid.). Both women and men who were engaged in outdoor field agricultural labour, as well as domestic work, wore headkerchiefs. While the headkerchief was a link to Africa, it also became symbolic of the "happy darky"—a figure of docile, uncritical, and even thankful acceptance of the conditions of enslavement—and especially the mammy in the mythology of the Old South created in the post–Civil War years (Goings 1994: 66).

Not only is the head-tie seen as a sign of inferiority from the hegemonic standpoint of racist constructions, it is also viewed as a sign of devaluation within African-American communities themselves. It signifies a black person who is acquiescent and servile to the desires of white Europeans, often at the expense of their own personal, as well as their black community's, desires. This person may also act in ways that are counter to political initiatives to eradicate the racial inequality of black people. Geneva Smitherman in *Black Talk: Words and Phrases from the Hood to the Amen Corner* notes that the term "handkerchief head" is indicative of this standpoint in African-American English (AAE) (1994: 131). A "handkerchief head" is defined as

> An Uncle Tom–type person who defers to European Americans and their authority; may also act against the interests of Black people. Also *Tom, Uncle Tom, Uncle Thomas; Aunt Thomasina, Aunt Jane.* (1994: 131)

The head-tie is also "read" within black communities as a sign of the "conjurer" or "doctor" of the spirit—those women who can "work" in order to intervene in matters of the spirit on behalf of those in the material world. This particular reading is ambivalent for it could be regarded as either a positive or negative valuation depending on the context.

Spiritual Baptist women with whom I spoke in Toronto mentioned their awareness of the ambivalent stereotype of being associated with "obeah"[12] and "devil work" within black community environs while at the same time also being seen as a resource for addressing personal problems when conventional spiritual and medical means were deemed ineffective or in need of boosting. In the following excerpt, Mother Victoria discusses this ambivalent position and its relationship to being identified by attire and the head-tie, in particular:

> Sister, if your husband gi'ing yuh problem, kneel down and pray to God. 'Cause sometimes people only come to you, the Christian person, or the converted person in a church because they now meeting *trouble*! Without trouble they ain't coming by you 'tall! Right? Because some people might say, "*Them Baptist people they's devil people, me ain't business with them because they does tie they head*!" Right [hand clap]? But when they start meeting presha and trouble is you-self they come—*they doesn't study how you dress*, if you burn a candle, if you ring a bell! They ain't business that. They coming. [my emphasis]

While there is a negative valuation of the tied head as symbolic of being either a "sellout" or of doing "devil work" within black communities, a competing meaning coexisted that positively valued the head-tie as one of the tangible signs, in this case, cloth, of ties to an African cultural past and as a symbol of feminine power.

In the 1960s and early 1970s, civil rights and Black Power years, there was a reclaiming of the head-tie in North America as is evidenced through photographs taken of young black women during those years. Along with the wearing of the Afro, cornrows, and other "natural"[13] hairstyles that were not dependent on chemical or hot-comb straightening, the head-tie resurfaced as a sign of pride in an aesthetic that valued blackness and connections to Africa. This reclamation can be linked to an aspect of the Black Power movement that placed aesthetics as an important part of a revolutionary political agenda. This initiative is epitomized by singer James Brown's chart-topping soul-music hit "Say It Loud—I'm Black and I'm Proud" of the era.

The reclaiming of the head-tie has also been publicized through some contemporary black women celebrities such as Maya Angelou, celebrated poet, writer, teacher, and actor who appears from time to time on national televised broadcasts in a head-tie. Although her head-tie is not referenced, directly, in her televised comments, the visual image that Angelou presents is one that situates her as a mother of the community. The head-tie is not Angelou's usual style of dress and when she is wearing it, it has been on occasions where she is speaking from a place of moral authority.

In the 1990s, particularly in association with hip-hop culture, there has been a resurgence of the head-tie as a sign of cultural pride and affirmation of ties to a valued African identity. Hip hop, the predominant youth culture that originated among inner-city African-Americans in the late 1970s, is now international in its effects on the music, fashion, linguistic patterns, and other consumer choices of youth. The resurgence of what have been referred to as "afrocentric" fashions in the last decade, particularly among some sectors of urban African-American youth culture, including hip hop, is another instance in which the head-tie makes an appearance.

African-American woman singer Erykah Badu, a major star in hip hop, came to prominence in the entertainment industry with her debut album, *Baduizm* (1994). Badu wore a headwrap, an extended visual riff on the head-tie, whose length and height, in contrast to Badu's petite frame, draw considerable attention. Badu's reputation as a singer is closely associated with her visual representation of an ancestral past as signified by the headwrap, and her wearing of pieces of jewellery, such as the ankh, that signify her presence as a "roots" woman—an Afrocentric diva who is tapped into a pipeline directly connected with an African-American and African past. Erykah Badu's visual image represents another vision of invented Africa, but one that is particularly New World connected with an eclectic postmodern sensibility in the way that her Billie Holiday–inspired jazz vocal riffs meet extended headwrap dreadlocks, gigantic afro and Southern African-American–inflected speech patterns.

The head-tie worn by Spiritual Baptist women in Toronto is likely to be subject to a number of cultural significations, including those that arise out of North American, African-American, and African-Canadian experiences and those from Caribbean as well as African cultural contexts. With regard to the latter, the presence in Toronto of women from continental African countries such as Ghana and Nigeria in West Africa, and Ethiopia and Somalia in East Africa, due to immigration in the last two decades, has contributed to the variety of fashion and style of black women in Toronto. Many of these black women can be observed on Toronto streets wearing head coverings such as head scarves and head-ties. These are often worn for reasons of religious observance by Muslim women, but may also be worn as fashion statements. Indeed, there are parallels between what has been the wearing of the veil by Muslim women (wearing of several forms of concealing clothing including head covering and long, loose outfits) and the use of the head-tie by Spiritual Baptist women. The similarity rests in the differential valorizing of the clothing worn by Spiritual Baptist and Muslim women that on one hand serves to mark these women as racially and culturally different and therefore inferior at the same time that the women themselves may use forms of dress to assert their identities in full view.

A renewed influence of the style and fashions of African women and men is evident in a number of the Spiritual Baptist women and men I met who often wore African and African-inspired clothing to church or social functions such as tea parties, or Christmas dinners. Some of these clothes were purchased from clothing stores and independent vendors who specialized in importing clothing and fabrics from African countries such as Nigeria and Ghana. These outfits almost always featured a matching head-tie to complement the ensemble. The importance of these, to borrow Mercer's term, "syncretic products of New World stylization" (1994: 115) was noted, for example, in the staging of events such as a fashion show featuring African fashions at events such as the annual Christmas dinner party of a Toronto-area Spiritual Baptist Church that I attended in November 1994 and other events since then.

HEAD-TIES AND THE SOCIAL CONSTRUCTION OF IDENTITY

The head-tie has a variety of significations among Spiritual Baptist women in Toronto. The most obvious, it would seem, is its signalling of an adherence to the Jewish, Christian, and Muslim practice of women covering their hair as a sign of modesty and religious observance. While this particular meaning is important, the head-tie also simultaneously signifies a variety of meanings that connect contemporary Spiritual Baptist women with an African-Caribbean archetype in the form of the Creole woman, their own individual female ancestors, and the legacy which fashioned in cloth. In addition to these multiple reference points, the head-tie serves as a visible sign of identity of a Spiritual Baptist woman, and it can function, ritually, in curative and restorative ways.

What I am pointing to here specifically, in the last instance, is the use of the head-tie to signify a binding of the head as a securing of the woman's consciousness. This practice is reminiscent of African-American Yoruban priestess and spiritual counsellor Iyanla Vanzant's entreaty to "save yourself" by holding the head with one hand on the forehead and the other at the back of the head during a potentially consciousness-changing moment such as contentious, heated exchanges. Vanzant, who has gained international recognition and celebrity status through the sales of her books[14] and her past appearances on the long-running *Oprah Winfrey Show*, was observed leading Oprah Winfrey and the studio audience in this gesture of holding the head to "save themselves" during broadcasts in the 1998–99 television season. The shows are dubbed by Winfrey herself as "Save your life TV."[15] I interpret this gesture as a symbolic act of "holding the head," which is akin to using the head-tie to quite literally "keep it together" in potentially "mind-blowing" situations.

In the following, we will revisit Bishop Mother Patricia's journey that led to her becoming a Spiritual Baptist in Toronto in the 1970s. On the way, she used her head-tie to "save her head" on numerous occasions. Many Spiritual Baptists were careful to note the difference between "the power of manifestation" and the onset of mental illness from a Western, medical model. The head-tie enabled her to "save her head" in light of the significant, and sometimes debilitating, shifts and changes she experienced in her spiritual call to the religion. What is apparent in the following, which took place in 1972 in Toronto, is that the head-tie was one of the means that enabled Mother Pat to literally keep her "head" in the material world when the Spirit called her:

So, I started going back to Anglican Church. It was nothing new to me and it was fine. But I was going to a lot of parties in the nights but by one o'clock, twelve o'clock in the nights, I don't know. I dance, I went into the spirit or whatever ... but at dance I took very sick, I collapse and I always end up in hospital; I never forget. Every Sat'day night before the party was just getting hot ... and all you had to do was give me a glass of water and wrap my head. And I was fine.

So I met this lady, she was Guyanese and she said, "Pat, you're crazy." And I was getting sicker and sicker and sicker. And she said Patl, "You're really, really crazy. You don't know what's happening to you?" And I said, "Kind of, but I'm not too sure." She said, "You're one of *those people!*" I said, "What do you—those people?" She said, "Those guys that wrap they head and give messages and do different things. You are!" I said, "Me? No way! I'm not doing that. Uh-uh, forget it." She said, "Pat you have to."

So one day I left work and I was down at the Eaton Centre. And while I was at the Eaton Centre, I was frazzled out. I started fainting. I hold on and everything. And then it came back to me, Pat, get your head wrap, get some water and get out of Eaton Centre. But in my purse, in detail, I'm telling you, was only my Eaton's account card. The only thing I had—I had no money! So, I take the Eaton's and I go to the material store at Eaton's and they cut me a piece of blue cloth, yellow. And they hand it to me. And I stand up in there, say "The Lord my shepherd" and wrap my head and I was fine. Then I walked up the road and from that day I just—but people were just staring at me with this wrap on my head.

Following this incident, Mother Pat spoke to a woman friend who suggested that she speak with an "old spiritual woman" in the United States who recommended that Mother Pat attend a church where "you could wrap your head." Mother Pat, however, was resistant to the idea at first because she saw head-wrapping as antithetical to her aims as a "career woman":

So, I told my girlfriend, uh, what was happening to me. And she said, Pat, you gotta—you gotta check this thing out so she took me to the States. There was a old lady. And she was a old spiritual woman. She said, "You'll *never* get better because the spirit of the Lord need to use you. You're too proud. You're too—" I really never want to get into this. If I had a choice, I would not do anything. But I said to her, "Okay fine, if that's what you want me to do" and stuff like that, "I will go back and I will do it." She said, "You gotta go find that church where you could wrap your head, where you could do stuff. Where you could wrap your head, where you could do stuff, and you could do anything you want." And she says, "You gotta go back and do that 'cause you'd never get better." And my 'termination is that I could do it. But I don't have to wrap my head. You don't have to do it. I still was stubborn.

However, um, I took sick meanwhile. Doctors didn't know what were happening to me. And somebody took me to this Jamaican lady and she was a revivalist. 'Cause I mention—I think that was in '74 … but … that was in '74, yeah … about '73, '74. Suffering for a year and a half or two. And she look on me and she said to me, "Wow this is ripe! She's just ready to work. She's young, she's vibrant. She have the spirit. But you don't want to go into it." And I said, "No. I'm not wrapping my head. I'm not gonna be crazy like these people. I'm going to be a career woman and I'm not getting involved with this period." And she say, "You gonna have no choice, dear. Else you gonna lose everything." I had a fancy car, I had an apartment. I had everything. I was a spoilt child. And so I make myself spoil. So it was materialistic.

Mother Yvonne, another woman leader of a church, also expressed a similar reluctance and resistance to wearing a head-tie in describing her first visit to a Spiritual Baptist Church in Toronto. In the following excerpt from an interview I conducted with Mother Yvonne, she describes her transformation through the wearing of a head-tie:

MY: Maybe I should go and visit the Baptist Church. It's not as if I didn't want to get involved. And the Saturday, I got home—I know you have to tie your head so I was gonna go buy something to tie my head and I didn't bother. You know? And I didn't bother to go and I thought that I wouldn't go. So, anyway, Sunday morning, Tony said to me, you better go to church. We got up early and cooked and everything. She told me what time service starts and I decide I was gonna go. And I was a very particular person.

CBD: Mmmmhmmm.

MY: My high shoes. Heels was this high [indicates a four-inch pump heel height with her fingers].

CBD: [laughter]

MY: Everybody knows me by my hat and my gloves.

CBD: Mmmmhmmm.

MY: You understand?

CBD: Mmmmhmmm.

MY: And that was the type of person I am. Everybody think I am. But a little more down to earth, perfect.

CBD: Mmmmhmmm.

MY: [laughter with CBD] You know? And um always well dressed, always well-groomed.

CBD: Mmmmhmmm.

MY: Go to the hairdresser every week.

CBD: Mmmmhmmm.

MY: Wouldn't miss the Thursday hairdresser.

CBD: Mmmmhmmm.

MY: You know? You know that type?

CBD: I know!

MY: Right? [laughter with C] Who is going to tie their head? [laughter with C] You understand?

CBD: I understand. That's me! [laughter] Somewhat. So … [laughter]

MY: I got in the car and I drove. I had the number … And Carol … I saw the number of the church and I sat in the car. Oh, I'm not gonna get involved in the Baptist Church in Toronto! I'm going home! That's how confident I was. Then I decided. I just turn the car around and go back [home].

CBD: Mmmmhmmm.

MY: I knew I said that to myself but when I catch myself again I was right at the church door. Don't ask me how I got there. And when the service finish, I had to stand up in front of that church door and think which direction I came from. But anyway, when I stood in front of this door—

CBD: Mmmmhmmm.

MY: I heard it too. And I never forget that voice, when I grew up. They used to pray sweet. You really have Baptist in Toronto! I never involve in it.

CBD: Mmmmhmmm.

MY: You know? And he say, "Yes." Listen to the prayers. And I open di door and went into di church—the church is different now because they pray at the front—

CBD: Mmmmhmmm.

MY: —now, right? And I started for the back and Mother was looking for me because she's really hoping that I would come. And her daughter—I had my nice black felt hat, my high-heel boots. [laughter] And I took a scarf, a silk scarf and put it in my purse and when I get there I put that over my head and I'll put my hat back on. 'Cause I wasn't into Baptist. You know? And nobody could tell me I am, you know? Unconsciously. [The daughter] came to me and tells me, "Are you gonna come and sit with me?" And I says, "Why? I'm gonna sit right there." She say, "Sister, I have a seat over there for you."

CBD: Mmmmhmmm.

MY: Then she turn around and she says, "How dare you come here without the head-tie. You come with a hat." And I says to her, "How dare you tell me that! I'm not a Baptist!" [laughter with CBD] "Why would I tie my head? I have a scarf, if it would please you, I'll put it on my head."

CBD: Mmmmhmmm.

MY: So, I open my purse, take out the scarf, put it over my head, tie it with this, put my hat back on—can you see it?—and then followed her back to my seat. And Carol, I was not in my seat for five minutes there and I saw the bishop coming up from the altar. And then I realized that he was coming to me.

CBD: Mmmmm.

MY: And he came to me and he made the sign of the cross on my fore-head. I took off my hat and he gave it to Susan and he turn around to someone and he said, "Get me a red something." And I don't know what they got; they brought something and they fold it. And he did like this and I went wild! … That was it! They had to hold me down to tie the head. [whispering] And I went down … and jump and shout and take the whole service! [uproarious belly laugh with CBD]

CBD: My goodness!

MY: When I finish, I went what's wrong with me? You know?

CBD: Mmmmhmmm.

MY: Susan say to me, "I thought you said, you wasn't a Baptist." [belly laugh with CBD] It was like my spirit was just bursting—

CBD: Mmmmhmmm.

MY: —to come out.

In Mother Yvonne's final statement, "It was like my spirit was just burst-ing to come out," she alludes to the significance of wearing the head-tie, which signalled a change in her identity and her religious life and the begin-ning of her religious life within the church. Mother Yvonne further attests to this signification of the red head-tie in describing her visit to her spiri-tual mother and father in Trinidad following her introduction to the Spir-itual Baptist Church in Toronto:

MY: I told them what was happening and she laughed and she said, "My little red rose. The rose is finally going to bloom." And I didn't even understand what she meant when she said that. And I stayed with her.

Then I had this red head-tie. Tie my head. I spent two weeks in Trinidad and I couldn't take it off. I practically got on to the plane with it! [belly laugh with C] I had to put another on my head. I couldn't open my head. Once my spiritual mother tie my head, I couldn't untie it. And that was part taking my shame away. I went all over Trinidad with this big, red head-tie on my head. Everywhere. You know?

Sister Asha, unlike Mother Pat and Mother Yvonne, grew up as a young girl in Trinidad who liked to tie her head. Though she was a member of the Roman Catholic Church at that time, her liking for head-ties and long, "modest" clothing was seen by people who knew her as a sign that she was destined to become a Spiritual Baptist in the future:

But back home, my mom used to say you know, "You would become a Baptist." They used to say it because like my head is always tied the way they tie their heads and you know long skirts and you know what have you. I never used to get involve or get caught up with the short mini and the shorts and exposin' my body. No never, you know. So, as my mom says, you know, it's there but just time would tell, right.

The head-tie also serves as a marker of spiritual gifts within the Spiritual Baptist Church hierarchy of offices and roles occupied by women. Mother Ruth, in her conversations with me, discussed the significance of styles of head-ties among Spiritual Baptist women pointing out that the "fancy" head-ties, the ones that are wrapped high, signify the rank of a church mother, whereas the more modestly tied head-ties signify that the woman is a "sister" or "baptismal candidate" rather than a "mother."

CONCLUSION

I will return to the question posed in the subtitle of this chapter: is Aunt(y) Jemima's status that of "spiritual mother or servile woman"? This chapter has argued that the figure of Aunt(y) Jemima in Spiritual Baptist experiences clearly situates her within the church as a spiritual mother figure worthy of respect. However, the unequal race, class, and gender power relations that structure labour in North America and the continuing impact of stereotypes that have their origins in the construction of a mythic Old South continue to have an impact on Spiritual Baptist women in their work lives even north of the U.S. border.

The attire of Toronto Spiritual Baptist women, the iconic presence of Aunt(y) Jemima in a Spiritual Baptist church in Toronto, and her appearances in some of the women's dreams and mourning experiences are interpreted in this chapter as not only a recasting of Aunt(y) Jemima and the stereotypic image of Mammy, but also as a way of connecting the lives of contemporary black women with black women ancestors. These ancestors span not only the women's biological ancestors but also include biblical women such as St. Anne, mother of Mary; Mary, mother of Jesus; and Roman Catholic saints such as St. Catherine of Siena and St. Filomena. Aunt(y) Jemima, referenced by name, is also included in this pantheon of female religious figures in some Toronto Spiritual Baptist women's lives.

Historically, in the Americas, black women were largely barred from literacy both through law and custom during plantation slavery and later through class, gender, and colour oppression within colonial and post-colonial societies. Nonetheless, Spiritual Baptist Church women were able to fashion, through cloth and thread, a rich symbolic system in which they wrote the past—both their own personal histories and the history of their relationship to biblical women and men. Through the clothing they made they created their own empowering iconic images of themselves.

Importantly, the clothing—long skirts and dresses, aprons, and head-ties—provides a tangible link between the world of the spirit and the world of the living through the use of cloth and colours that symbolize the women's spiritual gifts and roles in the church. The clothes also provide a link between an ancestral past, shared by women in the Caribbean, and other black women in the Americas. This affirmative valuation of the clothing associated with the dominant culture's images of black women as servile women accomplishes the miracle that Goings noted of being able to "see" the real people trapped by the "junk" of the Aunt Jemima stereotype (1994). In embracing clothing historically associated with servitude and one of the most pervasive stereotypic images of black women in North America as a type of ritual performance, church members are able to celebrate their lives and the lives of other Spiritual Baptist women by breaking the mould of a stereotype fired in the kiln of sexist-racist iconography.

NOTES

1 From the first decade of the twentieth century until as late as the 1950s, a number of black women were actually hired to portray Aunt Jemima (Goings 1994). Further contributing to the "true to life" imagery of Aunt Jemima as a real person, a Mammy figurine based on actor Hattie McDaniels, famed for her portrayal of Mammy in *Gone With the Wind*, was also created in the 1940s (Goings 1994). These efforts helped to foster a biography for Mammy and give her a "real" life in the world. Deloris S. Williams in *Sisters in the Wilderness: The Challenge of Womanist God-talk* notes that some black women in the antebellum south appropriated the style of the mammy in exercising female authority in the home and community (1993: 80).

2 Personal communication with Dr. Gary Woodill (Department of Early Childhood Education, Ryerson Polytechnic University, Toronto) in August 1999.

3 My grandmother, Dorothy Sebastian Prince, would often use this term to distinguish those items that were manufactured and purchased in a store from those that were fashioned by hand. More than this seemingly simple distinction about the process of labour, the term "ready-made" also implied class divisions and aesthetics as those who preferred and could afford "ready-made" goods aspired to, or had already attained, a middle-class standard of living. In addition, in the context of Caribbean economies in which, historically, the black poor and working class had to produce their own subsistence, the emergence of this term "ready-made" goods, goods shipped from "overseas," signalled a shift in the domestic political economy of subsistence. Thus Aunt Jemima was "ready-made" not only as a mass-produced symbol but she was "ready-made" seemingly without the roots and family history that "home-made" would imply.

4 Quotation from collectors cited in "Cookie Jars of Oppression: Shades of Jim Crow Make It Big as Collectible," *Newsweek*, 16 May 1987, 75–76.

5 In *The History of Mary Prince*, the first slave narrative of a black woman, Bermudian-born Mary Prince notes that after she had been sold into slavery in Antigua, away from her family, she developed a close relationship with another slave woman, Hetty, a French black woman, whom she called Aunt: "Poor Hetty, my fellow slave, was very kind to me, and I used to call her my Aunt; but she led a most miserable life, and her death was hastened (at least the slaves all believed and said so), by the dreadful chastisement she received from my master during her pregnancy" (1987: 194).

6 Here Sister Maria is referring to Mary, mother of Jesus, as being "with her ever since."

7 Luke 1:27–45.

8 Luke 1:46–55.

9 See, for example, the image of Bennett on the cover of *Aunty Roachy Seh*.

10 To *teck bad sinting meck* laugh is Jamaican Creole or patois that translates literally as "to make light of a bad situation." The expression points to a deeper meaning, which is the strategy of addressing difficult topics through the use of humour.

11 Miss Lou, in her oral presentations and writings based on them, often prefaces her statements with references to her "Aunty Roachy." Aunty Roachy serves as the authorial voice in Miss Lou's pronouncements and commentary: "My Aunty Roachy seh dat it bwile her temper an really bex her fi true anytime she hear anybody a style we Jamaican dialec as 'corruption of the English language'" (1993: 1). Aunty Roach represents an older time and an elder's voice on which Miss Lou draws to substantiate her commentary. Note the similarity in naming between Miss Lou's Aunty Roachy and the Aunty Jemima of Sister Maria's mourning experiences.

12 Obeah is popularly and pejoratively associated with "sorcery" and "black magic" in the Caribbean. The obeah man or obeah woman is a shaman-like intermediary who intervenes on behalf of their "clients" in matters ranging from health to financial affairs and relationships. Many do not see any contradiction between consulting obeah practitioners and being Christian. However, in spite of the pejorative image, obeah is still a widely regarded practice with people seeking services from obeah men and women from all walks of life. So influential was obeah that after 1760 in colonial Jamaica the practice was punishable by death for the enslaved. Planters feared that it would incite rebellion (Bisnauth 1996: 83).

13 Kobena Mercer (1994) questions the positioning of "natural" black hairstyles as more "ideologically right-on" (99) in comparison to chemically processed styles such as the "conk" of the 1940s and the popular "curly perm" hairstyle of the 1980s. He suggests that "natural" styles such as the Afro and Dreadlocks also require techniques of stylization. They are in effect "worked on," although the ways in which they are styled differ from chemically processed styles. Mercer acknowledges the political importance of these styles in the 1960s and 1970s in positing a valuation of black aesthetics in the face of overwhelmingly "Eurocentric" notions of beauty. However, he calls for a recognition of the hybridity of contemporary "black practices of stylization" that draw on both European and African stylistic influences from the past and the present (124–25). Similarly, the head-tie as worn by Spiritual Baptist women is also an example of "creolizing stylization" (125) in incorporating an "African" element, the head-tie, with dress styles that are European in origin. They are very similar to, if not identical, in some cases, to eighteenth- and nineteenth-century styles of dress of enslaved and free black women and women of colour in the Caribbean (Honychurch 1984: 61).

14 See for example *Faith in the Valley*.

15 Interestingly, Oprah Winfrey's new talk-show format combines conventional talk-show fare featuring celebrity interviews and "human interest" stories about "ordinary" Americans in "extraordinary" circumstances along with a focus on spirituality. Winfrey has drawn both criticism and praise for her new show format, especially with regard to the incorporation of spirituality on a daily basis with such segments as "Remember Your Spirit."

Conclusion

... she [Mother Yvonne] close it off down here but not up
where she is in Canada.   —MOTHER RUBY, *Trinidad*

As far as I understand, our ancestors was Christian. My
ancestors was Christian, awright? For instance, in the slavery days when they were there and they were on the plantation, right? although they were slaves they were still
practisin' what they believe in which is prayin' and you know
in the nights when the white man would go sleep, I understand that they would, you know, meet secretly, and you
know, um experiment is not the word but, practise their
drums and their dance and their cultural, you know, beliefs
and um, you know, it all has to do with Christianity, right?
It all has to do with God. Because as far as I understand, they
had like the rain god or the sun god, just like the Indians, all
right. So it was, you know, passed down from generation to
generation. So, you know, it's up to me now, you know, to
pick it up and take it forward so when I have kids, my kids
would know more or less their background, you know?
                                      —SISTER ASHA, *Toronto*

"To Pick It Up and Take It Forward"

The Toronto Spiritual Baptist Church is a continuation of religious and cultural forms that have their basis in an over-four-hundred-year-long tradition of resistance to slavery and colonialism in the Americas by Africans and their descendants. The British transatlantic slave trade was officially ended in 1807, followed by the abolition of slavery in all British territories, including the Anglo-Caribbean and British North America in 1834, the places of "origin" and "new home," respectively, of Toronto Spiritual Baptists. However, religious and cultural forms like the Spiritual Baptist Church that emerged out of enslaved Africans' attempts to understand, accommodate, and resist their condition of enslavement continue to have salience for their descendants in the twenty-first century in metropolitan cities like Toronto to which Caribbean people have emigrated. Racism, the legacy of the slave trade, slavery, and colonialism, continues to be a salient feature in contemporary societies, having a profound impact on notions of identity and nation. It is within this wider socio-historical framework that the history of Toronto Spiritual Baptists, the vast majority of whom are African-Caribbean migrants to Canada, has been conceptualized in this research.

A key contribution of this study is the development of a framework for analysis that is particularly suited to Spiritual Baptist experiences and worldview. The history of Spiritual Baptists is linked fundamentally to migration, first the Middle Passage transporting Africans to the Americas and then subsequent journeys within the Caribbean region and the Americas. Spiritual journeying through dreams, visions, and the mourning ritual is another dimension of movement. In discussing Spiritual Baptist experiences in Toronto, I have incorporated these various movements as an integral part of the narrative.

I have also emphasized the intersection of auto/biography and wider social events in articulating a multi-voiced story. The sociological theories of Mills on the importance of the "sociological imagination" (1959) and Smith on the "everyday world as problematic" (1988; 1990) have been important in underscoring the importance of doing sociological analysis that pays attention to the ordinary as a site of analysis. In this study, the figure of the *travessao*, a "spirit walker," in the Spiritual Baptist tradition provides the basis for an approach that accommodates Spiritual Baptist experiences in spiritual as well as carnal or material terms. As in Gates's articulation of an African-American theory of literary criticism based on the black vernacular itself in the figure of the "signifyin' monkey" (1988), I have turned to the Spiritual

Baptist tradition's internal strategies of critique in basing my approach on the figure of the *travessao*. As an indeterminate, liminal figure, the *travessao*, characterized as being in perpetual movement, provides the basis of a critical approach to Spiritual Baptist experiences of emigration to Toronto.

A central theme explored throughout the study is the importance of the phrase "so spiritually, so carnally." The Spiritual Baptist Church is characterized by a worldview in which the spiritual (the world of spirit) and carnal (the material world and human relationships) are intrinsically linked. "So spiritually, so carnally" encapsulates this viewpoint. Thus, Spiritual Baptists, though firmly rooted in the world of spirit, are also deeply concerned with the material and political circumstances in which they live their everyday lives. Spiritual Baptists in Toronto engaged their religious practice as a way of dealing with the challenges of immigration, namely racism and discrimination in employment and other areas of their lives. As a result, the tradition has been adapted to meet their changing life circumstances on both individual and communal levels, particularly in ritual contexts.

It has been noted that in a similar context—the migration of Converted from St. Vincent to Brooklyn, New York—religion "needs to stay the same" as it represents "home" for practitioners (Zane 1999). However, my research on Toronto Spiritual Baptists has shown that while this may be the case for some individual churches and members, there is also the opposing impulse to seek and implement *change* in response to the current circumstances. These two impulses that often occur simultaneously are summarized in Sister Asha's assertion that it is up to her to "pick it up and take it forward" to subsequent generations. Her claim resonates with the notion of sankofa, the idea of "looking back toward the future."

With regard to "looking back toward the future," I am aware of the popularity of the concept of sankofa in black communities in the African Diaspora in Canada, the United States, and the United Kingdom. For some, the term "sankofa" refers to a reclamation of an "African" past in order to move "forward" in the future. I wish to underscore the continued presence of an "African" (as understood and articulated by the practitioners) past in Spiritual Baptist worship experiences. This has been a salient feature of the religion before the current renaissance in black arts and culture that has taken place since the 1980s in major urban centres such as New York City and London, England. In other words, before it was fashionable or a part of contemporary black cultural parlance, Spiritual Baptists were already "looking back toward the future" as a central value of the tradition. In fact, in

many ways, it is their backward-looking glance toward Africa, however it was
reconstructed, that was often at the basis of discriminatory attitudes toward
Spiritual Baptists in the colonial period in the Caribbean.

In picking it up and taking it forward, Spiritual Baptists draw on the
spiritual beliefs and ritual repertoire developed in the Caribbean during
slavery and in the early decades of the twentieth century, adapting and shaping these rituals to their present life circumstances. In their dress, particularly women who wear the long skirts, head-ties, *duiettes* (an overskirt), and
fulas (a neck scarf) of eighteenth-century African women in the Caribbean,
they visually invoke the past into a Canadian present. In this way, clothes
become not only a marker of identity as a Spiritual Baptist but also, as discussed in Chapter 6, a tangible, material link to a creolized Caribbean past.

As I sat with church mothers and sisters on Toronto buses and subway
trains as we returned from church services, I was acutely aware not only of
looks from other passengers on the bus but of being part of a historical trajectory that extends itself through time and space in the world of spirit but
also very visibly in the material world through the my presence and that of
the churchwomen.

In Toronto, where the vast majority of Spiritual Baptists are women and
many of whom currently work or who have worked in the past in paid
domestic service, the church is especially important in meeting spiritual
and social needs. The mothers of the church have played a crucial role in
the development of the church. Conservative definitions of gender placing
women in inferior positions relative to their male counterparts continue to
influence church organization and ritual practices. However, these are being
challenged both in the interpretation of biblical scriptures that have been used
to substantiate the subordination of women as well as in leadership roles of
women in the church. On this last point, the "mothers of the church" have
been especially crucial in the development of the Spiritual Baptist community in Toronto, and in this study I have focused on their significance as
both spiritual and community leaders.

My research on the Toronto Spiritual Baptist Church also points to the
practice of the religion as the emergence of a part of the Caribbean Diaspora in Canada. This dual trajectory is perhaps best symbolized by recent
developments in church organization. While most churches remain fairly
autonomous with small congregations, since 1997 concrete steps have
been taken to create umbrella organizations for Spiritual Baptists in Toronto. The Canadian branch of the Shouters Evangelical Baptist faith was

established in 1997 under the leadership of Bishop Mother Deloris Seiveright, with direct ties to Trinidad Spiritual Baptists.[1] In August 1998, the Spiritual Baptist Faith of Canada was established in Toronto under separate leadership.[2] Bishop Mother Yvonne Drakes serves as its secretary. She noted that the establishment of Spiritual Baptists as a Canadian organization was especially important in laying a foundation for the continuation of the Spiritual Baptist Church as a part of the Canadian religious landscape. The ability of the newly created diocese to ordain ministers was especially significant as a Canadian-trained ministry would be a possibility for the future development of the religion.

While Spiritual Baptists face formidable barriers in mainstream society through racist, sexist, and class-based discrimination, they nevertheless envision themselves as having a future in Canada. "This Canada is supposed to be a land of opportunity, right? You know, you could become anything you wanna become, right?" says Sister Asha. One notable exception was one church mother who saw going "home" to the Caribbean as an alternative to continuing to live in Canada. One brother, Brother Tee, actually tried to return "home" to the Caribbean but discovered that in his over twenty years out of his country of birth, he had changed and so had the society: "I went and I spent four months—actually I wanted to stay down there, but the atmosphere wasn't conducive. The way of life is so different...."

Spiritual Baptists envisioned their goals for the future as located both within the spiritual context of the religion's continuity and development in Canada as well as intrinsically connected to development of the wider black community in Toronto. Some of the people I interviewed mentioned specific, personal goals such as advancing their educational qualifications in order to secure better-paying jobs. Indeed, the two younger women, Sisters Asha and Louise, then in their twenties, were working part-time on completing high school diplomas in 1994 and 1995 while working full-time in paid, commercial domestic service and office work. Sister Maria, a former live-in domestic worker, had completed a university B.A. and had moved on to working in a commercial day care. I also met a few other sisters who were enrolled in both full-time and part-time post-secondary programs of study. Among the men, some like Bishop Dickson, a registered nurse, had acquired professional qualifications in Canada. Others, like Brother James and Brother John, had acquired qualifications in skilled trades, although they had experienced racial discrimination in finding full-time, permanent employment.

Other Spiritual Baptists saw the development of autonomous institutions as key for the development of the black community. Bishop Dickson, for instance, saw the development of a retirement home for black seniors as particularly important, clearly indicating that he sees Caribbean black people in Toronto as staying around long enough to age in Canadian society. In addition, care for elders was linked with the survival of Caribbean cultural traditions, including religion and cuisine:

> Watch the world today, you will find a lot of us in Canada in years, but you're not going to find a lot of black people in nursing homes, in hospitals, and so forth. What happens when we reach to that stage? Our culture, our culture and food, our religion, our way of worship would be taken away from us if we are not watchful and careful.

The youth in the church were encouraged by Dickson to "hold on to the vine" and to "place [themselves] in the core of one of the branches." Archbishop Dickson's future vision for Spiritual Baptists is one that simultaneously looks back to the past and the future as he sees the care of the young and the elders as intrinsically linked to the continuity of not only the Spiritual Baptists, but also the wider black community in Toronto.

In addition to a focus on personal development as represented by educational achievement and institutional development in the form of autonomous community organizations such as a home for the aged, there were others who focused on changing the underlying power structure as key to their full participation in mainstream Canadian society. For these Spiritual Baptists, such as Brother Tee, the lack of access to participation in arenas of power such as the legal system, business, and politics was responsible for placing black people at a structural disadvantage:

> The big issue that I find is that people—people in our black community who should be in positions of power they're not getting it. They're fought in every way. They may put one in just to say, well, here we have your token black person. But theoretically, they don't have that much more. And if they try to confront it, they're branded as, you're not a team player, you know, you know that sort of thing? ... I mean what this guy said is true about the police.

In addition, Brother Tee points to "criminalization" of black people, especially, young black men as extremely detrimental:

We—to me, Carol, from what I'm experiencing and what I've seen and what I've read of how—um, especially, young black men are treated in this city alone, I find you have more bloody policemen who are criminals than the so-called criminal on the street. This system is designed— the judicial system is designed, to me, to put black people in their place and to put all black men, especially younger guys, in jail. And do not forget that the police in North America was founded on the premise that black people—to look after black people, to keep them where they are. It was founded in the Southern states.

The "solution" for Brother Tee, lies not in "rhetoric," as he calls it, but in closer ties between black parents and their children.

Toronto Spiritual Baptists have both maintained *and*, in doing so, simultaneously created a vital religious tradition drawing on beliefs and ritual practices that have their basis in the history of resistance to slavery and colonialism. Post–Second World War Caribbean immigration to metropolitan countries such as Canada has resulted in the creation of innovative cultural and religious forms forged in the context of "making a way" in the host country. Though often told as a story that focuses on the barriers encountered in securing employment, educational, and other goals—carnal, or material, aspects of Caribbean immigrants' lives—this study has included a focus on the religious. In this regard, I aimed to contribute to feminist sociological perspectives that have not always integrated the religious dimensions of work, family, and immigration, as a central part of their analysis. Spiritual Baptist rituals and beliefs, especially mourning, provide a countercultural perspective on nation and national identity. Though rooted in a Caribbean past, the multicultural worldview of the Spiritual Baptist Church offers insight into the way in which Africans and their descendants in the Americas interpreted their historical experiences of estrangement and exile in a way that also profoundly referenced "home."

Childhood and adolescent experiences of girls and young women remain largely unexplored in a Canadian context, especially as the basis of the development of critical feminist consciousness. This study's analytical framework was informed, in part, by my reflections on my life experiences as a child and adolescent shortly after immigrating to Canada. The dearth of theorizing that includes the experiences of girlhood as a basis for feminist theorizing as well as those that position women's religious experiences as the basis for social science analysis probably exists because of the overwhelmingly secular focus of contemporary Women's Studies and the accompanying focus on women's rather than girls' experiences. These developments reflect a wider trend in the North American academy and indeed a Western worldview in which sacred and secular are regarded as opposite halves of a dualistic pair and in which children's views on serious topics are generally regarded as less "right on" than those of adults. Following from this viewpoint, the religious is discussed in theological or academic study of religion contexts while domestic work is discussed in social science. While my views here may be regarded as polemical by some, my intent has been non-polemical in that I have attempted to underscore the importance of integrated analyses from a variety of standpoints.

In this study, I have aimed to redress both omissions in feminist sociological analyses. The study's research and writing was not initiated with these specific goals in mind. However, it became apparent that childhood experiences, as well as relationships with elder women such as grandmothers, were relevant in the conceptualization of the study. In addition, many of the Toronto Spiritual Baptists who joined the religion in Toronto did so many years after hearing about it during their own childhood. Brother James's pronouncements about the passing down of values that he associated with his mother being a Spiritual Baptist in St. Vincent, through the bloodline to children exemplifies this idea. Thus I presented an analysis of Toronto Spiritual Baptist experiences that integrates Spiritual Baptist perspectives in all of their liminality and hybridity as a part of its analytic framework, and I have drawn on various childhood as well as adult experiences in the conceptualization and analysis.

In a short period of only twenty years, from 1975 to 1995, the Spiritual Baptist Church was established in Toronto as part of the community development of African-Caribbean immigrants. The church remains almost exclusively African-Caribbean in membership, with a few Indo-Caribbean members. Middle-aged women, forty to seventy years, are overwhelmingly predominant in congregations. Recent developments in the Spiritual Baptist Church organization since 1997 point to the development of a more centralized form of organization than that of the autonomous churches that first emerged out of home churches in the mid-1970s. As well, women church leaders have emerged who are challenging conventional notions of gender both in theological and practical terms related to the carrying out of spiritual work. The impact of these recent changes remains to be seen.

Will Spiritual Baptists achieve their personal and communal goals of fighting racial discrimination and establishing a strong foundation, both spiritually and carnally, in Canada? Will the Spiritual Baptist religion survive or develop into another tradition in response to the social conditions of Toronto? At the close of this book, these questions emerge as the counterpoint to the ones I asked in the Introduction concerning the significance of the Spiritual Baptist religion for Caribbean immigrants to Toronto. What is new about them is that they require an orientation outward to the wider Toronto black community and Canadian society in contrast to the early days of the church when it developed as a kind of mobile sanctuary moving from home to home.

My current research explores the development of community outreach activities and social activism primarily through feeding at a homeless shelter by one Spiritual Baptist Church in the Toronto area. I have also expanded the exploration of the significance of the aesthetic culture begun in Chapter 6, with a focus on the design of ritual space, altars, and specifically clothing worn in ritual contexts. These two foci intersect in the exploration of ritual garments, referred to as "spiritual clothes," within the tradition, and their significance as markers of identity, power, and a call to social action. I have also begun explorations on the practice of the tradition beyond the first generation of Caribbean-born practitioners in Toronto and on its practice in Diasporic contexts linking Toronto with cities in the United States, the United Kingdom, and the Caribbean. It is in this nexus of transnational networks that the exploration of Sister Asha's charge, to "pick it up and take it forward," are ultimately grounded.

NOTES

1 Personal communication with Bishop Mother Deloris Seiveright, June 1997.
2 Personal communication with Bishop Queen Mother Yvonne Drakes, April 2000.

Bibliography

Anderson, Benedict. *Imagined Communities: Reflections on the Origin and Spread of Nationalism*. London; New York: Verso, 1996.

Angelou, Maya. *I Know Why the Caged Bird Sings*. New York: Random House, 1970.

Anzaldúa, Gloria. "La Conciencia de la Mestiza: Towards a New Consciousness," in Carole R. McCann and Seung-Kyung Kim (eds.), *Feminist Theory Reader: Local and Global Perspectives*. New York: Routledge, 2003, 179–87.

———. "Speaking in Tongues: A Letter to 3rd World Women Writers," in Gloria Anzaldúa and Cherríe Moraga (eds.), *This Bridge Called My Back: Writings by Radical Women of Color* (2nd ed.). New York: Kitchen Table Women of Colour Press, [1981] 1983.

———. *Borderlands: The New Mestiza*. San Francisco: Aunt Lute, 1987.

Armstrong, Pat, and Hugh Armstrong. "Women and the Economic Crisis," in Charlene Gannagé and D.W. Livingstone (eds.), *Working People and Hard Times*. Toronto: Garamond Press, 1987, 225–46.

Arnopolous, Sheila McLeod. *Problems of Immigrant Women in the Canadian Labour Force*. Ottawa: Canadian Advisory Council on the Status of Women, 1979.

Asante, Molefi Kete. *The Afrocentric Idea*. Philadelphia: Temple University Press, 1987.

———. *Afrocentricity*. Trenton, NJ: African World Press, 1988.

Baer, Hans A., and Merrill Singer. *African-American Religion in the Twentieth Century: Varieties of Protest and Accommodation*. Knoxville: University of Tennessee Press, 1992.

Bannerji, Himani. "But Who Speaks for Us: Experience and Agency in Conventional Feminist Paradigms," in *Thinking Through: Essays on Feminism, Marxism, and Anti-Racism*. Toronto: Women's Press, 1995, 55–95.

———. "Re:Turning the Gaze," in *Thinking Through: Essays on Feminism, Marxism, and Anti-Racism*. Toronto: Women's Press, 1995, 97–119.

Bell, Catherine. "Constructing Ritual," in Ronald L. Grimes (ed.), *Readings in Ritual Studies*. Upper Saddle River, NJ: Prentice Hall, 1996, 21–33.

Benítez-Rojo, Antonio. *The Repeating Island: The Caribbean and the Postmodern Perspective* (2nd ed.). Trans. James Maraniss. Durham, NC: Duke University Press, 1996.

Bennett, Louise Coverleigh. *Aunty Roachy Seh*. Kingston, Jamaica: Sangster's Book Stores, 1993.

Berdichewsky, Bernardo. *Racism, Ethnicity and Multiculturalism*. Vancouver, BC: Future Publications, 1994.

Best, Wallace. *Passionately Human, No Less Divine: Religion and Culture in Black Chicago, 1915–1952*. Princeton, NJ: Princeton University Press, 2005.

Beverley, John. "The Margin at the Center: On *Testimonio* (Testimonial Narrative)," in Sidonie Smith and Julia Watson (eds.), *De/Colonizing the Subject: The Politics of Gender in Women's Autobiography*. Minneapolis: University of Minnesota Press, 1992, 91–114.

Bhabha, Homi. "DissemiNation: Time, Marrative, and the Margins of the Modern Nation," in Homi Bhabha (ed.), *Nation and Narration*. London: Routledge, 1990, 291–322.

Bisnauth, Dale. *History of Religions in the Caribbean*. Trenton, NJ: Africa World Press, 1996.

Black Girls, The (eds.). *Black Girl Talk*. Toronto: Sister Vision Press, 1995.

Bolaria, B. Singh, and Peter S. Li. *Racial Oppression in Canada* (enlarged 2nd ed.). Toronto: Garamond Press, 1988.

Brand, Dionne. *Bread Out of Stone: Recollections, Sex, Recognitions, Race, Dreaming, Politics*. Toronto: Coach House Press, 1994.

———. *In Another Place Not Here*. Toronto: A.A. Knopf Canada, 1996.

———. *Older, Stronger, Wiser*. Dir. Claire Prieto. Prod. Rina Fraticelli. Videocassette. National Film Board of Canada, 1989.

Brand, Dionne, and Krisantha Sri Bhaggiyadatta. *Rivers Have Sources, Trees Have Roots: Speaking of Racism*. Toronto: Cross-Cultural Communication Centre, 1986.

Brantlinger, Patrick. "Victorians and Africans: The Genealogy of the Myth of the Dark Continent," in Henry Louis Gates, Jr. (ed.), *"Race," Writing and Difference*. Chicago: University of Chicago Press, 1986, 185–222.

Brathwaite, Edward. *History of the Voice: The Development of Nation Language in Anglophone Caribbean Poetry*. London: New Beacon Books, 1984.

Brereton, Bridget. *A History of Modern Trinidad, 1783–1962*. Kingston; Port of Spain; London: Heinemann, 1981.

Brown, Elsa Barkley. "Mothers of Mind," in Patricia Bell-Scott et al. (eds.), *Double Stitch: Black Women Write About Mothers & Daughters*. New York: Harper Perennial, 1993, 74–93.

Bunyan, John. *The Pilgrim's Progress*. Oxford and New York: Oxford University Press, 1988.

Butler, Octavia E. *Wild Seed*. New York: Popular Library, 1980.

———. *Kindred*. Introd. Robert Crossley. Boston: Beacon Press, 1988.

———. *Parable of the Sower*. New York: Warner Books, 1993.

Callahan, Allen Dwight. *The Talking Book: African Americans and the Bible*. New Haven, CT: Yale University Press, 2006.

Calliste, Agnes. "Canada's Immigration Policy and Domestics from the Caribbean: The Second Domestic Scheme," in Jesse Vorst et al. (eds.), *Race, Class, Gender: Bonds and Barriers,* 2nd (rev.) ed. Toronto: Garamond Press, 1991, 136–68.

Cannon, Dale. *Six Ways of Being Religious: A Framework for Comparative Studies of Religion*. Belmont, CA: Wadsworth, 1996.

Carty, Linda. "Black Women in Academia: A Statement from the Periphery," in Himani Bannerji et al. (eds.), *Unsettling Relations: The University as a Site of Feminist Struggles*. Toronto: Women's Press, 1991.

Chevannes, Barry. *Rastafari: Roots and Ideology*. Syracuse: Syracuse University Press, 1994.

Christiansen, Juliette M., Anne Thornley-Brown, and Jean A. Robinson (Project Supervisor). *West Indians in Toronto: Implications for Helping Professionals*. Toronto: Family Service Association of Metropolitan Toronto, 1974.

Clarke, George Elliott. "Treason of the Black Intellectuals?" McGill Institute for the Study of Canada, Working Papers, 1998.

Clifford, James. *Predicament of Culture: Twentieth-century Ethnography, Literature and Art*. Cambridge, MA: Harvard University Press, 1988.

———. "Diasporas," *Cultural Anthropology* 9(3) (1994): 302–38.

Code, Lorraine. *What Can She Know? Feminist Theory and the Construction of Knowledge*. Ithaca; London: Cornell University Press, 1991.

Collins, Patricia Hill. *Black Feminist Thought: Knowledge, Consciousness, and the Politics of Empowerment*. New York: Routledge, 1991.

Cone, James H. *God of the Oppressed*. New York: Seabury Press, 1975.

———. *For My People: Black Theology and the Black Church*. Maryknoll, NY: Orbis, 1984.

"Cookie Jars of Oppression: Shades of Jim Crow Make It Big as Collectible," *Newsweek*, 16 May 1987, 75–76.

Cooper, Afua. *Memories Have Tongue: Poetry*. Toronto: Sister Vision Press, 1992.

Cooper, Carolyn. *Noises in the Blood: Orality, Gender and the "Vulgar" Body of Jamaican Popular Culture*. London: Macmillan Caribbean, 1993.

Corke, Penny (prod.). *Caribbean Crucible*. Dir. Dennis Marks. Video recording. UK: Third Eye Productions Ltd. for Channel Four in association with RM Arts, 1984.

Coverleigh, Louise Bennett. *Aunty Roachy Seh*. Kingston, Jamaica: Sangster's Book Stores, 1993.

Craton, Michael. *Testing the Chains: Resistance to Slavery in the British West Indies*. Ithaca, NY: Cornell University Press, 1982.

Crowley, Terry. "The French Regime to 1760," in Terrence Murphy and Roberto Perin (eds.), *A Concise History of Christianity in Canada*. Toronto: Oxford University Press, 1996, 1–55.

Davies, Carole Boyce. "Collaboration and the Ordering Imperative in Life Story Production," in Sidonie Smith and Julia Watson (eds.), *De/Colonizing the Subject: The Politics of Gender in Women's Autobiography*. Minneapolis: University of Minnesota, 1992, 3–19.

———. *Black Women, Writing and Identity: Migrations of the Subject*. London; New York: Routledge, 1994.

Davis, Kortright. *Emancipation Still Comin': Explorations in Caribbean Emancipatory Theology*. Maryknoll, NY: Orbis Bools, 1990.

Deikman, A.J. "Bimodal Consciousness." *Archives of General Psychiatry* 25: 481–89.

Denniston, Dorothy Hamer. "Recognition and Recovery: Diasporan Connections," in *The Fiction of Paule Marshall: Reconstructions of History, Culture, and Gender*. Knoxville: University of Tennessee Press, 1995, 126–45.

Dickson, Angela Y. *Women, Race and Class*. New York: Vintage Books, 1983.

Dickson, Kortright. *Emancipation Still Comin': Explorations in Caribbean Emancipatory Theology*. Maryknoll, NY: Orbis Books, 1990.

Douglass, Frederick. "Narrative of the Life of Frederick Douglass, an African Slave," in Henry Louis Gates, Jr. (ed.), *The Classic Slave Narratives*. New York: Penguin Books, 1987, 243–331.

Driedger, Leo. *Multi-Ethnic Canada: Identities & Inequalities*. Toronto; Oxford; New York: Oxford University Press, 1996.

Du Bois, W.E.B. *The Souls of Black Folk: Authoritative Text, Contexts, Criticism*, ed. Henry Louis Gates, Jr., and Terri Hume Oliver. New York: W.W. Norton, 1999.

Eastman, Rudolf, and Maureen Warner-Lewis. "Forms of African Spirituality in Trinidad and Tobago," in Jacob K. Olupona, ed., *African Sprituality*. Crossroads Publishing, 2000, 403–15.

Elkins, Stanley. *Slavery: A Problem in American Institutional and Intellectual Life*. Chicago: University of Chicago Press, 1959.

Employment and Immigration Task Force on Immigration Practices and Procedures. *Domestic Workers on Employment Authorizations*. Ottawa: Minister of Supply and Services Canada, 1981.

Equiano, Olaudah. "The Interesting Narrative of the Life of Olaudah Equiano or Gustavus Vassa, the African," in Henry Louis Gates, Jr. (ed.), *The Classic Slave Narratives*. New York: Penguin Books, 1987, 1–182.

Fanon, Frantz. *Black Skin, White Masks*. New York: Grove Press, 1967.

———. *The Wretched of the Earth*. New York: Grove Press, 1963.

Farrell, Susan A. "Introduction: The Search for a Feminist/Womanist Methodology in Sociology," in Sue Rosenberg Zalk and Janice Gordon-Kelter (eds.),

Revolutions in Knowledge: Feminism in the Social Sciences. Boulder, CO: Westview Press, 1992, 57–62.

Flynn, Karen. "Proletarianization, Professionalization, and Caribbean Immigrant Nurses," in Nuzhat Amin et al. (eds.), *Canadian Woman Studies: An Introductory Reader.* Toronto: Inanna Publications and Education, 1999, 243–49.

Ford-Smith, Honor. *Lionheart Gal: Lifestories of Jamaican Women.* Toronto: Sister Vision Press, 1987.

Game, Ann. *Undoing the Social: Towards a Deconstructive Sociology.* Toronto: University of Toronto Press, 1991.

———. "Sociology's Emotions," *Canadian Review of Sociology and Anthropology* 34(4) (November 1997): 383–99.

Gates, Jr., Henry Louis. "Introduction," in *The Classic Slave Narratives.* New York: Penguin Books, 1987, ix–xviii.

———. *The Signifying Monkey: A Theory of Afro-American Literary Criticism.* New York; London: Oxford University Press, 1988.

Gilkes, Cheryl Townsend. "The Sanctified Church," in Darlene Clark Hine, Rosalyn Terborg-Penn, and Elsa Barkley Brown (eds.), *Black Women in America: An Historical Encyclopedia.* Brooklyn, NY: Carlson Publishing, 1993, 1005.

———. "The Roles of Church and Community Mothers: Ambivalent American Sexism or Fragmented African Familyhood," in *African-American Religion: Interpretive Essays in History and Culture.* New York; London: Routledge, 1997, 365–88.

Gilroy, Paul. *The Black Atlantic: Modernity and Double Consciousness.* Cambridge, MA: Harvard University Press, 1993.

Glazier, Stephen D. "Heterodoxy and Heteropraxy in the Spiritual Baptist Faith," in *Journal of the Interdenominational Theological Center* 8 (Fall 1980): 89–101.

———. "African Cults and Christian Churches in Trinidad: The Spiritual Baptist Case," in *Journal of Religious Thought* 39(2) (Fall–Winter 1982–83): 17–25.

———. "Caribbean Pilgrimages: A Typology," in *Journal for the Scientific Study of Religion* 22(4) (1983): 316–25.

———. "Syncretism and Separation: Ritual Change in an Afro-Caribbean Faith," in *Journal of American Folklore* 98(387) (January–March 1985): 51–62.

———. "Mourning in the Afro-Baptist Traditions: A Comparative Study of Religion in the American South and in Trinidad," in *Southern Quarterly* 23 (1985b): 141–56.

———. *Marchin' the Pilgrims Home: A Study of the Spiritual Baptists of Trinidad.* Salem, WI: Sheffield, 1991.

God's Gonna Trouble the Water. Video recording. ETV, South Carolina, 1997.

Goings, Kenneth W. *Mammy and Uncle Mose: Black Collectibles and American Stereotyping.* Bloomington; Indianapolis: Indiana University Press, 1994.

Gone with the Wind. Dir. Victor Fleming. Screenplay by Sidney Howard. Prod. David O. Selznick. Video recording. Selznick International Pictures, 1939.

Green, Herb. "Turning the Myths of Black Masculinity Inside/Out," in Becky Thompson and Sangeeta Tyagi (eds.), *Names We Call Home: Autobiography on Racial Identity*. New York; London: Routledge, 1996, 253–63.

Haley, Alex. *The Autobiography of Malcolm X*. Introd. M.S. Handler. New York: Ballantine Books, 1992 [1964 Alex Haley and Malcom X; 1965 Malcolm X and Betty Shabazz].

——. *Roots*. Garden City, NY: Doubleday, 1976.

Harris, Michael W. *The Rise of Gospel Blues: The Music of Thomas Andrew Dorsey in the Urban Church*. New York; Oxford: Oxford University Press, 1992.

Henry, Frances. *The Caribbean Diaspora in Toronto: Learning to Live with Racism*. Toronto: University of Toronto Press, 1994.

Herskovits, Melville J. *Life in a Haitian Valley*. Garden City, NY: Anchor Books, 1971.

Herskovits, Melville J., and Frances S. Herskovits. *Trinidad Village*. New York: Octagon Books, 1964 [1947].

Hill, Clifford S. *West Indian Migrants and the London Churches*. London; New York: Oxford University Press, 1963.

Honychurch, Lennox. *The Dominica Story: A History of the Island*. Roseau, Dominica, Windward Islands, W.I.: Dominica Institute, 1984.

Hood, Robert E. *Must God Remain Greek? Afro Cultures and God-talk*. Minneapolis: Fortress Press, 1990.

hooks, bell. *Ain't I a Woman?* Boston: South End Press, 1981.

——. *Feminist Theory from Margin to Center*. Boston: South End Press, 1984.

——. *Talking Back: Thinking Feminist, Thinking Black*. Boston: South End Press, 1988.

——. "The Politics of Radical Black Subjectivity," in *Yearning: Race, Gender and Cultural Politics*. Boston: South End Press, 1990, 15–22.

——. "Postmodern Blackness," in *Yearning: Race, Gender and Cultural Politics*. Boston: South End Press, 1990, 23–31.

——. "Homeplace: A Site of Resistance," in *Yearning: Race, Gender and Cultural Politics*. Boston: South End Press, 1990, 41–49.

——. "Black Women Intellectuals," in *Breaking Bread: Insurgent Black Intellectual Life*. Toronto: Between the Lines, 1991, 147–64.

——. *Sisters of the Yam: Black Women and Self-Recovery*. Toronto: Between the Lines, 1993.

——. *Bone Black: Memories of Girlhood*. New York: Henry Holt, 1996.

Houk, James T. *Spirits, Blood, and Drums*. Philadelphia: Temple University Press, 1995.

Hurston, Zora Neale. *Dust Tracks on a Road*. New York: Harper Perennial, 1991 [1942].

——. *Mules and Men*. Bloomington: Indiana University Press, 1978 [1935].

Jackson, Bruce. "The Other Kind of Doctor: Conjure and Magic in Black Folk Medicine," in Timoth E. Fulop and Albert J. Raboteau (eds.), *African-American*

Religion: Interpretive Essays in History and Culture. New York; London: Routledge, 1997, 415–31.

Jacobs, C.M. *Joy Comes in the Morning: Elton George Griffith and the Shouter Baptists.* Port-of-Spain, Trinidad: Caribbean Historical Society, 1996.

James, C.L.R. *The Black Jacobins: Toussaint L'Ouverture and the San Domingo Revolution.* New York: Vintage Books, 1963.

James, Carl E. *Making It: Black Youth, Racism and Career Aspirations in a Big City.* Oakville, ON: Mosaic Press, 1990.

Jewell, K. Sue. *From Mammy to Miss America and Beyond: Cultural Images and the Shaping of U.S. Social Policy.* London and New York: Routledge, 1993.

Johnson-Hill, Jack A. in *I-Sight: The World of Rastafari: An Interpretive Sociological Account of Rastafarian Ethics.* Evanston, IL: American Theological Association; and Metchen, NJ: Scarecrow Press, 1995.

Jonas, Joyce. *Anancy in the Great House: Ways of Reading West Indian Fiction.* New York: Greenwood Press, 1990.

Jones, Arthur C. *Wade in the Water: The Wisdom of the Spirituals.* Maryknoll, NY: Orbis, 1993.

Julien, Isaac. *Frantz Fanon: Black Skin, White Mask.* Video recording. London: Normal Films Production for BBC and Arts Council of England, 1995.

Kincaid, Jamaica. *Annie John.* New York: New American Library, 1986.

Kymlicka, Will. *The New Debate over Minority Rights.* Robert F. Harney Professorship and Program in Ethnic Immigration and Pluralism Studies, University of Toronto. Lectures and Paper in Ethnicity, Number 26, December 1997.

Lacelle, Claudette. *Urban Domestic Servants in Nineteenth-Century Canada.* Ottawa: Minister of Supply and Services, Canada, 1987.

Li, Peter S., and B. Singh Bolaria. *Racial Oppression in Canada.* Toronto: Garamond Press, 1988.

Lorde, Audre. *Zami: A New Spelling of My Name.* Freedom, CA: Crossing Press Series, 1994, 1982.

———. *Sister Outsider.* Freedom, CA: Crossing Press Series, 1984.

Lum, Kenneth Anthony. *Praising His Name in the Dance: Spirit Possession in the Spiritual Baptist Faith and Orisha Work in Trinidad, West Indies.* Routledge, 2000.

Luxton, Meg. *More Than a Labour of Love: Three Generations of Women's Work in the Home.* Toronto: Women's Educational Press, 1980.

Macklin, Audrey. "On the Inside Looking In: Foreign Domestic Workers in Canada," in Wenona Giles and Sedef Arat-Koç (eds.), *Maid in the Market: Women's Paid Domestic Labour.* Halifax: Fernwood Publishing, 1994, 13–39.

Marshall, Paule. *Praisesong for the Widow.* New York: Penguin Books, 1983.

Mbiti, John S. *African Religions and Philosophies.* Rev. ed. New York: Anchor Books, 1970.

McCarthy-Brown, Karen. *Mama Lola: A Voudou Priestess in Brooklyn.* Berkeley: University of California Press, 1991.

Mercer, Kobena. *Welcome to the Jungle: New Positions in Black Cultural Studies*. New York: Routledge, 1994.

Mills, C. Wright. *The Sociological Imagination*. London; Oxford; New York: Oxford University Press, 1959.

Mintz, Sidney W., and Richard Price. "The Birth of African-American Culture," in Timothy E. Fulop and Albert J. Raboteau (eds.), *African-American Religion: Interpretive Essays in History and Culture*. New York; London: Routledge, 1997, 37–53.

Morrison, Toni. *The Bluest Eye*. New York: Plume Book, 1970.

———. *Song of Solomon*. New York: Plume, 1977.

———. *Beloved*. New York: Signet, 1987.

Ng, Roxana. "Sexism, Racism, Canadian Nationalism," in Himani Bannerji (ed.), *Returning the Gaze: Essays on Racism, Feminism and Politics*. Toronto: Sister Vision Press, 1993, 182–96, 255–61.

Niehoff, A., and J. Niehoff. *East Indians in the West Indies*. Milwaukee: Milwaukee Public Museum, 1970.

Painter, Nell Irvin. "Soul Murder and Slavery: Toward a Fully Loaded Cost Accounting," in Linda Kerber (ed.), *U.S. History as Women's History: New Feminist Essays*. Chapel Hill: University of North Carolina Press, 1995.

Prince, Althea (Althea Trotman). *How the East Pond Got Its Flowers*. Toronto: Sister Vision Press, 1991.

Prince, Dorothy Mathurin Sebastian. *The Life of Dorothy Mathurin Sebastian-Prince: A Twentieth Century Antiguan Woman*. Toronto: Althea Prince, 1992.

Prince, Mary. "The History of Mary Prince, A West Indian Slave," in Henry Louis Gates, Jr. (ed.), *The Classic Slave Narratives*. New York: Penguin Books, 1987, 183–242.

Raboteau, Albert J. *Slave Religion: The "Invisible Institution" in the Antebellum South*. New York: Oxford University Press, 1978.

Ramcharan, Subhas. *The Adaptation of West Indians in Canada*. Thesis, York University, 1974.

———. *Racism: Non-White Immigrants in Canada*. Scarborough, ON: Butterworths, 1982.

Razack, Sherene. "Storytelling for Social Change," in Himani Bannerji (ed.), *Returning the Gaze: Essays on Racism, Feminism and Politics*. Toronto: Sister Vision Press, 1993, 83–100.

———. *Looking White People in the Eye: Gender, Race, and Culture in Courtrooms and Classrooms*. Toronto: University of Toronto Press, 1997.

Reagon, Beatrice Johnson. "Coalition Politics: Turning the Century," in Barbara Smith (ed.), *Homegirls: A Black Feminist Anthology*. Albany: Kitchen Table Women of Color Press, 1983.

———, with Bill Moyers. *The Songs Are Free*. Dir. Gail Pellett. Prod. Public Affairs Television. Films for the Humanities and Social Sciences. Videocassette. 1997.

Rey, H.A. *Curious George*. Boston: Houghton Mifflin, 1969.

Richmond, Anthony. *Caribbean Immigrants: A Demo-economic Analysis*. Ottawa: [Statistics Canada], 1989.

Riggs, Marlon. *Black Is ... Black Ain't*. Prod./dir. Marlon T. Riggs. Co-prod. Nicole Atkinson. Co-dir./ed. Christiane Badgley. Video recording Mongrel Media, Toronto; California Newsreel, San Francisco 1995.

————. *Ethnic Notions*. Video recording. [United States]: KQED in association with M. Riggs, 1986.

Shadd, Adrienne. "'The Lord Seemed to Say "Go"': Women and the Underground Railroad Movement," in Peggy Bristow et al. (eds.), *'We're Rooted Here and They Can't Pull Us Up': Essays in African Canadian Women's History*. Toronto: University of Toronto Press, 1994, 41–68.

Silvera, Makeda. *Silenced: Makeda Silvera Talks with Working Class Caribbean Women about Their Lives and Struggles as Domestic Workers in Canada*. Toronto: Sister Vision Press, 1989.

————. *Remembering G and Other Stories*. Toronto: Sister Vision Press, 1991.

Simmons, A., and Dwaine Plaza. "International Migration and Schooling in the Eastern Caribbean." Toronto: Centre for Research on Latin America and the Caribbean, York University, 1991.

Simpson, George Eaton. *Religious Cults of the Caribbean: Trinidad, Jamaica, and Haiti*. Rio Piedras: Institute of Caribbean Studies, University of Puerto Rico, 1980.

Smith, Dorothy E. *The Everyday World as Problematic: A Feminist Sociology*. Milton Keynes, UK: Open University Press, 1987.

————. *The Conceptual Practices of Power: A Feminist Sociology of Knowledge*. Toronto: University of Toronto Press, 1990.

Smitherman, Geneva. *Black Talk: Words and Phrases from the Hood to the Amen Corner*. Boston; New York: Houghton Mifflin, 1994.

Spelman, Elizabeth. *Inessential Woman: Problems of Exclusion in Feminist Thought*. Boston: Beacon Press, 1988.

Spivak, Gayatri Chakravorty. *The Post-Colonial Critic: Interviews, Strategies, Dialogues*. Ed. Sara Harasym. New York and London: Routledge, 1990.

Staal, Frits. "The Meaninglessness of Ritual," in Ronald L. Grimes (ed.), *Readings in Ritual Studies*. Upper Saddle River, NJ: Prentice Hall, 1996, 483–94.

Talbot, Carol. *Growing Up Black in Canada*. Toronto: Williams-Wallace Publishers, 1984.

Tambiah, Stanley J. "A Performative Approach to Ritual," in Ronald L. Grimes (ed.), *Readings in Ritual Studies*. Upper Saddle River, NJ: Prentice Hall, 1996, 495–511.

Taylor, Charles. *Multiculturalism and "The Politics of Recognition."* Essay by Charles Taylor with commentary by Amy Gutmann, ed., Steven C. Rockefeller, Michael Walzer, and Susan Wolf. Princeton, NJ: Princeton University Press, 1992.

Taylor, Patrick. *The Narrative of Liberation: Historical Consciousness in the Afro-Caribbean.* Diss. Ottawa: National Library of Canada, 1985.

Taylor, Patrick. *The Narrative of Liberation: Perspectives on Afro-Caribbean Literature, Popular Culture, and Politics.* Ithaca, NY: Cornell University Press, 1989.

Thistlethwaite, Susan. *Sex, Race, and God: Christian Feminism in Black and White.* New York: Crossroad, 1989.

Thomas, Eudora. *A History of the Shouter Baptists in Trinidad and Tobago.* Ithaca, NY: Calaloux Publications, 1987.

Thompson, Becky, and Sangeeta Tyagi. "Introduction: Storytelling as Social Conscience: The Power of Autobiography," in *Names We Call Home: Autobiography on Racial Identity.* New York; London: Routledge, 1996, xi–xvii.

Thornhill, Esmeralda. "Focus on Black Women!" in Jesse Vorst et al. (eds.), *Race, Class, Gender: Bonds and Barriers.* Toronto: Garamond Press, 1989, 27–38.

Tompkins, Jane. "'Indians,' Textualism, Morality and the Problem of History," in Henry Louis Gates, Jr. (ed.), *"Race," Writing and Difference.* Chicago: University of Chicago Press, 1986, 59–77.

Toni Morrison: Profile of a Writer. Video recording. London Weekend Television, US, 1987.

Townes, Emile M. *In a Blaze of Glory: Womanist Spirituality as Social Witness.* Nashville: Abingdon Press, 1995.

Tully, James. *Strange Multiplicity: Constitutionalism in an Age of Diversity.* Cambridge: Cambridge University Press, 1997.

Turner, Victor. "The Center out There: Pilgrim's Goal." *History of Religions* 12 (1973): 191–230.

———. *Dramas, Fields and Metaphors.* Ithaca, NY: Cornell University Press, 1974.

———. *Image and Pilgrimage in Christian Culture.* New York: Columbia University Press, 1978.

———. "Liminality and Community," in Ronald L. Grimes (ed.), *Readings in Ritual Studies.* Upper Saddle River, NJ: Prentice Hall, 1996, 511–19.

Turritin, Jane. "Doing Domestic-Work Relationships in a Particularistic Setting," in Katherina L.P. Lundy and Barbara D. Warme (eds.), *Work in the Canadian Context: Continuity Despite Change.* Toronto: Butterworth (Canada), 1981, 93–108.

Van Gennep, Arnold. "Territorial Passage and the Classification of Rites," in Ronald L. Grimes (ed.), *Readings in Ritual Studies.* Upper Saddle River, NJ: Prentice Hall, 1996, 529–36.

Vanzant, Iyanla. *Faith in the Valley: Lessons for Women on the Journey Toward Peace.* New York: Simon and Schuster, 1996.

Ward, Colleen, and Michael Beaubrun. "Trance Induction and Hallucination in Spiritual Baptist Mourning," *Journal of Psychological Anthropology* 2 (1979): 479–88.

Weil, Susan. "From the Other Side of Silence: New Possibilities for Dialogue in Academic Writing," *Changes* 14(3) (1996): 223–31.

West, Cornel. "The Dilemma of the Black Intellectual," in *Breaking Bread: Insurgent Black Intellectual Life*. Toronto: Between the Lines, 1991, 131–46.

———. *Race Matters*. Boston: Beacon Press, 1993.

———. "Foreword," in Madeleine Burnside and Rosemarie Robotham, *Spirits of the Passage: The Transatlantic Save Trade in the Seventeenth Century*. New York: Simon and Schuster, 1997.

———. *The Cornel West Reader*. New York: Basic Civitas Books, 1999.

Williams, Delores S. *Sisters in the Wilderness: The Challenge of Womanist God-talk*. Maryknoll, NY: Orbis Books, 1993.

Williams, Eric. *Capitalism and Slavery*. London: Andre Deutsch, 1964.

Wish, H. *Slavery in the South*. New York: Noon Day Press, 1968.

Wolf, Eric. *Europe and the People Without History*. Berkeley: University of California Press, 1982.

Zane, Wallace W. *Journeys to the Spiritual Lands: The Natural History of a West Indian Religion*. New York; Oxford: Oxford University Press, 1999.

Zong, Li. "New Racism, Cultural Diversity and the Search for a National Identity," in Andrew Cardozo and Louis Musto (eds.), *The Battle Over Multiculturalism: Does It Help or Hinder Canadian Unity?* Ottawa: Pearson-Shoyama Institute, 1997, 115–26.

Index

Note: "Church" refers to the Spiritual Baptist Church; individual Church leaders and members (Mothers, Sisters, and Brothers) are indexed under their names.